THE INDIVIDUAL AND THE POLITICAL ORDER
An Introduction to Social and Political Philosophy

Second Edition

NORMAN E. BOWIE
University of Delaware

ROBERT L. SIMON
Hamilton College

Prentice-Hall, Inc., Englewood Cliffs, New Jersey 07632

Library of Congress Cataloging-in-Publication Data

Bowie, Norman E., date
  The individual and the political order.

  Includes bibliographies and index.
  1. Liberty.   2. Equality.   3. Justice.
I. Simon, Robert L., 1941-   .   II. Title.
JC571.B675 1986   323.4′01   85-12444
ISBN 0-13-457151-7

Editorial/production supervision and
  interior design: Kate Kelly
Cover design: Lundgren Graphics, Ltd.
Manufacturing buyer: Harry P. Baisley

Printed in the United States of America

10 9 8 7 6 5

ISBN 0-13-457151-7   01

Prentice-Hall International (UK) Limited, *London*
Prentice-Hall of Australia Pty. Limited, *Sydney*
Prentice-Hall Canada Inc., *Toronto*
Prentice-Hall Hispanoamericana, S.A., *Mexico*
Prentice-Hall of India Private Limited, *New Delhi*
Prentice-Hall of Japan, Inc., *Tokyo*
Prentice-Hall of Southeast Asia Pte. Ltd., *Singapore*
Editora Prentice-Hall do Brasil, Ltda., *Rio de Janeiro*
Whitehall Books Limited, *Wellington, New Zealand*

To Joy, Marc, Bruce, Brian, and Peter
for their help, encouragement and patience.

CONTENTS

PREFACE

Nearly a decade has passed since the publication of the first edition of *The Individual and the Political Order*. The climate of America and the attitudes of students have changed markedly in this period. Yet, despite these changes in attitude, we noted in preparing the second edition of *The Individual and the Political Order* that the basic issues of political philosophy have remained constant. Questions remain as to the proper authority of the state, the definition of the public interest, the means for resolving conflicts among rights, for strengthening democracy, the appropriate way to provide justice, be it distributive or retributive, and whether or not affirmative action programs are a proper means for redressing discrimination against minorities and women. Hence readers familiar with the first edition will find many welcome landmarks.

In addition to changes in detail, the second edition contains two major changes. We have combined the chapters on Justice and Economic Justice into one chapter. Secondly, we have added a chapter on International Affairs which discusses the uses and limits of morality in international affairs, the obligations of affluent nations to impoverished countries, global justice with respect to natural resources and the morality of nuclear deterrence.

We would like to thank readers of the first edition for helpful comments on how to improve *The Individual and the Political Order*. In addition,

Robert Simon is grateful for the support he received from the Rockefeller Foundation and the National Humanities Center for work on a project on ethics and international affairs, of which one of the results is the last chapter of this book. We would like to thank Professor Alan Wertheimer for his many helpful comments, as well as the anonymous Prentice-Hall referees. We would also like to thank Sandy Manno for assisting us with the typing and editing of our manuscript, and to Philosophy Editor Emily Baker and Production Editor Kate Kelly for shepherding the manuscript to publication.

INTRODUCTION

In a moving article entitled "Bicentennial Blues in Boston," Jonathan Kozol describes as follows his encounter with a poverty-stricken black child in Boston:

> One day I am forced to realize that Peter is no longer growing at a normal rate. . . . Brain growth was impeded prior to birth or else in infancy: he will not grow up to normal size. . . .
>
> The doctor is firm. We ask if this is common and we ask . . . what causes something of this sort. Prenatal care. The mother is poor, or ill or underfed. . . . Peter's mother *was* in fact extremely ill. His infancy was lived in almost unabated hunger.
>
> The doctor goes on, ". . . It hardly happens in white neighborhoods. . . . It is a problem of the poor, of rural slums and of impacted sections in the cities. With the right kind of care this could be totally eliminated [someday]."
>
> Someday, but we are alive on this day. . . . And Peter will not be born someday, will not be crippled one day. He is a real boy in the real world with a real curse.[1]

Consideration of tragic cases such as this can lead us to consider and examine the social and political arrangements that may contribute to these evils. One might ask, for example, whether the state should take income from the rich and powerful and redistribute it to the poor and disadvantaged. Other related questions may arise. Should everyone be guaranteed adequate medical care, regardless of ability to pay? Should everyone, or at least every qualified person, have access to a college education at government expense? Does unjust discrimination in the past against women and certain minorities justify preferential treatment for them now?

These and other related questions are hotly debated, not only in the press and by political leaders, but by ordinary citizens as well.

Very often, however, the philosophical issues underlying these debates are lost in the heat of controversy. Yet political positions rest on philosophical presuppositions; presuppositions which often are never made explicit or even subjected to rational examination. Consider, for example, the following dialogues.

> **Citizen A:** This new tax law is unjust. The government has gone too far when it taxes me to provide medical care for others.
>
> **Citizen B:** But proper medical care clearly is a necessity. Given the high cost of health care, many citizens just cannot afford to pay for adequate medical attention. Only a strong nationwide health plan, financed out of tax revenues, will provide the needed care.
>
> **Citizen A:** It isn't the government's job to undertake every project that leads to a social good. Indeed, such social projects are to be avoided. The result is the creation of giant but inefficient bureaucracies that waste money and represent a threat to liberty—including the individual's liberty to spend his hard-earned money as he sees fit.
>
> **Citizen B:** But doesn't every citizen have a right to adequate health care?
>
> **Citizen A:** I don't accept that. If people won't work or if they squander their resources, why should I be forced to bail them out?
>
> **Citizen C:** All candidates for the position are about equally qualified, so either a woman or a minority group member should be hired.
>
> **Citizen D:** But that's unjust. After all, if it is unjust to discriminate against persons simply because they are women or members of a minority group, it is surely unjust to discriminate in their favor for the same irrelevant reason.
>
> **Citizen C:** But the best way to overcome the insidious effects of past discrimination is precisely to discriminate in favor of the victimized group.

Debates such as these raise the kinds of issues that will be considered here. In each exchange, fundamental philosophical positions are being appealed to. Citizen A, for example, holds that there are certain limits on the rightful exercise of government authority and that such limits prohibit redistribution of an individual's earnings to others. But how can A *justify* his views on the limited role of government? If pressed, he may appeal to a general account of the purpose or role of the state. Such a general theory, he will hold, explains why the state that governs least governs best. In developing such a theory, he may be led to consider the rights of individuals; rights that set moral limits on the scope of government authority. But then, he will be led to explore various questions that arise concerning rights. Does everyone have the right to vote? The right to free medical care? If people have the former right but not the latter one, what accounts for the difference? What are rights anyway and how can we tell when people have them?

Similarly, Citizen D implicitly appeals to a conception of justice that itself requires clarification and defense. Does justice require simply that everyone be judged on their merits? Is evaluation by merit appropriate when not everyone has had an equal or fair chance to acquire merit? What if some persons or groups were systematically denied the opportunity to develop their talents and capacities? Or what if they were denied the fruits of whatever merit they did manage to exhibit? What of the effects of pervasive and systematic discrimination directed against blacks and members of other minority groups? Is it enough to apply normal standards of merit as usual in light of past inequalities? Or does compensatory justice require that some special form of redress be made?

It is the task of political and social philosophy to grapple with the issues, theoretical and specific, raised by questions considered in the preceding paragraphs. How these and related issues are dealt with will affect us all. Accordingly, if we are to do more than merely express our subjective likes and dislikes, we must subject such policies to critical evaluation.

Political decisions can determine the opportunities that will be open to us, the resources that will be available for our use, the kinds of legal redress to which we can appeal, and even, in time of war, whether we will live or die. Yet, all too often, individual claims are ignored or swept away when they come into conflict with those of powerful economic, social, and political institutions or groups. Whether it is the bureaucracy of a large university that must deal with students only through impersonal computers, the large corporation that promotes potentially harmful products to maximize profits, or the nation-state that sends an unwilling citizen off to a war in which he does not believe, the individual often seems lost in the shuffle. The need is as great as it ever was, then, to assess critically the political order itself. It is important not only to understand how the political order *does* work but also to formulate criteria for determining how it *ought* to work. Otherwise, criticisms of existing institutions or proposals for change are without rational foundations.

There are at least two ways in which political philosophy can contribute to political evaluation. First, it can clarify the concepts and arguments employed in political discourse. Unless such notions as "authority," "rights," "justice," and "liberty" are analyzed it is far from clear that parties to the sorts of disputes exemplified in our sample dialogues even understand just what it is they are arguing about. It is easy, for example, simply to claim that one has a right to something. It is quite another thing to explain what it is to have a right or to give a plausible account of just what rights people have. A similar point can be made about the other concepts characteristically employed in political arguments.

Conceptual analysis is of great importance since it helps us to understand what the political claims before us mean, as well as to disentangle separate issues that all too often get blurred together in the heat of debate. But while it surely is important to be clear about what it is that we (or others) are saying, it is at least equally important that we use our concepts to say something defensible. We want to know, for example, not just how to understand talk about liberty, but also how much liberty people are entitled to. Political philosophy can contribute to questions of the second sort by formulating, assessing, and applying criteria for evaluating the political and social order.

Our goal in this work is to use the tools of conceptual analysis on questions of theory and practice, not only to contribute to the clarification of political discourse, but also to evaluate particular political positions. We intend to investigate some of the principal problems of political and social philosophy and apply our results to the examination of selected issues in the area of public affairs.

As it is sometimes helpful to know where one is going before one sets out, the following remarks may prove helpful. Our first task will be to consider various proposals for evaluating that most powerful of political institutions, the nation-state. If a defensible set of criteria can be found, it will indicate the proper function of government and the limit of the government's legitimate authority over the individual. In formulating and evaluating proposed criteria, we discuss not only competing views of the nature and function of the state but also utilitarianism, natural or human rights, justice, democracy, and the grounds of political obligation. As a result of this inquiry, which takes up our first five chapters, we develop a political perspective of our own, directed toward protection of individual rights and implementation of certain principles of justice, which can be applied to concrete policy issues.

In the subsequent chapters, we investigate in light of our earlier discussions issues arising within the political order. Particular attention is paid to the nature, grounds, and possible limits of individual liberty and to the justifiability of various principles of law.

Later chapters consider issues that arise when charges of injustice are brought against the political order. Special attention is paid to the justifiability of civil disobedience, the issue of whether government should tolerate certain forms of law breaking, and to the claims of compensatory justice made on behalf of wronged groups, and to international affairs.

Our aim throughout this work is to present an introduction to political and social philosophy that illustrates how philosophical analysis and inquiry can illuminate areas of pressing political and social concern.

Throughout this work, the principal concern is to delineate the proper relation of the individual to the political order and to the institutions that make up that order. We hope, through consideration of alternate views, to develop, defend and apply the principle so eloquently stated by John Rawls that "Each person possesses an inviolability . . . that even the welfare of society cannot override. . . . the rights secured by justice are not subject to political bargaining or to the calculus of social interests."[2] But whichever political position turns out to be most defensible, perhaps the study of political philosophy itself is of the highest value, for it can lead to critical and reflective evaluation of that great leviathan, the political order, which can so significantly affect our lives.

NOTES

[1]Jonathan Kozol, "Bicentennial Blues in Boston," *The New York Times,* Oct. 20, 1975, p. 33. © by *The New York Times* reprinted by permission.

[2]John Rawls, *A Theory of Justice* (Cambridge, Mass.: Harvard University Press, 1971) pp. 3-4.

SELECTED READINGS

Each chapter of this book will be followed by a short list of suggested readings. While these lists are not intended to be comprehensive or exhaustive, we believe that the materials included will be of special use and interest to readers. Additional bibliographic information may be found in the notes following each chapter.

General introduction to social and political philosophy

Barry, Brian. *Political Argument.* London: Routledge and Kegan Paul, Ltd., 1965.
Benn, S. I. and **Peters, R. S.** *The Principles of Political Thought: Social Foundations of the Democratic State.* New York: The Free Press, 1965.
Bluhm, William T. *Theories of the Political System: Classics of Political Thought and Modern Political Analysis.* 3rd ed. Englewood Cliffs, N.J.: Prentice-Hall, 1978.
Feinberg, Joel. *Social Philosophy.* Englewood Cliffs, N.J.: Prentice-Hall, 1973.
Fowler, Robert Booth and **Orenstein, Jeffrey R.** *Contemporary Issues in Political Theory.* New York: John Wiley, 1977.
Held, Virginia. *Rights and Goods.* New York: The Free Press, 1984.
Lucas, J. R. *The Principles of Politics.* Oxford: Clarendon Press, 1966.
Raphael, D .D. *Problems of Political Philosophy.* New York: Praeger Publishers, Inc., 1970.
Sabine, George H. *A History of Political Theory.* 4th ed. Revised by Thomas Landon Thorson. Hinsdale, Il: Dryden Press, 1973.
Taylor, Richard. *Freedom, Anarchy and the Law.* 2nd ed. Buffalo: Prometheus Books, 1982.

Anthologies

Diggs, B. J., ed. *The State, Justice and the Common Good.* Glenview, Illinois: Scott, Foresman, 1974.

Flathman, Richard E., ed. *Concepts in Social and Political Philosophy.*New York: Macmillan, 1973.

Murphy, Jeffrie G., ed. *An Introduction to Moral and Social Philosophy: Basic Readings in Theory and Practice.* Belmont, California: Wadsworth, 1973.

Schwartz, Thomas, ed. *Freedom and Authority: An Introduction to Social and Political Philosophy.* Encino, California: Dickenson, 1973.

One

LOVE IT OR LEAVE IT? INDIVIDUAL CONSCIENCE AND POLITICAL AUTHORITY

We live in an age of political turmoil. Internationally, the superpowers rely mainly on a balance of nuclear terror to keep what peace there is. The poor and the disadvantaged cry out for a more equal distribution of the world's wealth at both the national and international level. Domestically, controversy rages over the size of government and the effect of big government on individual freedom. There is little consensus on how major social problems are to be resolved. Can the mixed economy of the welfare state best handle problems of poverty and unemployment? Or should we turn to socialism, on the one hand, or the unregulated free market on the other? How are we to deal with crime in the streets and in the executive suites?

It is evident that the way major social and political problems are dealt with will profoundly affect us all. The wise use of political power can benefit millions while the unwise or immoral use of political power can cost the lives of millions more. Hence, it is important not just to *describe* how the political order *does* work. It also is desirable to determine how it *should* work. One of the principal tasks of social and political philosophy is to formulate, clarify, and assess criteria for *evaluating* political institutions. Accordingly, political philosophy is a critical activity in at least the sense that it subjects political and social institutions to intensive scrutiny.

It is characteristic of many such institutions that they claim to have *authority* over individuals who stand in certain relationships to them. For example, a college or its faculty may claim the authority to establish requirements for graduation. If individuals wish to graduate from that institution, they must satisfy whatever requirements have been duly promulgated by the institution. Dominant among political institutions is the nation-state. Such states claim to have authority over their citizens in the strong sense of having the *right* to be obeyed. If states simply required obedience on the grounds that they are sufficiently powerful to make their subjects obey, their commands would lose all moral legitimacy. Their behavior would be no different in principle from that of the bully who forces smaller and weaker children to carry out his commands. Normally, states do not claim merely to be the biggest bully of them all.

When a college or university claims to have the authority or right to set graduation requirements, it need not also claim that every individual is obligated to enroll in an institution of higher learning in the first place. The graduation requirements of the institution function as *enabling* rules. They tell us what we are to do if we wish to secure the degree, and so enable us to graduate. Many of the state's laws and edicts are not like that, however. Rather, such laws and edicts are thought to impose an *obligation* to obey. The United States government, for example, does not hold that it is up to the individual whether he or she obeys the tax laws. This strong sense of authority in which the having of authority generates the obligation to obey leads to problems. The problem of concern here arises from the conflict between the claims of authority, on the one hand, and those of individual conscience and judgment, on the other.

Consider, for example, the problem which at one time faced the kind of large hospital to which many patients came for treatment of kidney failure. Unfortunately, the number of patients far exceeded the number of spaces available on kidney-dialysis machines. Yet without access to the machines, many patients surely would die. Other hospitals had the same problem so the overload could not be sent elsewhere.

Physicians and hospital administrators agreed that some procedure was needed for determining who would have access to the machines. Since, as individuals, the staff did not agree on who should and who should not be treated, no one would have been treated unless such a procedure was instituted. It was often agreed that a panel consisting of physicians, administrators, nurses, and representatives of the general public make the decisions and that all decisions of this committee would be authoritative.

Suppose under this procedure, a certain patient, A, comes up for treatment. A would not have needed treatment at this time had he but followed his doctor's orders about diet and medication. Because of his own negligence, he did not obey instructions and so needs treatment now. He is a prominent research scientist whose work, if carried to fruition, may be of great benefit to humanity.

However, a second person, B, also needs immediate treatment. Unfortunately, there is space for only one more patient on the machine. B, whose work is of no special benefit to others, needs treatment now only because he obeyed his physician's instructions so faithfully. By being so careful, he postponed the time when he would need dialysis as long as possible, thereby freeing the machine for use by others. The problem facing the committee is whether A or B should receive treatment.

The committee decides that A should receive treatment, because of the great value of his research for humanity. However, those directly involved in administering dialysis treatment regard the decision as grossly unfair. The committee responds to their protest by pointing out that, by common agreement, it and it alone has the authority to make the decision. The protestors reply that their consciences will not allow them to carry out the decision.

This case is a paradigm illustration of how the claims of authority can conflict with those of individual conscience and judgment. One issue raised by the case is, of course, that of whether the dialysis committee made the right decision.[1] The issue of present concern, however, is somewhat different. It is the issue of whether it is possible to acknowledge the claims of political authority *and* the claims of individual conscience and autonomy as well.

Particularly where the authority of the state is concerned, many are inclined to give *absolute weight* to its claims to authority. Particularly in times of crisis, it is felt that criticism of leaders and decisions (let alone actual protest or disobedience) is dangerous if not downright subversive. In this view, the attitude of citizens toward their leaders should be analogous to that of players on a team toward their coach (on at least one traditional view of that relationship). That is, once one is a member of a team, one should not challenge directives from the top. Imagine what would happen, for example, if during a crucial break in a basketball game, each player debated with every other player what the team should do next. On the political level, the slogan "Love it or leave it," which was so frequently directed against critics of the Vietnam War, quite clearly expresses the attitude that criticism of the political order is incompatible with allegiance to it.

While some persons are disposed to give absolute weight to the claims of authority, others are equally disposed to go the other way. Consider, for example, Henry David Thoreau's reaction to what he considered an unjust war. Rather than pay taxes that would have supported the Mexican War effort, he refused to pay and was subsequently imprisoned. That he was *legally* obligated to pay was in his view an insufficient reason for obedience.

For him, the crucial issue was the *moral* acceptability of compliance. According to Thoreau:

> Laws never made men a whit more just: and, by means of their respect for it, even the well disposed are daily made instruments of injustice. A common and natural result of an undue respect for law is, that you might see a file of soldiers . . . marching in admirable order over hill and dale to the wars, against their wills, ay, against their common sense and consciences . . . . [2]

It appears as if there is great tension between the claims to authority made by political and social institutions, particularly the nation-state, and the claims of individual conscience and autonomy. As one contemporary writer puts it:

> The defining mark of the state is authority, the right to rule. The primary obligation of man is autonomy, the refusal to be ruled. It would seem, then, that there can be no resolution of the conflict between autonomy . . . and the putative authority of the state. [3]

The implications of this purported conflict are enormous. If the conflict is indeed genuine, we are faced with a momentous choice. If, on the one hand, we are impressed with the need for authority, we may be led to stifle exercise of independent critical judgment. But as a result, we may end up with the abhorrent picture of "good Germans" engaging in genocide at the command of their Nazi superiors. If, on the other hand, we assign absolute weight to individual conscience, we may lose all the advantages that settled political decision procedures can provide.

A major goal of political philosophy is to formulate defensible criteria for assessing the political order, particularly as it is embodied in the nation state. However, as the preceding discussion indicates, it is first important to consider what actually is involved in accepting political authority and whether the costs of such acceptance might be prohibitive. We begin by examining a classic defense of the necessity of absolute political authority, that provided by Thomas Hobbes. Then, we will consider whether the only alternative to absolute authority is abandonment of the state and the political order. In the concluding section of this chapter, we will develop a strategy for evaluating the state, for distinguishing good states from bad ones and for determining under what conditions the former might come to have some form of authority over their citizens. So it is to the political theory of Thomas Hobbes that we now turn.

AUTHORITY VS. AUTONOMY AND CONSCIENCE

Thomas Hobbes (1588–1679)—The Case for Absolute Authority

The two great influences on Hobbes's political philosophy are its author's horror of war, particularly civil war, and his reliance on individualist methodology. The former is not surprising. Hobbes was born as the Spanish Armada was approaching England. The reigns of Elizabeth and James I, the Civil War, the rule of Cromwell, and the Restoration all occurred within his lifetime.

Educated at Oxford, within the Scholastic tradition (which he later repudiated), Hobbes spent most of his life as tutor and later adviser to the children of the noted Cavendish family. His employment provided time for reading, writing, and thinking. Moreover, through the Cavendish family, he was able to meet many of the great thinkers of his own time. Because of his political views, he feared the outcome of the Civil War and so, before the outbreak of the conflict, left England for Paris. There, he tutored the Prince of Wales, who was later to become Charles II. However, the publication of his major work, *Leviathan* (1651), made him unpopular with the Royalists. Its naturalistic, scientific approach to political thought left him open to charges of atheism and anti-Royalism. So he made his peace with Cromwell and returned to England. When Charles II took the throne after the fall of Cromwell's government, he remembered Hobbes with affection. The last years of Hobbes's life were spent in philosophical reflection and conversation, with financial support provided by the throne.

Perhaps the key to understanding Hobbes's political thought is his philosophical method. Sometimes called the "resolutive-compositive" method, it requires that explanation involves breaking wholes down into parts. Once the atomic or basic elements of a process or state of affairs are isolated and their workings understood, the whole can be explained as the sum total of the parts and the laws governing their behavior. For example, expansion of a heated gas can be understood simply as the result of changes in the behavior of its simple constituents, molecules, when exposed to increasing amounts of energy. Likewise, the existence of a traffic jam might be explained by an account of the decisions of individual drivers (none of whom intended to produce the jam) along with an account of available highway space.

Once the atomic elements of a situation have been isolated and understood, Hobbes thought that one could then proceed *geometrically*, deducing the nature of the whole from the nature of the parts. Hobbes's friend Aubrey reports on Hobbes's discovery of geometry as follows:

Being in a gentleman's library, Euclid's *Elements* lay open, and twas the 47th [theorem of Book I]. He read the proposition. "By God," said he, "this is impossible . . ." So he reads the demonstration of it which referred him back to such a proposition: which proposition he read. That referred him back to another, which he also read. At last (after referring all the way back to the axioms) he was demonstratively convinced of that truth. This made him in love with geometry.[4]

Hobbes's goal, then, was to explain that great leviathan the state solely by reference to its elements, the individual citizens out of which it was composed. Once the laws governing individuals were specified, the job would be to proceed geometrically (deductively) to the nature and function of the state.

Hobbes's political philosophy   Hobbes's political philosophy rests upon his psychology, his view of human nature. His psychology, in turn, rests upon his physics. His physics is roughly that of the science of his time—that reality is ultimately nothing but minute material particles in motion. Human behavior, as a part of nature, is to be explained purely mechanically, as the result of the influence of external particles upon that collection of other particles that constitute the human being. "The small beginnings of motion, within the body of man, before they appear in walking, speaking, striking and other visible actions, are commonly called Endeavor."[5] Endeavors, or motives, are the causes of action and are themselves nothing but particles in motion.

Motives are of two basic sorts. Either we are attracted toward something, which we therefore call good, or we are repelled by something, in which case we call it bad. "But whatsoever is the object of any man's appetite or desire, that is it which he for his part calleth good: and the object of hate or aversion evil . . ."[6] Hobbes explains all human action in purely mechanistic terms. Persons, when they act voluntarily, are moved to satisfy their appetites either by securing the objects of their desires or by avoiding the objects of their aversions. All action is egoistic, directed ultimately at satisfying the agent. However, agents are normally (or at least have the potential to be) efficient rational calculators—they can select the best means to their chosen aims and so are rational in choosing among alternatives.

Here then is Hobbes's individualist starting point. It is a conception of human nature as it would be independent of the existence of any political order. The proper function of the state is to be deduced from the characteristics of egoistic but rational individuals. What ends or goals could such individuals secure through the state that they could not (or could not so efficiently) secure without it?

Life without the state, Hobbes tells us, would be "solitary, poor, nasty, brutish and short."[7] This conclusion is to be justified by appeal to Hobbes's conception of human nature. If there were no state, if humans lived in a so-called state of nature, then given selfishness, scarcity of resources, and approximate equality in strength, cunning, and personal resources, the end result would be a war of all against all. For if there were not enough to go around, and everyone always acted to satisfy their desires, then (since anyone, given strength or sufficient cleverness, can hope to kill anyone else) the "haves" and "have-nots" would be at one another's throats. Consequently, if it is reasonable to accept Hobbes's postulates—that humans are rational egoists, that they are approximately equal in their capacity to harm one another, and that not everyone's desires can be satisfied—we can conclude that the state of nature would be one of anxiety, violence, and constant danger.

Hobbes's argument, as reconstructed here, does not presuppose that there ever was an actual state of nature.[8] The actual existence of such a state of affairs is irrelevant to Hobbes's purpose. What Hobbes is trying to do is to justify the state by showing how bad life would be *if* the state did not exist. Since his point is hypothetical—*if* the state did not exist, look how bad things *would* be—the actual existence of the state of nature is not required for the success of his argument.

Hobbes described humans as sufficiently rational to realize that the state of nature, one of war of all against all, was contrary to their interests, especially their overriding concern with self-preservation. For whatever else people want, they need personal security as a prerequisite of their enjoyment of anything else:

> The passions that incline men to peace are fear of death; desire of such things as are necessary to commodious living; and a hope by their industry to obtain them. And reason suggesteth convenient articles of peace . . . which otherwise are called Laws of Nature.[9]

According to Hobbes, "A LAW OF NATURE . . . is a precept or general rule, found out by reason, by which a man is forbidden to do that which is destructive of his life, or taketh away the means of preserving the same. And consequently, that every man ought to endeavor peace, as far as he has hope of obtaining it; and when he cannot obtain it, that he may seek . . . all help and advantages of war."[10]

We have already seen that the Hobbesian state of nature, being a state of war of all against all, is a disaster for all concerned. Hence, we can see that it is in the rational self-interest of the inhabitants to form a state. Thus, the first law of nature, which enjoins peace, implies the second; namely, that when others are willing, all parties to the state of war contract together to set up a supreme authority over them. By doing so, the evils of the war of all against all can be avoided.

The function of the state, in Hobbes's view, is to provide the security sufficient to protect us from the egoism of our fellows. Everyone's pursuit of their immediate self-interest is not in the enlightened self-interest of anyone. The state is an instrument to keep egoism in check.[11]

Given his view of human nature, Hobbes concludes that only an absolutist state can provide security. Only a government in which the state has complete authority and the individual has virtually no rights or autonomy can hope to avoid the state of nature:

> covenants without the sword, are but words, and of no strength to secure a man at all . . . if there be no power . . . every man will rely on his own strength and art . . . against all other men.[12]

Since they are rational, inhabitants of the state of nature will understand that if the individual is given too much leeway within the state, the state of nature will simply reappear in new guise. Since only an absolute, common power can prevent reversion to the war of all against all, that is exactly the kind of state they will create:

> The only way to erect such a common power . . . is to confer all power . . . upon one man or upon one assembly of men that they may reduce all their wills, by plurality of voices unto one will . . . and he that carrieth this [power] is called SOVEREIGN . . . and every one besides his SUBJECT.[13]

Hobbes believes that authority and individual autonomy are incompatible. Indeed, Hobbes allows concern for self-preservation and order to take precedence over any other values a state might be thought to secure. Little, if any, room is left, for example, for individual rights. In spite of its gloomy conclusions, however, Hobbes's approach has several significant merits. In particular, it is an attempt to explain the basis for political authority in scientific, naturalistic terms. No recourse is made to controversial moral assumptions or to such questionable doctrines as that of the divine right of kings. Rather, what Hobbes does is to isolate what he takes to be the basic unit of political analysis—the individual—and ground his political philosophy on a view of human nature.

Evaluation of Hobbes's political theory Hobbes views the state as an instrument for providing those basic primary goods without which even a minimally satisfactory human life is impossible. These primary goods, he claims, are peace and security. And in his view, only an absolute authority can provide them.

Those who wish to avoid Hobbesian conclusions might begin by questioning his view of human nature. Even if it is true, as Hobbes maintains, that people always act to satisfy their desires, it does not follow that those desires are always *selfish* ones. The parent who acts for the benefit of his or her child, the soldier who sacrifices himself for his comrades, the lover who acts for the happiness of the beloved all count as examples of agents who at least sometimes act unselfishly. A Hobbesian might reply that such actions must *really be selfish* after all. The parent gets personal satisfaction from helping the child, the soldier really wants to be remembered as a war hero, and the lover wants to bask in the affection of the beloved. But surely such a reply will not do. One might just as well say that all apparently selfish actions are *really altruistic,* and then proceed to explain away whatever counterexamples are proposed.

If one discounts a priori any data that conflict with a pet theory, it will be possible to hold that theory come what may. But such a path is open not only to those who hold that all actions are selfish but also to those who hold that all actions are altruistic. Rather than adopt such a dogmatic policy, it seems much more reasonable to distinguish acting on our desires from acting on selfish desires in such a way that the claim "All desires that lead to human action are selfish ones" becomes susceptible to test. Once the possibility of counterexample is allowed, it seems likely that at least some of the ordinary day-to-day cases of apparently altruistic behavior will turn out to be actually altruistic as well. Consequently, Hobbes's view of human nature as entirely egoistic seems altogether too pessimistic to withstand examination.

Moreover, even if we concede to Hobbes his view of human nature, he still faces serious difficulty. For given that all human actions are selfish, the Hobbesian state would itself seem to be an impossibility. For the sovereign to have the kind of absolute power Hobbes assigns it, it must have a powerful coercive apparatus under its control, e.g., a strong police force or army. But, given Hobbes's psychology, who will coerce the coercers? The police and soldiers will act in their own interest in cases where it conflicts with that of the sovereign. That is, the sovereign and its agents will be in a state of nature with respect to one another, resulting in a breakdown of the very coercive apparatus that is supposed to preserve law and order. Hobbes's psychology undermines his own political theory.

A second sort of internal criticism questions the Hobbesian derivation of an absolute sovereign. As the seventeenth-century philosopher John Locke argued, Hobbesian egoists would be irrational to set up such a totalitarian political order:

> though men when they enter into society give up the equality, liberty and executive power they had in the state of nature into the hands of society . . . yet it being only with an intention in every one

> the better to preserve himself, his liberty and property—for no
> rational creature can be supposed to change his condition with an
> intention to be worse.[14]

Surely it would be irrational to leave the approximate equality of the state
of nature simply to create a sovereign more powerful than any of one's
previous enemies. If so, Hobbes's deduction of the absolute supremacy of
the state over the individual seems invalid.

Indeed, one can follow Locke in denying that absolute authority is
needed to prevent chaos. Hobbes is committed to the incompatibility of
authority and autonomy. His philosophy reveals the danger to which such
a belief can lead when authority and law and order are given absolute
weight over individual rights. Hobbes's leviathan state is deficient on moral
grounds. As we will argue later, a state that violates the basic rights of its
citizens has no moral claim to authority to begin with.

For Hobbes, power relations are central. The state is simply a mechanism for avoiding the disastrous consequences of the use of power by all
against all. The Hobbesian emphasis on power may well explain the kind of
motivation that can produce a Watergate or CIA abuses but it hardly shows
that such a view of the political order is morally acceptable. Indeed, as we
have argued, if Hobbesian assumptions are correct, the authoritarian state
cannot work and the social contract that creates it cannot rationally be
signed.

A Hobbesian may respond, however, by pointing to the lack of alternatives. Reminding us of the alleged conflict between autonomy and
authority, he may claim that we abandon the authoritarian state only at the
price of individual anarchy and chaos. Since we have been given no good
grounds for accepting absolute authority, let us examine whether abandonment of the political order is the only option left.

The Supremacy of Conscience—
Robert Paul Wolff

It is possible to construct an argument for the abandonment of political authority by appeal to the work of a contemporary philosopher, Robert
Paul Wolff. Wolff argues that by analyzing the *meaning* of "authority" and
"autonomy" we can see that the two are incompatible. Given that authority
must be absolute and that we are not justified in acknowledging absolute
authority, it follows that no political authority ought to be acknowledged.

According to Professor Wolff, whose position here seems close to an
interpretation of the work of Immanuel Kant, when a person adopts a
moral position, he is acting as a legislator. That is, he is determining on
which rules or policies he is to act. As Kant argued, "moral autonomy is a
combination of freedom and responsibility: it is a submission to laws which

one has made for oneself."[15] Another way of putting this point emphasizes that there is a sense in which we cannot delegate our individual moral judgment to others. If we are faced with a moral dilemma, say whether to betray a personal trust in order to prevent great harm, we can of course decide to accept the advice of others. But so long as we function as moral agents, we must decide for ourselves if it is good advice, advice which ought to be followed. Being autonomous, then ". . . means making the final decisions about what one should do."[16]

"Authority" as we have already seen, refers to the *right* to command. Here we want to distinguish between the state actually having authority and merely claiming to have it. Just because people may believe that a particular state has authority does not mean that the state really does have authority. Believing something is the case does not make it so.

In a passage quoted earlier, Wolff formulates the conflict between authority and autonomy:

> The defining mark of the state is authority, the right to rule. The primary obligation of man is autonomy, the refusal to be ruled. It would seem, then, that there can be no resolution of the conflict between autonomy . . . and the putative authority of the state.

Wolff then concludes that "it would seem that anarchism is the only political doctrine consistent with the virtue of autonomy."[17]

The argument here, on at least one plausible reading, can be unpacked as follows:

1. If the state has authority over the citizen, then the state has the right to command the citizen.
2. If the state has the right to command the citizen, the citizen has the obligation to obey the state just because it is the state.
3. But if the citizen is obligated to be autonomous, then he is obligated to act only from reasons he himself regards as good.
4. If the citizen is obligated to act only for reasons he himself regards as good, he cannot be obligated to obey the state just because it is the state.
5. Therefore, it cannot be the case *both* that the citizen is autonomous *and* under the authority of the state.

If we add to this argument Professor Wolff's belief that our highest obligation is to be autonomous, it follows that we should object to being ruled and so reject the state's claim to authority over us.

Professor Wolff performs a valuable task in emphasizing the importance of individual judgment and autonomy. Note, however, that he accepts the very same assumption that underlies the Hobbesian view. That is, both Wolff and Hobbes could accept premise 4 above. Hobbes agrees that autonomy and authority can conflict—indeed *must* conflict—and fearing anarchy opts for absolute authority. Wolff too sees the conflict between authority and autonomy as inevitable and fearing absolute authority opts for autonomy and anarchism. But are Hobbesian absolute authority and Wolffian anarchism the only two alternatives? Must we either "Blindly obey it or leave it," on the one hand, or abandon the advantages of a political decision procedure on the other? It is to this issue we now turn.

RECONCILING AUTHORITY AND AUTONOMY

The reasoning in Wolff's argument appears cogent. *If* the premises are true, the conclusion must be true. But are the premises true?

One plausible response is to reject premise 2 on the grounds that in a democratic state at least, autonomy and authority are compatible. While 2 may hold in totalitarian societies, it does not seem to apply to democracies, where the people themselves govern.

Professor Wolff himself agrees that in a certain kind of democratic state, 2 would not apply.[18] In a direct democracy, governed by the rule of unanimity, each citizen would vote on all proposals of the state and the opposition of a single citizen would be sufficient to veto any proposal. Given such a system, autonomy could not conflict with authority since the (presumably autonomous) consent of every citizen would be required before any proposal would be carried out by the state.

As a matter of fact, however, there are no direct democracies operating under the rule of unanimity. Rather, existing democracies are representative in character and generally proceed by majority rule. Moreover, there is good reason to believe that direct unanimous democracy is grossly impractical. The vast bureaucracy and efficient technology needed to count votes on every issue are, at best, excessively costly and cumbersome. Moreover, as issues become more and more complex, there may well be need for a class of people able to devote full-time attention to political issues. Hence, there may be a need for representatives of the people who, in theory at least, devote more time to consideration of political and social issues than the average citizen is able to afford. Finally, since there hardly will be unanimous agreement on most political questions, a state governed by a unanimity rule would be virtually ineffectual. One dissenting voice on a given policy would be sufficient to block it, regardless of the degree of support it commanded.

Wolff grants, then, that under some conditions the democratic rejoinder is successful. His reply is that such conditions do not apply to the real world. Consequently, although the concept of the state having authority over the individual may be coherent, it has no application to reality.

Perhaps we should take another tack and challenge the belief that our highest obligation is to be autonomous. But, unfortunately, this would take us from the frying pan into the fire. The alleged incompatibility of authority and autonomy would have been left to stand unchallenged. Hence, no reply would have been made to those who would trample upon autonomy in their rush to protect authority. What we would like to show is that contrary to Wolff, on the one hand, and the authoritarians on the other, it is *possible* to acknowledge the state's authority and retain one's autonomy as well. (Whether one *ought to* acknowledge any state's claim to authority is another question.)

Our attention, then, will remain on premise 4. A plausible objection to 4 is that the obligation to be autonomous is not the sort of thing that can conflict with our obligation to obey the state's commands. Since each kind of obligation operates at different levels, conflict is impossible and 4 is false. All that being autonomous involves is exercising our own judgment, making up our own minds about what to do. Surely, then, we can decide for ourselves to accept the authority of the state.

To put the same point in another way, the obligation to be autonomous is not an obligation to decide in any particular way. It does not require a particular decision, only a decision. Thus, it does not rule out the autonomous acceptance of the state's authority.[19] We can be obligated to do what the state commands if we *autonomously* determine that there are good reasons for putting ourselves under the authority of the state and then proceed to do so. Consequently, we can acknowledge authority autonomously, so the two are not incompatible after all.

Such an objection, while it at least begins to clarify the relationship between autonomy and authority, is not decisive. More needs to be said. For even if we can autonomously place ourselves under the state's authority, it does not follow that we can *keep* our autonomy after having done so. That is, Wolff might argue that just as one can, by one's free choice, sell oneself into slavery, one can freely submit to the state. But then, so the argument goes, one is no longer autonomous. The slave is a slave, not a free person, even though he freely became a slave. Similarly, the citizen is no longer autonomous even though he autonomously assumed the obligations of citizenship. What we have shown, it appears, is only that one can decide for oneself to regard the state's commands as authoritative. What we have not shown is that once such a decision has been made, personal autonomy is still retained.

What we must still show is that autonomously placing oneself under the state's authority is or can be relevantly different from freely contracting into slavery. The difference emerges, we suggest, from consideration of what it is to acknowledge the state's authority and to accept the obligation to obey it. According to Professor Wolff:

> Obedience is not a matter of doing what someone tells you to do. It is a matter of doing what he tells you *because he tells you to do it*.[20]

We can see why Wolff regards obedience to authority with such distaste. It is because he equates it with blind subservience.

However, it is far from clear that such an identification always holds. Thus, there may be *good reasons* why each of us would favor general compliance with the dictates of some collective decision procedure. In our hospital example, if the physicians could not collectively agree on who should be treated, all the patients would die. In the political realm as well, the consequences of everyone generally acting on their individual judgment would be disastrous.

> . . . political systems *begin* from the assumption that some areas of behavior are too crucial to the mutual well-being and survival of the community to be left to the conscience of its members. . . . Hence, the starting point of a political system is the fallibility of conscience.[21]

One may regard the state's commands as binding, then, not simply because they are the state's commands but rather because there are good reasons for following the edicts of a collective decision procedure. Where one does obey, it is because there are reasons one has arrived at oneself for giving great weight to the edicts of the state.

Moreover, recognition of political authority does not preclude disobedience of at least some of that authority's commands. That is, one can acknowledge the need for a collective political decision procedure, recognize one such procedure as authoritative, yet correctly hold that its commands are *overridden* on a particular occasion. As many theorists of civil disobedience have claimed, it is possible to disobey particular laws or commands without calling the authority of the state into question. We will defend such a view later in our discussion of civil disobedience and protest. For now we note that it is far from clear that acknowledgment of authority requires obedience to each of the authority's commands or edicts. Rather, the authority's commands can be taken as only prima facie binding. That is, they are absolutely binding only in the absence of overriding factors. As one of Wolff's critics puts it,

> the citizen does agree [in a representative democracy governed by majority rule] . . . to comply with decisions that he himself may think wrong or unwise. But his agreement to do this is conditional, and it is he himself who is to judge whether the condition of legitimacy is met.[22]

At this point, one might want to object that a crucial question has been begged. Even if recognition of the state's authority need not involve blind subservience to its commands, it still requires that the individual give some weight to those commands in advance of consideration of particular cases.

Isn't the commitment to assign *automatically* great weight to the state's edicts itself an abandonment of individual judgment and autonomy?

It surely is true that if we decide in advance to give special weight to the dictates of authority when considering particular cases, then if we stick to that decision, we can no longer consider in each individual case whether to assign such weight. We cannot both accept and not accept authority. But if that is all Professor Wolff means to say, his victory may be a hollow one. Authority may be incompatible with a kind of autonomy, but the kind in question is trivial. In this trivial sense, we lack autonomy in writing a paper if we decide in advance to count the ungrammaticalness of a sentence as a strong reason for reformulating it. However, we still retain autonomy in the sense of retaining the prerogative to decide whether ungram- maticalness is a decisive reason for revision.

Professor Wolff seems to think that judgment is exercised only if we approach each case with no prior commitments about what factors are relevant to deciding it. But if we had no idea in advance on consideration of particular cases what is to count as a reason for decision, how could we possibly select which of the indefinitely many features of the situation are of significance? Moreover, once a selection had been made, wouldn't we be logically committed to assigning the same significance to similar features in similar situations? That is, wouldn't we be committed to a rule? If an autonomous decision is equated with a decision in which rules or pro- cedures play no role, then such a decision seems totally irrational. It must be based on whim alone for nothing else is left.

Consequently, one can acknowledge the authority of the state and retain one's autonomy as well if one does not follow the state's commands blindly or mechanically, if one is willing to override such commands when the situation warrants, and if one understands and accepts the reasons supporting such acknowledgment.

What we are suggesting is that in acknowledging political authority, one need not assume a commitment to obey its edicts blindly. Rather, what one may do is decide in advance of consideration of particular cases to assign special weight to the authority's commands, edicts, or policies. In our hospital illustration, for example, what made the dissenting physicians' dilemma so poignant is that they had agreed to regard the dialysis commit- tee's decisions as authoritative, and thought there were good reasons for doing so. Thus, on our analysis, the difference between one who recognizes the authority of the state and one who refuses to do so *is not* the difference between blind subservience and exercise of independent judgment. Rather, it is a difference in what one regards as the factors that ought to be considered in deciding what to do. The person who accepts the state's authority need only decide in advance of consideration of particular cases to assign a special weight to the edicts of the state. The person who refuses to acknowledge the state's authority does no such thing. Acknowledgment of political authority is not a matter of blind subservience. Rather, it is a matter of widening the sphere of what counts as relevant to the decision-making process.

In this connection, it may be helpful to consider David Lewis's example of the convention to the effect that if one is disconnected during a telephone conversation, the party who originally placed the call should call back.[23] There obviously are reasons for accepting *some* such convention here. What if both parties tried to call back at the same time? But to accept the convention is not necessarily to commit oneself to following it blindly regardless of circumstances. Rather, it is to acknowledge that in the absence of overriding circumstances, if one places a call and is disconnected, one should call back.

Professor Wolff's argument, then, is open to serious objection. Premise 4 ignores the possibility of autonomous commitment to a decision procedure. Such a commitment is incompatible with authority only if Wolff's conception of authority, as stated in premise 2, is acceptable. But, as we have argued, that view is itself dubious. Hence, while acknowledging the ingenuity of Professor Wolff's argument as well as its significance in forcing us to be clear about the concepts involved, we conclude that at best it is far from decisive and at worst seriously mistaken.

Accordingly, those who equate dissent from authority with disloyalty simply are in error. "Love it or leave it" does not cover all the relevant alternatives. Indeed, one can acknowledge and respect a given state's authority even while disobeying it, as we will argue later. Likewise, if criticism and dissent or disobedience are compatible with acknowledgment of authority, Professor Wolff's case for anarchism surely fails. The choice between Hobbesian absolute authority and Wolffian repudiation of political authority restricts the alternatives too narrowly.

Of course, none of this implies there actually is any state worthy of our respect—one whose authority we ought to acknowledge. However, it at least indicates that an inquiry into the conditions under which states might justifiably claim authority, and citizens correctly acknowledge an obligation to obey, is not necessarily pointless. It is to that inquiry that we now turn.

EVALUATING THE POLITICAL ORDER

Even if acceptance of political authority does not entail commitment to an authoritarian "love it or leave it" philosophy, it does not follow that we ought to acknowledge any actual institution's authority. Consider particularly the state. All too many evils, including the practice of genocide and slavery, have been carried out with the direct support of the state. Democracy itself is not immune to the grave misuse of power, either through the manipulation of the citizenry by unscrupulous leaders, the poor judgment or ignorance of the citizenry, or the tyranny of the majority. As the power of such states becomes greater and greater, it becomes more and more urgent to determine how such power may be properly or legitimately used. Accordingly, it is crucial that the state and its claims to authority be subjected to critical scrutiny.

Such critical inquiry might fruitfully pursue three lines of investigation. First, we should investigate under what conditions a state actually does have authority over its citizens. Suppose, for example, that an elected government is overthrown by a military rebellion that was to some degree the beneficiary of foreign interference. The new military government institutes a dictatorship and tortures members of the opposition. It claims to be the legitimate government and to have authority over the citizenry. Are these claims justified? If so, what sorts of considerations must be appealed to in the justificatory process? If not, what rules them out? If such a government lacks authority, how much different from it must other governments be if they are to have a legitimate claim to authority?

Moreover, even if we had a plausible account of the ground or justification of political authority, we would still want to know over how wide a domain such authority extends. May the state require a citizen to fight in a war he regards as evil? May it require citizens to pledge allegiance to its flag even though their religion forbids the making of such pledges? May it tax some citizens simply in order to make other less fortunate citizens better off? Presumably, even the most devoted advocate of law and order would wonder whether the state were exceeding the limits of its authority if it were to command him to adopt a particular religion or set of moral values.

Thus, even if we knew what conditions must hold for a state to have authority over its citizens, we should still want to know the proper *extent* of that authority. If such authority is limited, if it holds only within certain boundaries, we should also want to know just what such limits might be.

Finally, there is the issue of how the state should deal with violation of law. Are criminals to be punished or are they better regarded as "sick" individuals who require treatment and rehabilitation? Is civil disobedience sometimes justifiable, as Thoreau seems to have thought? Must law violators always be punished? For example, might the granting of an unconditional amnesty to those who oppose and refuse to fight in a particular war for moral reasons sometimes be warranted? And, in cases where the state itself has been in error or has tolerated injustice or is faced with the consequences of past injustice, what compensation might be due the victims?

Three distinct lines of inquiry concerning authority have been identified, as expressed in the following questions:

1. Under what conditions should the state's claim to authority be accepted?
2. How wide should that authority extend?
3. What are the obligations of a citizen to the state and its laws? What is the proper response of political authority to lawbreaking, on the one hand, and past injustice, on the other?

Each of these questions is important in its own right. Moreover, as we will see, each is closely connected to other important problems of political and social philosophy. Suppose, for example, that in answer to question 1, it was claimed that a state has authority over its citizens only if its treatment of them is at least minimally *just.* If such a position is to be sufficiently clear to serve as a guide for action, a clear defensible account of justice is required. Consequently, it is important to consider answers to questions 1, 2, and 3 not only because of their own importance but also because consideration of proposed answers will lead to exploration of equally important questions as well.

Identifying the Good State

One strategy for answering at least two of the questions asked above begins by considering what the state is for, what functions it serves, what individuals get out of it that they would not get without it. Hobbes, for example, believed that it was the function of the state to provide peace and security, even if this meant suppressing individual freedom in the process. Other thinkers have identified the end of the state with protection of human rights, the maximization of human welfare, or provision of opportunities for self-realization, to cite only some of the principal alternatives.

In our own time, much debate in the United States has centered on the role of the state in providing minimal material prerequisites of well-being for the citizenry. The extent of poverty in an affluent society has aroused considerable concern. Black persons, Indians, and members of certain other minorities have borne a disproportionate share of the burdens of poverty, unemployment, ill health, and malnutrition. In response, liberal advocates of the welfare state have supported "Great Society" programs as part of a war on poverty. Big government has been the source of food stamp programs, welfare payments, unemployment compensation, and Medicaid, to name just a few of the campaigns in the assault on poverty.

Others, arguing from a conservative point of view, have objected to big government. They maintain that welfare programs of the sort described are not only a threat to individual liberty but also are inefficient, wasteful, and do not do the jobs they were designed to perform. Not only are many persons legally required to pay for programs that they philosophically oppose but in addition they find a larger and larger share of their income going to others.

Liberals reply that government surely has some responsibility to those who cannot provide for themselves. At the very least, children, the disabled, and the aged would seem to fall into such a category. How can children through no fault of their own be doomed to a life of poverty? What of those who cannot support themselves? Isn't it the state's job to distribute resources so that hardship and suffering are eliminated or reduced to the extent humanly possible?

Our first task, then, is to ask what purposes the state should serve. In dealing with such a problem, we hope to shed light on the contemporary debate over the alleged evils of big government.

Moreover, if good states are those that perform their functions well, it can then be argued that the good state is precisely the kind of state that has the strongest claim to political authority, at least under certain conditions. What those conditions are and what degree of goodness is required are questions that also warrant further inquiry. It also seems plausible to argue that the limits of the state's authority are set by its function. That is, the state's authority would seem to extend only so far as is necessary to enable it to perform its function. In all other areas, the individual would be free of obligations to the state. Accordingly, we propose to explore responses to our first two questions by investigating what the function(s) or end(s) of the state might be.

In the next few chapters, we examine various criteria for evaluating the state. One criterion often appealed to is that of social utility. The good state is the one whose actions or policies produce as good or better consequences than those of alternate acts or policies available to it. It is to the ethical theory of utilitarianism and its application in political philosophy that we now turn.

NOTES

[1] For an excellent discussion of some of the issues involved, see Nicholas Rescher, "The Allocation of Exotic Medical Lifesaving Therapy," *Ethics 79*, no. 3 (April 1969): 173–84.

[2] Henry David Thoreau, "Civil Disobedience," in Thoreau's *A Yankee in Canada* (Boston: Ticknor and Fields, 1866), p. 125. Thoreau's essay is widely reprinted and is available, for example, in Hugo A. Bedau's collection, *Civil Disobedience: Theory and Practice* (New York: Pegasus, 1969).

[3] Robert Paul Wolff, *In Defense of Anarchism* (New York: Harper & Row, 1970), p. 18.

[4] Quoted by L. Stephen in *Hobbes* (London: Macmillan, 1904), pp. 17-18; parentheses ours.

[5] Thomas Hobbes, *Leviathan* (1651). Reprinted in Frederick J. E. Woodbridge, ed., *Hobbes Selections* (New York: Scribners, 1930), p. 186.

[6] Ibid., p. 188.

[7] Ibid., p. 253.

[8] Hobbes does suggest, however, that the nations of the world are in a state of nature with respect to one another.

[9] Hobbes, *Leviathan*, p. 257.

[10]Ibid., pp. 269–70.

[11]Some interpreters of Hobbes regard the Laws of Nature as moral rules rather than (as we suggest) prudential rules that it is in anyone's interest to support. We find such alternative interpretations unsatisfactory for ultimately some explanation must be given of why Hobbesian egoists would obey moral rules when it was not in their self-interest to do so. Usually, the reason given is fear of God's wrath. But that is just to introduce prudential considerations by the back door. For relevant essays and a helpful bibliography, see Bernard Baumrin, ed., *Hobbes's Leviathan: Interpretation and Criticism* (Belmont, Calif.: Wadsworth, 1969).

[12]Hobbes, *Leviathan*, pp. 335–36.

[13]Ibid., p. 340. Although Hobbes speaks of conferring all power on the sovereign, he does suggest that the individual always retains a right (or perhaps more accurately a power or ability) to attempt to preserve his own life.

[14]John Locke, *Second Treatise of Government*, 1690, chap. 9, sect. 13 (9, 13). This work is available in a number of editions, including that edited by Thomas P. Peardon (Indianapolis: Bobbs-Merrill, 1952), from which all quotations here are taken. Another useful edition is found in Peter Laslett, ed., *John Locke's Two Treatises of Government* (New York: Cambridge University Press, 1960).

[15]Wolff, *In Defense of Anarchism*, p. 14.

[16]Ibid., p. 15.

[17]Ibid., p. 18.

[18]Ibid., p. 22f.

[19]We owe this line of objection to Jeffrey H. Reiman, *In Defense of Political Philosophy* (New York: Harper & Row, 1972), p. 35, although Reiman makes different use of it than we do here.

[20]Wolff, *In Defense of Anarchism*, p.9.

[21]Reiman, *In Defense of Political Philosophy*, pp. 29, 31.

[22]Harry G. Frankfurt, "The Anarchism of Robert Paul Wolff," *Political Theory 1*, no. 4 (1974): 411.

[23]David Lewis, *Convention* (Cambridge, Mass.: Harvard University Press, 1969), p.43.

SUGGESTED READINGS

Baumrin, Bernard, ed. *Hobbes's Leviathan: Interpretation and Criticism.* Belmont, California: Wadsworth, 1969.

Benn, S. I. and **Peters, R. S.** *The Principles of Political Thought: Social Foundations of the Democratic State.* New York: The Free Press, 1965. Chapters 11-14.

Carter, April. *The Political Theory of Anarchism.* New York: Harper & Row, 1971.

Fishkin, James S. *Tyranny and Legitimacy.* Baltimore: The Johns Hopkins University Press, 1979.

Friedrich, C. J., ed. *Nomos I—Authority.* Cambridge, Mass.: Harvard University Press, 1958. A collection of articles by leading scholars.

Hart, H. L. A. *The Concept of Law.* London: Oxford University Press, 1961. Chapters II, IV, and VI.

Hobbes, Thomas. *Leviathan.* 1651. (Available in a variety of editions.)

Pennock, J. Roland and **Chapman, John W., eds.** *Nomos XIX—Anarchism.* New York: New York University Press, 1978. A collection of articles by leading scholars.

Reiman, Jeffrey H. *In Defense of Political Philosophy.* New York: Harper & Row, 1970.

Taylor, Richard. *Freedom, Anarchy and the Law.* 2nd ed. Buffalo: Prometheus Books, 1982. Chapters VII, VIII, XI, XII, and XIII.

Wolff, Robert Paul. *In Defense of Anarchism.* New York: Harper & Row, 1970.

———. *The Poverty of Liberalism.* Boston: Beacon Press, 1968. Chapter Two, "Loyalty."

Articles

Frankfurt, Harry G. "The Anarchism of Robert Paul Wolff." *Political Theory*, Vol. 1, No. 4 (1974), pp. 405–14.

Ladd, John. "Loyalty," in Paul Edwards, ed., *The Encyclopedia of Philosophy*. New York: Macmillan Publishing Company and the Free Press, 1967. Vol. 5, pp. 96–98.

Ladenson, Robert F. "Legitimate Authority." *American Philosophical Quarterly*, Vol. 9, No. 4 (1972), pp. 335–341.

Newton, Lisa. "On Reconciling Autonomy and Authority." *Ethics*, Vol. 82, No. 2 (1972), pp. 114–23.

Peters, R. S. "Authority." *Proceedings of the Aristotelian Society*, Vol. 32 (1958), pp. 207–24, reprinted in Richard E. Flathman, ed., *Concepts in Social and Political Philosophy*. New York: Macmillan, 1973, pp.146–56.

Two
UTILITARIANISM

Suppose one were to ask the following question of a cross section of American society: What should the United States government be doing for its citizens? Many people would answer in specific terms. For example, some would say that the United States government should be ever vigilant against the Russians; others would say that the government should lower taxes. Those who respond in more general terms, however, will say that the government should act in the general interest, the public interest, or that it should do what will benefit all Americans, not just the interests of business or labor, for example. Americans talk as if they want their elected leaders to serve all constituencies. A leader too closely identified with one faction or interest risks defeat at the polls. Many Americans, then, would argue that the purpose of government is to promote the general welfare or serve the public good.

Terms like "public interest" and "general good" have rich positive emotional associations. It may even be argued that such terms have more favorable connotations now than "motherhood" or "patriotism." Although everyone seems to be in favor of the public good or the general interest, it is very difficult to get everyone to agree as to what precisely promotes the public good. There is a tendency for each particular interest to claim that an activity or program that benefits its particular goal is really in the public interest while the activity or program that benefits a competing particular interest is not in the public interest. Each interest group has its own version of "What's good for business is good for America." Few, if any, interest groups have much of an idea of how to determine the public interest. However, there is a well-developed philosophical theory called utilitarianism, which does have a carefully worked out program for defining the public interest. The public interest is defined as the sum of individual interests. By examining this theory in some detail, the reader will see some of the advantages and disadvantages of a theory that sees the function of the state as a means for providing the aggregate welfare or public good, conceived of as the greatest good for the greatest number.

HISTORICAL BACKGROUND

Intellectual thought at the beginning of the nineteenth century could be characterized as a great battleground where various intellectual wars were waged simultaneously. There were battles between the defenders of the principle of the Enlightenment and the protagonists of the new vision of romanticism. Despite Kant, the war between those who believed reason was the proper path to knowledge and those who believed all knowledge was obtained through the senses continued to rage. With respect to political philosophy, the theory of individual natural rights and the utilitarian individualism of Hume were squeezed by followers of the conservative English political statesman Edmund Burke and by philosophers from Germany and France who argued for the supremacy of the state. During this period of great challenge to the individualist principles of political philosophy, three champions, Jeremy Bentham, James Mill, and the latter's more famous son John Stuart Mill, arose to carry the individualist banner. Their chief armor was their development and defense of the individualist theory known as utilitarianism. Utilitarian notions had played a part in the intellectual tradition of the West since the time of the Greeks, but Bentham was the first to develop utilitarianism into a full blown political-ethical theory. For this reason, we begin our discussion with Bentham's account.

Jeremy Bentham (1748–1832)

Jeremy Bentham was born in London and raised by a family with strict monarchical views. He studied law at Lincoln's Inn and during the course of his studies he was introduced to the contract theory of natural rights and obligations. However, he was also introduced to the legal works of the Italian writer Beccaria, the philosophical treatises of David Hume, and the economic writings of Adam Smith. As a result of these influences, he became skeptical of a contract theory as the basis for the legitimacy of the state because there was no empirical justification for asserting that any social contract ever existed. In addition he came to recognize that tradition, custom, and instinct had no foundation in reason. Indeed the blind adherence to tradition had created significant problems, Bentham believed. Hence, Bentham saw his task as one of reform. Using his individualistic utilitarianism, he believed he had the appropriate tool for the reformation of the major political institutions of his society.

Perhaps we can best understand utilitarianism if we consider a question that a legislator might well ask—"From among these competing policies, how can I choose the best one?" Bentham's answer was clear-cut. The legislator ought to choose the policy that leads to the greatest good for the greatest number. Indeed the test of the greatest good for the greatest number became Bentham's test for all social institutions. Upon applying his test, Bentham found many nineteenth-century English laws and institutions failing it. It is for this reason that Bentham's utilitarian principle was viewed as a principle of reform.

Bentham's earliest work, *Fragment on Government* (1776), provided a utilitarian critique of the British legal system and of its chief intellectual spokesman, Blackstone. In the criminal law, for example, Bentham believed that the traditional and formal classification of crimes and punishments should be given up. Crimes should be classified according to the amount of unhappiness they bring about. Punishments must be similarly classified to fit the crime. The basic rule is that the punishment must exceed the advantage gained by committing the offense. Penal institutions should make it likely that indeed crime does not pay.

Bentham's concern in punishment was not to set the moral order right, nor did he believe the infliction of punishment to be valuable because in some way the criminal was made to pay for his or her crime. Rather, Bentham argued that the infliction of pain was always an evil and hence was to be avoided unless it could bring about more good. One calculates the benefits of rehabilitation and deterrence that punishment effects and subtracts the pain that punishment causes. Punishment is justifiable only when the benefits exceed the pain. One should only punish up to that point where the infliction of pain brings about greatest benefits in rehabilitation and deterrence. Only in this way does punishment provide for the greatest good of the greatest number.

In order to apply utilitarianism, one must have an account of what is most valuable or intrinsically good. Bentham's view was based on his account of human psychology. He believed that human action was motivated by the seeking of pleasure and the avoidance of pain. He then concluded that individual happiness was the supreme good:

> Nature has placed mankind under the governance of two sovereign masters, pain and pleasure. It is for them alone to point out what we

ought to do, as well as to determine what we shall do. . . . The principle of utility recognizes this subjection, and assumes it for the foundation of that system, the object of which is to rear the fabric of felicity by the hands of reason and of law. . . . By the principle of utility is meant that principle which approves or disapproves of every action whatsoever, according to the tendency which it appears to have to augment or diminish the happiness of the party whose interest is in question.[1]

Having decided on what was most valuable, it was easy enough to formulate a utilitarian moral principle which stated that the right thing to do was to maximize that which was most valuable, namely, happiness. On utilitarian morality, one ought to act so as to produce the most happiness, the greatest good for the greatest number.

If one is to act on utilitarian morality, however, one has to have some way of measuring happiness so that the individual happiness or unhappiness created by any given act can be compared and summed up. Bentham is committed to a quantitative measurement of happiness whereby one computes the greatest total happiness by adding the quantitative units of individual happiness and by subtracting the units of individual unhappiness in order that one might arrive at a measure of total happiness. Bentham developed a device he called the hedonic calculus for measuring pleasure. The quantitative figure for any pleasurable experience is reached by considering its intensity, duration, certainty or uncertainty, propinquity or remoteness, fecundity, purity, and extent. Perhaps it is worth quoting Bentham's six-step process for evaluating any proposed action or event:

> To take an exact account then of the general tendency of any act, by which the interests of a community are affected, proceed as follows. Begin with any one person of those whose interests seem most immediately to be affected by it: and take an account,
>
> 1. Of the value of each distinguishable *pleasure* which appears to be produced by it in the *first* instance.
>
> 2. Of the value of each *pain* which appears to be produced by it in the *first* instance.
>
> 3. Of the value of each *pleasure* which appears to be produced by it *after* the first. This constitutes the *fecundity* of the first *pleasure* and the *impurity* of the first *pain*.
>
> 4. Of the value of each *pain* which appears to be produced by it after the first. This constitutes the *fecundity* of the first *pain*, and the *impurity* of the first *pleasure*.
>
> 5. Sum up all the values of all the *pleasures* on the one side, and those of all the pains on the other. The balance, if it be on the side of

pleasure, will give the *good* tendency of the act upon the whole, with respect to the interests of that *individual* person; if on the side of pain, the *bad* tendency of it upon the whole.

6. Take an account of the *number* of persons whose interests appear to be concerned; and repeat the above process with respect to each. *Sum up* the numbers expressive of the degrees of *good* tendency, which the act has, with respect to each individual, in regard to whom the tendency of it is *good* upon the whole: do this again with respect to each individual, in regard to whom the tendency of it is *bad* upon the whole. Take the *balance;* which, if on the side of *pleasure,* will give the general *good tendency* of the act with respect to the total number or community of individuals concerned; if on the side of pain, the general *evil tendency,* with respect to the same community.[2]

We now have a means for evaluating matters of policy and legislation. In facing a problem of what to do, e.g., staying with your sick mother or joining the Resistance to fight the Nazis, make your decision on the basis of the greatest happiness. Use the hedonic calculus to get a quantitative figure for the happiness of all relevant individuals affected by your act. Then, after adding the happiness and subtracting the unhappiness for each alternative act, perform the act that produces the most happiness.

In Chapter One, we maintained that three distinct kinds of questions could be raised about political authority. The first question asked under what conditions the state is morally entitled to authority. A Benthamite would argue that a state is entitled to authority if and only if the state promotes more happiness for the greatest number than alternative institutions, i.e., if and only if the state is justifiable on utilitarian grounds.

The second question asked what is the proper scope of the state or what is the extent of the state's authority. As a matter of consistency, utilitarian philosophy is compatible with a philosophy of a strong, socially oriented, paternalistic government. Since any state action that contributes to the greatest happiness of the greatest number is justifiable on utilitarian grounds, the logical justification for a strong central government is in hand. However, Bentham, influenced by laissez-faire economics, took a different route. He believed that the greatest happiness of the greatest number was best served by a very limited government. For Bentham, government action involved coercive action and coercive action created unhappiness. As England became a highly industrialized society in the first half of the nineteenth century, Bentham's empirical claim about the utilitarian contribution of limited government came to be increasingly challenged.

The third question asked about the citizen's obligation to obey the state and the appropriate response of a state to acts of lawbreaking. To the second part of this question Bentham's use of the utilitarian formula to reform the penal institutions has already been discussed. As for the first part of the question, Bentham seemed to believe that a citizen is morally obliged to perform any act that contributes to the greatest good. Bentham was quite unclear, however, on whether an individual was entitled to make claims against the state. Bentham does insist that the happiness of every individual affected by state action be considered in the formulation of state policy. However, Bentham provides no safeguards or guarantees that any particular individual's happiness will be achieved by any particular state action. The reason for this failure to provide any such guarantee for the individual will be discussed shortly. There is some evidence that Bentham feared that anarchy would result if each citizen were given the right to question whether this or that state action violated individual conscience.

Bentham's theory has been the target of vigorous and sustained criticism. We limit our discussion to three traditional critiques of Bentham's utilitarian political philosophy: a critique of its hedonism, a critique of its quantitative methodology, and a critique of utilitarianism as a normative test of state actions.

Bentham's hedonistic view that individual happiness was best understood in terms of pleasure soon came under ridicule. In fact his philosophy was sometimes referred to as the "pig philosophy." The difficulty centered on a conflict between the logic of hedonism and some commonly held beliefs on matters of value. In point of logic, under hedonism the pleasures of artistic creation may be no better than, or even inferior to, the pleasures of wine, sex, and song so long as the happiness of the latter is equal to or more than the former. It is charged that on hedonistic grounds it is better to be a satisfied pig than a dissatisfied Socrates. To see the force of this criticism the reader should ask whether he or she would willingly become a pig even with an ironclad guarantee that the life of the pig would be happier. Those who are still with us can see hedonism conflicts with our strong convictions that in fact some activities are better than others even if they are not more pleasurable.

It has also been objected that experiences of pleasure are not capable of quantitative measurement, that Bentham's hedonic calculus is really a useless device. How could one use the seven measuring devices of the calculus to compare quantitatively the pleasure of solving a difficult philosophical problem with the pleasures of a cool swim on a hot summer's day? Certainly Bentham's calculating tools are inadequate.

Even more serious are the moral objections that can be raised against utilitarianism. On moral grounds utilitarianism provides neither necessary nor sufficient conditions for justifying either state action or any of the institutions of government.

Utilitarianism cannot provide sufficient justification because some government decisions cannot be made on utilitarian grounds alone. For example, suppose a government could choose between two possible programs.

	PROGRAM ONE	PROGRAM TWO
Citizen One	3 units of pleasure	4 units of pleasure
Citizen Two	3 units of pleasure	5 units of pleasure
Citizen Three	3 units of pleasure	0 units of pleasure
	9	9

Since the greatest *total* happiness is identical for both programs, there is no basis on utilitarian grounds for choosing between them. However, other things being equal, most everyone would prefer Program One on egalitarian grounds. Equality provides an additional condition for evaluation.

Moreover, the traditional utilitarian formula "the greatest happiness for *the greatest number*" can provide conflicting results. Consider the following two government programs.[3]

	PROGRAM A	PROGRAM B
Citizen One	5 units of happiness	3 units of happiness
Citizen Two	4 units of happiness	3 units of happiness
Citizen Three	0 units of happiness	4 units of happiness
	9	10

Program A has more citizens happier than program B, but program B provides the greatest total happiness. Which program should the government provide?

A more important problem can be raised when one considers questions of population control. Consider the following situation, which reflects problems in the real world. If the government takes no steps to control population, 1,000,000 residents can be supported at a minimum standard of living. Let us say that such a minimum standard of living has a hedonic value of 10. Total utility for a population of one million would be 10,000,000, with the average utility for each person equal to 10. Suppose the population were limited by government action to ¾ of a million. This policy would enable each person to live a more comfortable life with an average utility value of 13. Total utility for the society would equal 9,950,000 utility units. Is it better to have a large population at a minimum standard of living or a small population that has a smaller total of happiness but where nonetheless each person is happier on the average? Utilitarianism seems to have nothing to say here. The reason for these paradoxes is clear. Bentham's utilitarianism is guilty of two sins of omission. It ignores the distribution of happiness and it ignores other values that should be considered when judging what a state ought or ought not to do. In the first of our examples above, the value of equality was ignored.

From our point of view, one of the most important values omitted from Bentham's utilitarianism is the value of individual rights. Indeed, failure to consider individual rights is one of the chief criticisms of utilitarianism today. We can illustrate this point with one of the most common and most persuasive objections against utilitarian analysis; the so-called punishment-of-the-innocent example. Consider the following situation:

A small city has been plagued by a number of particularly vicious unsolved crimes. The citizenry is near panic. All homeowners have guns; doors and windows are locked. The local police officer goes to the freight yards and arrests a tramp on a passing train. Investigation shows that although the tramp is innocent, he can be made to appear guilty. Without family or friends, utility, both total and average, could be increased if he were punished and the populace calmed. On utilitarian grounds the innocent man should be punished. But should he?

The objective illustrated in our story can now be generalized. None of our rights are safe from the measuring rod of utility. On the whole, our rights to freedom of the press, freedom of speech, and a trial by jury are consistent with utilitarian considerations but on occasion they are all subject to surrender. Indeed under utilitarianism there is nothing inconsistent in saying that a slave society is the best society. All one would need to show is that the happiness (total or average) of the slave society exceeds that of the nonslave society. Most of us, however, would not declare that the slave society is better even if it is happier. The utilitarians' lack of concern with rights offends some of our more firmly grounded moral insights.

Supporters of utilitarian theory denied that their theory had these undesirable consequences, or that at least Bentham's theory could be repaired so as to avoid them. These repairs began almost immediately and continue in the work of contemporary utilitarians discussed later in this chapter.

John Stuart Mill (1806–1873)

John Stuart Mill was stung by the barbs about the "pig philosophy" and one of his intellectual projects was to reformulate Bentham's utilitarianism so that it could avoid the objections of its critics.

Mill abandoned quantitative utilitarianism and the hedonic calculus that accompanied it for a qualitative utilitarianism. Mill vigorously maintained that some pleasures really are better than others. Pushpin is not as good as poetry. A dissatisfied Socrates' life is qualitatively better than the life of a satisfied pig:

It is quite compatible with the principle of utility to recognize the fact that some kinds of pleasure are more desirable and more valuable than others. It would be absurd that, while in estimating all other things quality is considered as well as quantity, the estimation of pleasure should be supposed to depend on quantity alone.[4]

Having introduced qualitative distinctions and having abandoned the hedonic calculus, Mill needed some other means for comparing and qualitatively ranking experiences. Mill claimed that we know one experience is better than another by consulting a panel of experts. Mill was not entirely clear as to how this panel of experts was to be composed, but one condition was that the members have had both the experiences in question. Having experienced both, they have met at least one of the conditions for making a qualified comparison:

> Of two pleasures, if there be one to which all or almost all who have experience of both give a decided preference, irrespective of any feeling of moral obligation to prefer it, that is the more desirable pleasure. If one of the two is, by those who are competently acquainted with both, placed so far above the other that they prefer it, even though knowing it to be attended with a greater amount of discontent, and would not resign it for any quantity of the other pleasure which their nature is capable of, we are justified in ascribing to the preferred enjoyment a superiority in quality so far outweighing quantity as to render it, in comparison, of small account.[5]

To those who might retort that such a panel of experts could not take the perspective of the pig, Mill argued that humans were qualitatively different from animals. Humans have a higher capacity that prevents them from desiring a lower grade of existence even if they would be happier. Mill refers to this capacity as man's sense of dignity. This sense of dignity provides the ground for qualitative distinctions among pleasures.

This reference to a human capacity might well provide the clue to Mill's answer to the moral objections to utilitarianism. It may well be that there are a number of human practices that if followed or human characteristics that if developed would lead to the greatest happiness. In other words, human rights are norms that are adopted because of their utilitarian value. It may well be that Mill was working toward a distinction that split utilitarianism into two camps. Today these two types of utilitarianism are most frequently referred to as act and rule utilitarianism.[6] Act utilitarians, like Bentham, argue that one ought to do those acts that produce the greatest good for the greatest number. On an act-utilitarian view, rules are mere shorthand devices that are suitable as rules of thumb but that are to be abandoned on those occasions where following them would not lead to the greatest good for the greatest number:

> Does the utilitarian formula leave any place for moral maxims like "Keep your promises" and "Always tell the truth?" Yes, these maxims can be regarded as directives that for the most part point out what is a person's duty. They are rules of thumb. They are properly taught to

children and used by everybody as a rough timesaving guide for ordinary decisions. Moreover, since we are all prone to rationalizing in our own favor, they are apt to be a better guide to our duty in complex cases than is our on-the-spot reflection. However, we are not to be enslaved to them. When there is good ground for thinking the maximum net expectable utility will be produced by an act that violates them, then we should depart from them. Such a rule is to be disregarded without hesitation, when it clearly conflicts with the general welfare.[7]

Under rule utilitarianism, however, rules have a very different status. On rule utilitarianism, the appropriate answer to the question "What ought I to do?" is, "You ought to follow the appropriate rule for that type of situation." However, the appropriate answer to the question, "What rules should one adopt?" is "One should adopt those rules which lead to the greatest good for the greatest number." Perhaps the difference between the two types of utilitarianism can be illustrated by an example. Consider the practice of grading college students for course work. Suppose that one of the rules for a grade of A in Mathematics 11 is a 90 average on quizzes and examinations. An act utilitarian would treat the rule of 90 for an A as a rule of thumb. In circumstances where utility would be maximized one could give an A for less than 90 or one could give a B for a grade of 90 or better. What determines each act of grading is the consequences of giving a certain grade in that particular case. The rule of A for 90 is a guide but it is not authoritative. For the rule utilitarian, things are different. A student with an 85 could not argue for an A on the basis of the special circumstances of his or her case alone. Rather, he or she would have to show that the grading rule of A for 90 does not provide the greatest good for the greatest number. The task of the moral philosopher, on the rule-utilitarian account, is to formulate those rules which pass the utilitarian test.[8] If Mill is interpreted as a rule utilitarian, individual rights can be construed as rules that protect individuals. These rights, however, are grounded on utilitarian considerations. Individual rights should be recognized only if by recognition of such rights the happiness of the greatest good for the greatest number can be secured. Whether or not Mill actually was a rule utilitarian is a matter of scholarly debate. However, interpreting him as a rule utilitarian enables us to see how Mill could construct a reply to those who criticized Bentham for ignoring moral rules, particularly rules for the distribution of happiness, and rules that protect individual rights. A society has such rules because they pass the utilitarian test.

Indeed one can more readily understand some of Mill's remarks on liberty, representative government, and laissez-faire capitalism from this rule utilitarian perspective. Mill saw the political philosopher's task as one of describing the procedures and institutions that make the realization of the greatest good for the greatest number most likely. In his writings on liberty, he attempted to describe the social and political conditions that must obtain, if individual liberty is to flourish. In his economic writings, he attempted to describe what social and political conditions are necessary to overcome the evils of industrialization, i.e., to increase the public good. For example, Mill's *On Liberty* discusses various institutional arrangements which support the free exchange of ideas. Mill was greatly concerned about the tyranny of public opinion—especially the tyranny of the opinions of the uneducated. Hence, one institutional safeguard he recommended in *Considerations on Representative Government* was weighted voting. The votes of the educated would count more than the votes of the uneducated.

In summary, one could argue that Mill strengthened utilitarianism by making qualitative distinctions among pleasures, by abandoning Bentham's simplistic hedonic calculus, and by finding a place for justice and individual rights within a utilitarian framework.

Criticisms of Mill   Mill's efforts, however, did not put an end to the critical commentary. Mill's critics argued that the attempt to make qualitative distinctions among pleasures was to concede that utilitarianism was inadequate. If the pleasure of listening to rock music is quantitatively greater than the pleasure of listening to Beethoven, even though Beethoven is better, what does the music of Beethoven have that rock does not have? Mill would say that Beethoven's music provides a higher pleasure. But surely Mill's response is deceptive. After all, how can pleasures differ except quantitatively. Beethoven's music must have some quality other than pleasure that makes us rate Beethoven's music higher than rock. Mill's appeal to higher pleasures is not an appeal to pleasure at all. Rather, by implication Mill concedes that there are some qualities that have value in addition to pleasure. In other words, there are a number of goods, in addition to pleasure, that are valuable.

In the late nineteenth and early twentieth centuries some utilitarians accepted this critique of Mill and formulated a new version of utilitarianism called ideal utilitarianism. Ideal utilitarianism asserts that there are many goods besides pleasure. What one ought to do is maximize the greatest goods for the greatest number. Ideal utilitarianism is not hedonistic but it still subscribes to the principle of maxima. In this view the function of the state is to maximize the total good.

Mill's substitution of the panel of experts for Bentham's hedonic calculus came under attack as well. Some argued that we could not say the life of a dissatisfied Socrates is better than the life of a satisfied pig since we could not get the opinion of the pig. At this level the objection misses the point since Mill stipulates that the panel of experts must have had both experiences. Of course, the panel could not literally live the life of the pig but, following Aristotle, the panel could contrast animal-like pleasures with the pleasure of rationality. This interpretation does not remove all the difficulties, however. Mill either assumes that the panel of experts will approach unanimity in their comparative judgments or that a majority opinion is sufficient to decide the question. Neither assumption would seem justified. Life styles are notoriously diverse even among the well-traveled and well-educated. There is no reason to think that a consensus would develop on anything but the most general value judgments. For example, most would probably say that the life of a dissatisfied Socrates is better than the life of a satisfied pig, but unanimity on much else is fairly unlikely. On the other hand the device of majority voting is hardly the self-evident correct device for deciding questions of this type. Finally, many objected to the elitism of Mill's panel of experts. Heavily influenced by the discipline of economics, which counted each person's desire as equal to every other, most utilitarians returned to a more refined hedonic calculus to measure and compare happiness. The economic theory of utility provided one such basis.

The most complicated exchange of ideas concerned the success or failure of Mill to find a legitimate place for rights and justice. Indeed, contemporary utilitarians have spent so much time discussing this issue that we should turn to their accounts of the matter. After a thorough analysis of these discussions we shall decide whether utilitarianism is able to provide the test for the justifiability of state actions.

CONTEMPORARY DISCUSSIONS OF UTILITARIANISM

Contemporary utilitarianism has developed considerably since the time of Bentham and Mill. Moreover, neither act nor rule utilitarianism has emerged supreme. An act utilitarian counterpart to Bentham is J.J.C. Smart.[9] A rule utilitarian counterpart to Mill is Richard Brandt.[10]

One of the challenges to contemporary utilitarians is to avoid counterexamples like the following:

> It implies that if you have employed a boy to mow your lawn and he has finished the job and asks for his pay, you should pay him what you promised only if you cannot find a better use for your money. It implies that when you bring home your monthly paycheck you should use it to support your family and yourself only if it cannot be used more effectively to supply the needs of others. It implies that if your father is ill and has no prospect of good in his life, and maintaining him is a drain on the energy and enjoyments of others, then, if you can end his life without provoking any public scandal or setting a bad example, it is your positive duty to take matters into your own hands and bring his life to a close.[11]

Act utilitarians believe that counterexamples like these are based on totally unrealistic situations. For example, the act utilitarian might say that it is extremely implausible to think that the decision to consciously punish an innocent person could remain secret. In addition, long-term consequences, such as the erosion of the sense of justice of the prosecuters, would work against the public interest in the long run.

On the other hand, suppose a careful act utilitarian does take account of such notions as justice, equity, and the dangers that result from breaking rules. Normally justice should be promoted, and well-entrenched moral rules should not be broken. But sometimes they should—namely in those rare cases where utility is maximized by breaking them and all the consequences of breaking the rules have been factored in.

But against such a response, consider that it may be extremely difficult to predict the consequences of acts, particularly those undertaken under pressure. At the very least, it seems to us that act utilitarianism does not offer sufficient protection for the innocent; the innocent are protected only in so far as complex calculations about consequences tend to come out the right way.

Considerations like these have encouraged other contemporary utilitarians to reformulate the rule utilitarianism of Mill. Richard Brandt's book, *A Theory of the Good and the Right*, is one such attempt. Brandt argues that utilitarians should advocate the adoption of a welfare maximizing moral system (or code of moral conduct). The rules in such a system would be suited to the nature of human beings and would take into account the intellectual capacities of the average person as well as the negative qualities the average human being possesses—negative qualities such as selfishness and impulsiveness. The code of moral conduct must be teachable and should have fairly concrete rules for frequent situations.[12]

Hence, Brandt thinks that utilitarianism is the principle which should serve as the moral guide for deciding what moral rules should be included in a moral system. Utilitarianism also urges us to consider psychological facts about human beings as various rules are proposed. Only in this way can you have a welfare maximizing moral system.

A similar argument can be made for the accommodation of individual rights. In fact, such an argument is found in David Braybrooke's *Three Tests for Democracy*. Indeed, Braybrooke refers to rights as rule-utilitarian devices. The chief purpose of rights in Braybrooke's view is to forestall some of the difficulties that attend act utilitarianism:

> However, one of the basic principles behind the practice of asserting and heeding rights is precisely to forestall general considerations of happiness or well-being and the like from being freely invoked to decide the particular cases embraced by rights. Neither the person asserting the right nor the agent or agents called upon to respect it

would normally be able in a particular case to review the alternative possibilities and their consequences really thoroughly. It would be dangerous to empower agents to act on such reviews as they can make: dangerous not only because the agents are liable to bias in their own interests, deviating from the demands of the asserted right in making the reviews; but dangerous also because the agents involved are out of communication with one another and do not have the information necessary to coordinate their actions.[13]

In this view rights are institutional safeguards to protect us from our own shortsightedness and bias in considering individual cases; rights protect us from the frailty of human nature. It does not seem wrong to conclude that in a world of perfectly rational and knowledgeable impartial observers there would be no rights at all. In the real world, utilitarians would argue that circumstances could arise in which we would want to say that rights should be given up in circumstances of that type; failure to give them up would lead to disastrous circumstances. However, for a few rights, the possibility of disastrous circumstances arising that would nullify the right are considered inconceivable. These rights, in Braybrooke's analysis, are inalienable and inextinguishable:

> Men may regard certain rights as inalienable, considering that the rights in question have emerged from profound social processes worth continuing respect. . . . There is, furthermore, an impressive empirical consideration that offers a strong defense, indefinitely continuing, for the inalienability of certain rights. Mindful of the weaknesses of human nature and aware of the imperfections of provisions for legislation, people believe that they will be safer if certain rights are kept out of reach. . . . Some rights, it might be said, are inalienable and inextinguishable for reasons that no empirical evidence could upset. Could the alienation or extinction of the right to a fair trial be accepted under any social conditions . . . if a society makes any use of the concept of rights to regulate its affairs then in that society there must be a right to a fair trial.[14]

Inalienable and inextinguishable rights are like other rights in having a ground in utilitarian considerations; however they differ from other rights in that empirical circumstances that would enable us to give up the practice are not a realistic possibility. In this respect inalienable rights are like basic laws of nature; falsification by empirical events is not to be expected.

The thrust of points of view like Brandt's and Braybrooke's is to find a place for our commonsense convictions about rights and justice within the structure of utilitarianism itself. Indeed the convictions and corresponding rights structure arise *because* adherence to justice and individual rights does work for the greatest good for the greatest number. If a system of rights did not work for the greatest good of the public it would soon be abandoned. Hence, the rights theorists are correct in emphasizing the importance of rights but they are incorrect in making them independent. We do not use rights to constrain utilitarianism; rather, utilitarianism is the justification for having rights in the first place.

CRITICISM OF CONTEMPORARY UTILITARIANISM

Perhaps the place to begin this aspect of the debate is with a hypothetical but very dramatic example described by Bernard Williams:

> Jim finds himself in the central square of a small South American town. Tied up against the wall are a row of twenty Indians, most terrified, a few defiant, in front of them several armed men in uniform. A heavy man in a sweat-stained khaki shirt turns out to be the captain in charge and, after a good deal of questioning of Jim which establishes that he got there by accident while on a botanical expedition, explains that the Indians are a random group of the inhabitants who, after recent acts of protest against the government, are just about to be killed to remind other possible protestors of the advantages of not protesting. However, since Jim is an honoured visitor from another land, the captain is happy to offer him a guest's privilege of killing one of the Indians himself. If Jim accepts, then as a special mark of the occasion, the other Indians will be let off. Of course, if Jim refuses, then there is no special occasion, and Pedro here will do what he was about to do when Jim arrived, and kill them all. Jim, with some desperate recollection of schoolboy fiction, wonders whether if he got hold of a gun, he could hold the captain, Pedro and the rest of the soldiers to threat, but it is quite clear from the set-up that nothing of that kind is going to work: any attempt at that sort of thing will mean that all the Indians will be killed, and himself. The men against the wall, and the other villagers, understand the situation, and are obviously begging him to accept. What should he do?[15]

It would seem that on any utilitarian analysis—even on the complex versions of Brandt and Braybrooke, Jim ought to kill one Indian so that nineteen others would be saved. A utilitarian of any stripe should find Jim's question rather easy to answer. A nonutilitarian might find Jim's question very difficult to answer, however. What makes the question difficult for the nonutilitarian is that something other than future consequences should be considered. Jim must consider not only the number of dead Indians, but the fact that if he chooses one way he is a killer, whereas if he chooses another way he is not. If Jim kills an Indian, then Jim himself has killed. However, if Jim refuses to kill an Indian then we cannot say that Jim has killed twenty Indians; perhaps we cannot even say that Jim caused the twenty Indians to be killed. What we think Williams is driving at is the fact that one's *position* in a situation makes a difference. There is an integrity of a position or role that cannot be captured under the utilitarian umbrella.

Jim does not have the same responsibility to the twenty Indians that Pedro would kill as Jim does to the one Indian he would kill. Of course, it may be that he should kill one to save nineteen, but there are *complications* in that question that no utilitarian can understand.

The utilitarian's failure to consider the position or role one holds in the chain of consequences is symptomatic of a serious deficiency in the way utilitarians consider individuals. John Rawls—at one time an adherent of rule utilitarianism—puts the criticism this way:

He charges the individualist theory of utilitarianism with ignoring the distinctions that exist among persons. Since utilitarianism has traditionally been viewed as an individualist theory par excellence, how is it possible that it ignores personalities? Rawls says that utilitarianism extends to society the principle of choice for one man:

> It is customary to think of utilitarianism as individualistic, and cer-
> tainly there are good reasons for this. The utilitarians were strong
> defenders of liberty and freedom of thought and they held that the
> good of society is constituted by the advantages enjoyed by individu-
> als. Yet utilitarianism is not individualistic, at least when arrived at by
> the more natural course of reflection, in that, by conflating all systems
> of desires, it applies to the society the principle of choice for one
> man. . . . There is no reason to suppose that the principles which
> should regulate an association of men is simply an extension of the
> principle of choice for one man.[16]

What Rawls seems to be saying is this. Under utilitarian theory, each person strives to maximize his net happiness with due account given to the intensity of his desires. So far, the utilitarian treats society as a single person. The satisfactions and frustrations of desires of the individuals in society are summed up, with the frustrations of some individuals canceling out the happiness of others. The policy that ought to be adopted is the one that maximizes net happiness. This answer looks at society as an individual who has balanced the gains and losses in order to achieve the greatest balance of happiness. Note the contrast in point of view, however. When Jones's desire for a third martini is denied because Jones wishes to avoid a headache tomorrow, both the desire frustrated and the desire fulfilled are desires of the same individual. However, when policy X, which leads to the greatest happiness on balance, cancels out the wants of Jones in favor of the wants of Smith, the analogy with a single individual is no longer legitimate. The frustration of Smith is not like the frustration of Jones's desire for a third martini.

Even though rule utilitarians and some antiutilitarians might endorse the same rules, the two schools look at the people governed by the rules in very different ways. The antiutilitarians do not treat people as means toward achieving maximum net satisfaction.

Just as the utilitarians make no distinctions among persons they also make no distinctions among desires. Utilitarians make much of the fact that utilitarianism is committed to equality, since each person's desires are given consideration. The important question, however, is how much each person's desires should count. The only factor most utilitarians consider is intensity. Those with more intense desires are provided with proportionately more pleasure. However, this is hardly the only difference that should enter in. Consider a racist society, for example. On strictly utilitarian grounds, the intense desires of the racist majority would count more than the more passive desires of the oppressed. Surely that is unjust. Indeed, the reader might ask, "Should certain desires be counted at all?" For example, would it be unjust not to count the racist's hatred? Many would think not:

> In utilitarianism the satisfaction of any desire has some value in itself which must be taken into account in deciding what is right. In calculating the greatest balance of satisfaction it does not matter, except indirectly what the desires are for. We are to arrange institutions so as to obtain the greatest sum of satisfactions, we ask no questions about their source or quality but only how their satisfaction would affect the total of well-being. Social welfare depends directly and solely upon the levels of satisfaction or dissatisfaction of individuals. Thus, if men take a certain pleasure in discriminating against one another, in subjecting others to a lesser liberty as a means of enhancing their self-respect, then the satisfaction of these desires must be weighed in our deliberations according to their intensity, or whatever, along with other desires.[17]

To conclude this discussion, one might ask what would motivate an individual to sacrifice his good for the public good even if those who gain are already better off. Traditionally the utilitarians have appealed to sympathy. However, to expect one to sacrifice further for those who are already better off is to place a heavy burden on sympathy indeed! Would not the less fortunate be extremely bitter at having to sacrifice even more for the benefit of the more fortunate? Rawls believes that sympathy cannot supply the complete motivation for utilitarian behavior on the part of individuals and that as a result a society with a utilitarian morality and political philosophy would be highly unstable.

In general we have criticized utilitarianism for failing to give an adequate account of how to insure protection of an individual's rights. The story of Jim's dilemma illustrates how utilitarians ignore the roles individuals play in the causal chain. One cannot say what a person ought to do by ignoring past obligations, commitments, and responsibilities. Neither can a state treat society as a superperson where canceling a desire of Smith to fulfill a desire of Jones is analogous to an individual's frustration of his one desire to fulfill another desire of his own. In addition, a state should not treat all desires of its citizens as equal. Moreover, it should not expect the less fortunate to make greater sacrifices for the more fortunate simply because total utility is thereby increased.

Utilitarians like Brandt and Braybrooke would respond that their more complex utilitarian formulas do take these complicating factors into account. They would argue that the more complex constructions of the utilitarian formula do not conflict with our widely cherished moral beliefs. For example, Brandt would argue that his formula allows utilitarianism to take account of such antiutilitarian sentiments.

Of course, one might refine utilitarianism so that rules and practices justified on utilitarian grounds were identical with the rules and practices that would be justified on some other nonutilitarian ethical theory. In other words, utilitarianism and at least one of its main rivals would sanction the same acts as morally right and condemn the same acts as morally wrong. To the reader, it might appear that we have a case of the chicken and the egg problem. However, that would be misleading. Even if the utilitarian and his rival agreed about what was right or wrong, they would continue to disagree on the reasons. For the utilitarian, the rules and practices that protect individual rights are justified because such rules lead to the greatest good for the greatest number. Should the world change and such utilitarian results no longer obtain, the rules and practices that protect individual rights would be surrendered. For the antiutilitarian the fact that the rules no longer bring about utilitarian results need not be a reason for abandoning them. The question now becomes what perspective should one take toward rules that protect individual rights and specify how happiness should be distributed.

CONCLUSION

We think the utilitarian perspective is inadequate and in the next chapter we develop a competing theory that places ultimate value on the rights of the individual. The answers to the questions of political philosophy are then assessed in terms of how well the rights of individuals are supported.

Even if a sophisticated utilitarianism such as Brandt's or Braybrooke's could give the same answers to these questions that we do, we would prefer our rights perspective to that of the utilitarian for two reasons.

First, the utilitarian support for rights rests on too shaky a foundation. As you recall, Braybrooke argued that there is "an impressive empirical consideration that offers a strong defense, indefinitely continuing, for the inalienability of certain rights. Mindful of the weakness of human nature and aware of the imperfections of provisions for legislation, people believe that they will be safer if certain rights are kept out of reach." From our point of view this provision for natural rights is too insecure. Let people's attitudes about the frailty of human nature become less pessimistic and human rights will be in danger.

Second, the very complexity of the utilitarian attempt to find a place for human rights suggests that we might do better to let human rights serve as the focal point at the outset. However, the reader is urged to wait until completing Chapter Three before making a final decision on the question. In concluding this chapter, let us return to at least two of our original questions concerning the state. Our first question asked under what conditions a state should actually have authority. A utilitarian would answer that the state should have authority to provide for the public good. Immediately one would then ask our second question: "What is the proper scope or extent of its authority?" To this question, a utilitarian would respond that the extent of the state's authority should be sufficient to enable it to provide for the public good as long as the cost of expanding state authority is taken into account. Let us now consider how an adherent of natural rights would delineate the function of the state and the scope of its proper authority.

NOTES

[1] Jeremy Bentham, *Principles of Morals and Legislation* (Garden City, N.Y.: Dolphin Books, 1961), p. 17.

[2] Ibid., pp. 38–39.

[3] This point, using the schema of both our examples, is made by Nicholas Rescher in his book *Distributive Justice* (New York: Bobbs-Merrill, 1966), chaps. 2 and 3. This problem could be avoided if the utilitarian simply used the greatest good as the criterion. There is some evidence that Bentham actually gave up the double criterion of the greatest good for the greatest number. See Bhikhu Parekh, ed., *Bentham's Political Thought* (London: Croom Helm, 1973), pp. 309–10.

[4] John Stuart Mill, *Utilitarianism* (Indianapolis: Bobbs-Merrill, 1957), p. 12.

[5] Ibid.

[6] Some philosophers like J.J.C. Smart use the term "extreme utilitarianism" to refer to act utilitarianism and "restricted utilitarianism" to refer to rule utilitarianism.

[7] Richard B. Brandt, *Ethical Theory* (Englewood Cliffs, N.J.: Prentice-Hall, 1959), p. 384.

[8] Some philosophers argue that a rule utilitarian who successfully formulated the rules that pass the utilitarian test would justify the same actions as an act utilitarian who successfully measured all the consequences of any individual act. The most outstanding book arguing for

this equivalence is David Lyons's *Forms and Limits of Utilitarianism* (London: Oxford University Press, 1965).

[9]See "An Outline of a System of Utilitarian Ethics" in *Utilitarianism: For and Against,* J.J.C. Smart and Bernard Williams, eds., (Cambridge: Cambridge University Press, 1973), pp. 3–74.

[10]See Richard B. Brandt, *A Theory of the Good and the Right* (Oxford University Press, 1979).

[11]Richard B. Brandt, "Toward a Credible Form of Utilitarianism" in Hector-Neri Castaneda and George Nakhnikian, eds., *Morality and the Language of Conduct* (Detroit: Wayne State University Press, 1963), pp. 109–10.

[12]Brandt, *A Theory of the Good and the Right,* p. 290.

[13]David Braybrooke, *Three Tests for Democracy: Personal Rights, Human Welfare, and Collective Preference* (New York: Random House, 1968), p. 39.

[14]Ibid., pp. 42–43.

[15]Bernard Williams, "A Critique of Utilitarianism," in *Utilitarianism: For and Against* by J.J.C. Smart and Bernard Williams, (New York: Cambridge University Press, 1973) pp. 98–99.

[16]John Rawls, *A Theory of Justice* (Cambridge, Mass.: Harvard University Press, 1971), pp. 28–29.

[17]Ibid., pp. 30–31.

SUGGESTED READINGS

Bentham, Jeremy. *Principles of Morals and Legislation* in *The Utilitarians.* Garden City, N.Y.: Doubleday, 1961.

Brandt, Richard B. *A Theory of the Good and the Right.* New York: Oxford University Press, 1979.

Braybrooke, David. *Three Tests For Democracy: Personal Rights, Human Welfare, and Collective Preference.* New York: Random House, 1968.

Frey, R.G., ed. *Utility and Rights.* Minneapolis: University of Minnesota Press, 1984.

Hare, R.M. *Moral Thinking: Its Levels, Method, and Point.* New York: Oxford University Press, 1981.

Haslett, D.W. *Moral Rightness.* The Hague: Martinus Nijhoff, 1974.

Lyons, David. *Forms and Limits of Utilitarianism.* Oxford: Clarendon Press, 1965.

Mill, John Stuart. *Utilitarianism.* Indianapolis: Bobbs-Merrill, 1957.

Narveson, Jan. *Morality and Utility.* Baltimore: The Johns Hopkins Press, 1967.

Sartorius, Rolf. *Individual Conduct and Social Norms.* Encino, California: Dickenson, 1975.

Sidgwick, Henry. *The Methods of Ethics.* 7th ed. Chicago: University of Chicago Press, 1962.

Smart, J.J.C. and Williams, Bernard. *Utilitarianism: For and Against.* Cambridge and New York: Cambridge University Press, 1973.

Articles

Brandt, Richard B. "Toward A Credible Form of Utilitarianism," in *Morality and the Language of Conduct.* Hector-Neri Castaneda and George Nakhnikian, eds. Detroit: Wayne State University Press, 1965, pp. 107-43.

Brock, Dan W. "Recent Work in Utilitarianism." *American Philosophical Quarterly,* Vol. 10 (1973), pp. 241–69.

Smart, J.J.C. "Extreme and Restricted Utilitarianism." *Philosophical Quarterly,* Vol. 6 (1956), pp. 344–54.

Three
NATURAL RIGHTS:
Meaning
and Justification

In his autobiography, the late black leader Malcolm X tells of an early experience that had a profound effect upon his life. At the time of the incident in question, Malcolm was one of the highest-ranking students in his largely white school. When a respected teacher asked him about his vocational plans, Malcolm replied that he would like to be a lawyer. The teacher looked surprised and replied that Malcolm needed to be realistic. "A lawyer," the teacher said, "that's no realistic goal for a nigger."[1] The teacher then advised Malcolm to think about carpentry as a career. Yet the very same teacher advised white students whose grades were far below Malcolm's to strive for success in the professions. It is quite evident that either because of his own prejudices or because of his beliefs about the prejudices of others, this teacher was willing to treat Malcolm in an unequal and degrading manner. It is just this kind of inequality and degradation that the doctrine of equal natural or human rights is designed to prevent.

However, before the natural-rights approach can be assessed, it must first be clarified. In particular, the concept of a right—and especially the concept of a natural right—must be explained and examined.

ANALYSIS

Rights

Compare two universities, which will be referred to as university A and university B. In each, it is sometimes the case that a professor grades a student's paper unfairly. The reasons for this vary from case to case and the incidence of unfairness is no greater at one institution than at the other. What does differ, however, are the methods and procedures for dealing with unfairness when it does arise.

In university A, if a student believes his paper has been unfairly graded and if he wishes to make an issue out of it all, he must *petition* the professor who graded the paper for an appointment. According to the rules of the university, however, it is entirely up to the professor whether such petitions are granted. Even if the petition is accepted, the rules of the university leave it entirely up to the professor whose fairness is being questioned as to whether the paper will be reviewed and the grade changed. There is no higher court of appeal. Of course, many faculty members at this university are conscientious and kind men and women. They will often call in colleagues to review a student's complaints and generally would not dream of turning down a student's petition for an appointment. However, according to the rules of the university, whether a professor chooses to act conscientiously and kindly is solely up to that professor. Students have no *claim* on the faculty nor are they *entitled* to impartial review. If some professors choose to act properly and others do not, then, as far as the rules of the university are concerned, it is a matter between them and their own conscience. At university A, then, faculty consideration of student complaints is a *gratuity* that may or may not be dispensed at will.[2]

In university B, things are quite different. Student complaints of unfairness in grading must be dealt with through established procedures. All complaints must be investigated by faculty previously uninvolved in the case. In university B, it is not up to the professor involved as to whether the grievance machinery is called into play. Rather, the student is entitled to impartial review upon request.

In university B, but not in university A, students have *rights* in the area in question. The example illustrates the difference between having and not having rights. The example also brings out the point that rights are *entitlements*. The students in university B are entitled to impartial review. Their claim to review is not dependent upon faculty good will or permission. Indeed, the domain of rights is to be contrasted with that of permissions, on the one hand, and benevolence, on the other.

The notion of an entitlement has justificatory import. If someone is entitled to something, his claim to it is justified, at least prima facie. The justification may be institutional, legal, or moral, depending upon the kind of right considered. Such a justification need not be conclusive. For one thing, rights may clash. My right to ten dollars from Jones and your right to ten dollars from Jones cannot both be honored if Jones has only ten dollars. Moreover, if Jones has only ten dollars, perhaps none of us is justified in claiming it in the first place, all things considered.[3]

If students in university B have a right to impartial review upon request, then they are entitled to such review. And if they are entitled to it, others—in this case, the faculty—are under at least a prima facie obligation to provide such a review. Rights imply obligations in the sense that if some person has a right to something, some other persons are under an obligation either to provide it or at least not interfere with the rights bearer's pursuit of it.[4]

Indeed, it is of crucial moral importance to distinguish obligations that arise from the rights claims of others from considerations of benevolence, charity, or noblesse oblige. A useful example has been provided by Richard Wasserstrom. Wasserstrom points out that during the civil rights struggles of the late 1950s and early 1960s, white Southerners frequently asserted that they had great concern for the welfare of "their Negroes." According to Wasserstrom:

> what this way of conceiving most denies to any Negro is the oppor-
> tunity to assert claims as a matter of right. It denies him the standing
> to protest the way he is treated. If the white Southerner fails to do his
> duty, that is simply a matter between him and his conscience.[5]

The white Southerner of Wasserstrom's example views kind treatment of blacks as a matter of personal benevolence. If indeed there are any obligations involved, as Wasserstrom's (perhaps confusing) use of the word "duty" may suggest, such obligations do not arise from the correlative rights of the blacks themselves. If we view persons as possessors of rights, we view them as agents, as makers of claims, as beings who are entitled to certain considerations whether or not others feel like going along. It is this aspect of the emphasis on rights which, as we will argue later, accounts for the important connection between natural rights, on the one hand, and human dignity, autonomy, and respect for persons on the other.[6]

It may be objected that to explicate rights in terms of entitlements is to offer a circular account. For what can it mean to say that someone is entitled to something other than that he or she has a right to it?

However, even if the analysis is circular, it is not necessarily unhelpful for our purposes. For our goal is not to offer a formal definition but rather to demonstrate the normative function of rights talk; namely to demarcate an area of individual inviolability which may not be invaded on grounds of benevolence, social utility, the public interest, or charity.

Perhaps a full analysis of rights would go on to explicate "X is entitled to Y" roughly as "X ought to have Y and it would be impermissible to deprive X of Y in the absence of a compelling justification." If moral rights were at issue, different kinds of moral theories could then provide different sorts of justifications for particular normative judgments about when X ought to have Y and why deprivations would normally be impermissible. Thus, rule utilitarians might see rights as institutional devices which forbid violation of the individual in direct pursuit of utility precisely because such a prohibition would indirectly promote the most utility in the long run. Nonutilitarians might argue, as we will do later in this chapter, that certain fundamental moral entitlements must be protected if persons are to be respected as rational autonomous agents.

For our purposes, then, rights are best construed as entitlements. Legal rights are entitlements that are supportable on legal grounds while moral rights are entitlements that are supportable, perhaps in the ways suggested above, on moral grounds. What then are natural rights?

Natural Rights

The doctrine of natural rights evolved over a long period of time and was often the center of political and philosophical controversy. The roots of the doctrine go back at least as far as debates among the Sophists of ancient Greece over whether justice is conventional or subject to objective warrant. Plato and Aristotle, as we shall see, argued that the nature of justice could be discovered by reason and so was accessible to all rational persons. And the later Stoic philosophers emphasized a natural law, binding on all men, that takes precedence over the particular laws embodied in human political institutions. As natural laws were held by the Stoics to be independent of existing legal principles, they constituted an Archimedean point from which the legal order could be evaluated.

The concern for the rule of law as manifested in ancient Rome led to further emphasis on the Stoic ideal of a law of nature. In A.D. 534 Emperor Justinian presided over the completion of the *Corpus Iuris Civilis,* a great codebook of Roman Law.[7] This codification of the law of the Roman Empire was to have remarkable influence, for one of the great gifts of Rome to later civilizations was appreciation of the significance of the rule of law. Justinian's law books claimed universal validity, and so reinforced the Stoic ideal of a law over and above the law of any particular community, applying equally to all. This conception of a "higher" law than that of one's community was acknowledged by many educated Romans during various stages of the Empire's development. Perhaps none expressed the idea as well as Cicero who declared:

> There is indeed a law, right reason, which is in accordance with nature; existing in all, unchangeable, eternal. . . . It is not one thing at

Rome, and another thing at Athens . . . but it is a law, eternal and immutable for all nations and for all time.[8]

This conception of natural law was further developed by Scholastic philosophers during the Middle Ages. The account defended by Thomas Aquinas has been especially influential. It fitted the Stoic belief in a rational moral order, analogous to an (allegedly) rational natural order, into the framework of Judeo-Christian theology, which sometimes identified moral laws with commands of God. This was done by identifying the natural laws with outpourings of divine reason which, being rational, were open to discovery by other rational beings. Aquinas maintained that:

> it is clear that the whole community of the universe is governed by divine reason. This rational guidance of created things on the part of God . . . we can call the Eternal Law. . . . But of all others, rational creatures are subject to the divine Providence in a special way . . . in that they control their own actions. . . . This participation in the Eternal Law by rational creatures is called the Natural Law.[9]

Aquinas emphasized that this natural law is a higher law than that of such man-made institutions as the state:

> And if a human law is at variance in any particular way with Natural Law, it is no longer legal but rather is a corruption of law.[10]

This conception of natural law, like that of the Stoics, provides an external, rational standard against which the laws and policies of particular states are to be measured.

The Scholastic conception of natural law, however, was intimately tied to a theological foundation and tended to be embedded in a theistic political framework. Although natural laws were held to be discernible by reason, they were also held to be promulgated by divine will. The political order, in turn, was held to serve a function determined by that will; namely, the development of distinctively human nature within a given social framework. However, in the seventeenth and eighteenth centuries, growing rationalism and growing individualism led to revision of the classical account of natural law and natural right. Such documents as the French Declaration of the Rights of Man and the American Declaration of Independence asserted the rights of humans *qua* humans against the state. The foundation of natural law and of the rights of the individual was placed in reason alone, rather than in theology. The political order, in turn, was viewed as an instrument through which diverse and essentially egoistic individuals could pursue their private ends and not as an agency for socialization through which the citizen would become fully human. Natural rights were appealed to in defense of human liberty and autonomy against what came to be perceived as the potentially (and often actually) oppressive power of the state.

However, with the rise of utilitarianism in the nineteenth century, the natural-rights approach entered into a long eclipse. Utilitarians, with their forward-looking consequentialist ethical theory, regarded only the effects of action or policy as relevant to moral evaluation. Right and wrong were held to depend on consequences, not on allegedly pre-existing natural rights. Thus, Jeremy Bentham helped to relegate the doctrine of natural rights to the graveyard of abandoned philosophies when he held that "Natural rights is simple nonsense: natural and imprescriptible rights, rhetorical nonsense—nonsense upon stilts."[11] Until recently, the doctrine of natural rights remained where the utilitarians had cast it.

But, as we have seen, a basic problem for utilitarian ethics is how to avoid permitting the oppression of a minority so long as the result is the production of the greatest overall good. The horrors of the Nazi Holocaust and the struggle for the civil rights of black persons in America seem to have motivated many to search for a normative political theory that asserts the inviolability of the individual. While utilitarianism, on any plausible interpretation, would condemn Nazi genocide, many reflective people have regarded the kind of protection utilitarianism provides for the individual as inadequate, resting at best on complex empirical calculations, and have tried to argue for the inviolability of persons on nonutilitarian grounds. Thus, the doctrine of natural rights has resurfaced, shorn of much of its excess metaphysical and theological baggage, in the form of a plea for human dignity and for the kind of treatment that makes at least a minimally decent human life possible.[12]

How then are we to conceive of natural rights? Traditionally, natural rights and natural law have been thought of as *independent* of any given social or political order. Thus, they can serve as external standards for the evaluation of such institutional frameworks. This explains the point of calling a certain class of rights natural ones. "Natural" has many opposites, including "artificial," "social," "conventional," "abnormal." In the context of natural rights, "natural" is in contrast with "social" and "conventional." Natural rights do not arise from any particular organization of society or from any roles their bearers may play within social institutions. They are to be distinguished from the rights of parents against children, teachers against students, and clients against their lawyers. Instead, they are rights possessed on grounds other than the institutional role of the holders or the nature of the society to which they belong. Conversely, natural rights impose obligations on anyone, regardless of rank or position. Since such rights are not held in virtue of social status, everyone is obliged to respect them.

Natural rights also are thought of as *morally fundamental*. That is, the justification of other rights claims ultimately involves appeal to them. They are the most general of our moral rights. Thus, the right to pursue a hobby in one's spare time can be defended as deriving from a more basic natural right to liberty from interference by others.

Moreover, natural rights are *general* rights, not *special* rights. Someone, for example, may have the right to limit your freedom because of some special arrangement to which you and he previously had agreed. Thus, if you promised Reed to carry his packages home, then he has the right to have you do your duty, even though you would rather do something else at the time. Such a right is a special right; one "which arises out of special transactions between individuals or out of some special relationship in which they stand to each other. . . ."[13] General rights, however, are rights that hold independent of the existence of such special arrangements. H.L.A. Hart has argued that special rights presuppose general ones.[14] For if one needs a special right in order to be justified in limiting another's freedom, then in the absence of such a special ground, others have the general right not to be interfered with. If Professor Hart is right here, we have at least part of the reason why natural rights are morally fundamental.

Natural rights are general rights, then, in that their existence is not dependent upon special relationships or previous agreements that rights bearers may have entered into. Natural rights are not only logically prior to social and political institutions, they are prior to human agreements as well.

In addition, many writers, including the authors of the Declaration of Independence, have held that such rights are inalienable. If this claim is taken to mean that it is always wrong to fail to honor a claim of natural right, the claim is mistaken. Since rights claims can clash, situations may arise in which we can honor the natural rights of some only at the expense of failing to honor the natural rights of others. Although this is lamentable, it hardly can be wrong if some such rights are not honored in this sort of context. No other alternative is available. (Perhaps, however, there is one right that is inalienable in this strong sense; namely, the metaright to have one's other rights counted in the moral decision-making process.)

More plausible interpretations of the claim that natural rights are inalienable are available. Perhaps they are inalienable in the sense that they must always be counted fully from the moral point of view, unless waived by the rights bearer under special sorts of circumstances. Thus, if there is a natural right to life, perhaps it cannot legitimately be disregarded unless the rights bearer himself decides that life is no longer worth living. Or perhaps natural rights are inalienable in the sense that rights bearers themselves cannot waive their claims of natural right. Thus, if someone were to say, "I give up my right to life, so go ahead and kill me," this would not entitle anyone to kill the speaker. However, requests for beneficient euthanasia in order to avoid the suffering of a terminal illness may constitute counterexamples to this formulation. Many of us are inclined to accept a waiver of the right to life in such circumstances. Perhaps, most plausibly, natural rights are inalienable in the sense that they cannot be waived except by the bearer and then only to protect another right of the same fundamental order. Thus, in the case of a request for beneficient euthanasia, we may view the patient as waiving the right to life in order to better implement the right to be free of purposeless suffering.

Someone has a natural right to something, then, if and only if *(a)* he or she is entitled to it; *(b)* the entitlement is morally fundamental; *(c)* it does not arise from the bearer's social status, the prescriptions of a legal system, or from any institutional rules or practices; and *(d)* it is general in the sense discussed above. In addition, natural rights may be inalienable in one of the several plausible senses mentioned. Condition *a* places natural rights within the broad category of rights while the other conditions identify natural rights as moral rights of a distinctive and fundamental kind.

THE STATE AS PROTECTOR OF INDIVIDUAL RIGHTS

As we have seen, utilitarian theorists regard the state as a maximizer of utility. But, as we have also seen, it is far from clear that utilitarianism provides sufficient protection for the individual. This leads to a non-utilitarian view of the state. For, from the point of view of the natural-rights tradition, it is the function of the state to protect and implement the natural rights of its citizens.

Perhaps the most influential spokesmen for this tradition in political philosophy was John Locke. As we will see, Locke, like Hobbes, used the social contract as a device to show that if the state did not exist, we would need to invent it. However, unlike Hobbes, Locke did not view all political and social relations as power relations. For Locke, human behavior was morally constrained by claims of natural rights. It was precisely the job of the state to secure such rights.

But just what rights do people have? It is an embarrassment to natural-rights theory that its proponents have been unable to agree on just which natural rights people possess. For example, the American Declaration of Independence speaks of the rights to life, liberty, and the pursuit of happiness. The French Declaration of the Rights of Man speaks of the natural right to security. Contemporary theorists defend rights to the material prerequisites of at least a minimal degree of well-being, e.g., the right to a guaranteed annual income. The Universal Declaration of Human Rights of the United Nations even includes the right to vacations with pay on its list.

Part of this divergence doubtless can be attributed to the fact that not every list is presented as a complete list. In addition, many lists do not distinguish fundamental from derivative rights. Thus, the right to paid vacations listed in the Universal Declaration probably can be best understood as a derivative right necessary to implement the more fundamental right to the minimal prerequisites of well-being.

Although some disagreement among the friends of natural rights can be explained away along such lines, deep differences remain. One such difference that is particularly fundamental concerns the shift in emphasis from negative rights to personal liberty—rights to do what one wills with one's own—to the positive rights to material prerequisites of well-being, which have been of concern to many contemporary defenders of human rights. Negative rights impose obligations on others to *refrain from interfering* with the rights bearer in the protected area. Positive rights, however, impose obligations *to provide* (or at least to support the sort of institutions that do provide) those goods and services necessary to secure at least a minimally decent level of human existence.

As many persons regard the positive variety of rights with grave suspicion, it will be worthwhile to examine both kinds of rights. The political philosophy of the seventeenth-century theorist John Locke is a paradigm example of a position that places nearly exclusive emphasis on negative rights. We will examine Locke's system in order to see if such an emphasis is justified. After considering Locke's position, we will go on to compare it with the expanded conception of natural rights suggested by the Universal Declaration of the United Nations. Next, we will consider the views of the critics of the modern expanded notion of rights. We will then be in a better position to decide just which fundamental rights, if any, the state ought to secure.

John Locke and the Referee State

John Locke (1633–1704) was not only an important political thinker of the first order, indeed one of the founders of the liberal tradition, but he also made important contributions to epistemology and metaphysics. In particular, his *Essay Concerning Human Understanding* is one of the classic texts of the empiricist tradition. The *Two Treatises of Government*, Locke's major work in political philosophy, is connected with the Revolution of 1688, serving both as a stimulus to and justification of it. The *Treatises*, particularly the *Second Treatise*, have exerted an important influence on liberal thought up to our own day, particularly through the United States Constitution, which embodies many Lockean ideas.

Both Locke's empiricism and his political philosophy were bulwarks in the seventeenth-century struggle against the entrenched privileges of the monarchy and nobility. Each stresses the tests of experience and reason in an attempt to question dogmatism in both epistemology and politics.

Locke's method in the *Second Treatise* (like that of Hobbes whom we discussed in Chapter One) is to postulate a state of nature within which no political sovereign exists. He then goes on to establish what sort of government the inhabitants of such a state could *rationally* establish. Locke may have thought there actually was such a state of nature. After all, as he points out, the different nation-states can be regarded as being in the state of nature with respect to one another. This, of course, is still the case. However, the actual existence of such a historical stage in human history is irrelevant to the force of his argument. Rather, we can analytically reconstruct Locke's purpose as that of showing what problems would arise if there was no state and hence why it would be rational to create one. Locke, like Hobbes, argues that if there were no such thing as the state, it would be necessary to invent it.

For Hobbes, the state of nature is one of war between each person and every other person. There are no reasons for obeying moral rules and life is depicted as "solitary, poor, nasty, brutish and short."

On the contrary, Locke's state of nature

> has a law to govern it which obliges everyone; and reason which is that law teaches all mankind who will but consult it that being all equal and independent, no one ought to harm another in his life, health, liberty or possessions.[15]

All men, then, are equal in possessing the natural rights to life, liberty, and property antecedent to the establishment of government. These rights are negative in that they impose obligations on others to *refrain from interfering* in the protected areas. Each person is given a sphere of autonomy that others may not violate. However, even though others may not deprive anyone of life, liberty, or possessions, they need not in addition take positive steps to provide property, or maintain life, or supply the conditions under which liberty may be meaningfully exercised. It is one thing, for example, to say that we may not prevent you from seeing a particular movie. It is quite another to say we must provide you with the price of admission. The equality of the state of nature is of the former sort, consisting only of "that equal right that each has to his natural freedom without being subjected to the will or authority of any other man."[16]

Locke then argues that rational persons in the state of nature would establish the institution of private property. This is important for, as we shall see, one of the terms of the social contract that establishes the state is that the state protect the private property of its citizens. The Lockean argument here is that the world is a storehouse created for the benefit of humans. Consequently, persons may appropriate the goods in the storehouse for their own use. The means of appropriation is labor:

> for this labor being the unquestionable property of the laborer, no man but he can have a right to what that is at once joined to, at least when there is enough and as good left for others . . .[17]

Property arises from labor, according to Locke. But, we are told, labor yields property only when there is "enough and as good left over for others." If we assume approximate equality of ability and need, this requirement seems to lead to a fairly egalitarian distribution of goods, where all those willing and able to work end up with about the same amount of possessions.

In the state of nature, the world is a storehouse for human use. If any person were to take more than could be used, the surplus would spoil, thus depriving others of their due. This spoilage problem could be avoided, however, if an imperishable medium of exchange were to be introduced. Money is precisely such a thing. If a farmer, for example:

> would give his nuts for a piece of metal, pleased with its color, or exchange his sheep for shells, or wool for a sparkling pebble or diamond, and keep these . . . he invaded not the right of others.[18]

For, as we have seen, Locke limits the property owner, not in the amount of possessions that can be accumulated, but rather to the accumulation of what will not spoil, so long as enough and as good is left for others. As long as one's possessions do not spoil and others have the liberty and opportunity to try to accumulate possessions of their own, no limit is set on the amount one might own. Consequently:

> it is plain that men have agreed to a disproportionate and unequal possession . . . having by tacit and voluntary consent found out a way how a man may fairly possess more than he himself can use the product of by receiving in exchange for the surplus gold and silver. . . .[19]

Through the introduction of money, the state of nature becomes one of *unequal* distribution in which some persons amass huge amounts of property through talent, effort, exchanges on the marketplace, and plain good fortune. Locke could have used his restriction on accumulation of personal property in defense of egalitarian distribution of wealth. Instead, he introduced inequality into the state of nature, thereby justifying inequality in civil society. Inequality results since people differ in talent, willingness to exert effort, business acumen in market transactions, and in good fortune. Such difference produces unequal possessions. And since, as we will see, people enter civil society to at least in part preserve their property, inequality carries over into the state itself.

The right to property, like the other Lockean rights we have considered, is negative. No one is obliged to provide property for anyone else. Rather, the only obligations are those of noninterference. Inhabitants of the state of nature are obligated not to deprive each other of the fruits of their labor or of possessions secured through contractual arrangements for the exchange of such possessions.

What rational consideration might induce an inhabitant of such a state to contract with others to establish political society? Several reasons are cited by Locke, although he does not always clearly distinguish them. For one thing, there is no impartial judiciary to enforce the law of nature. Consequently, persons become judges in their own case. Moreover, after such "judges" hand down their decisions, there is no one to enforce them save the parties to the dispute themselves. This hardly makes either for fair and impartial decision making, or for peaceful acceptance of decisions by all parties concerned. Even worse, everyone cannot be counted upon to obey the natural law at all times or to respect the rights of others. Indeed, any dispute might end in conflict. Consequently:

> to avoid the state of war—wherein there is no appeal but to heaven and wherein even the least difference is apt to end where there is no authority to decide between the contenders—is one great reason of men's putting themselves into society and quitting the state of nature.[20]

However, since "no rational creature can be supposed to change his condition for an intention to be the worse,"[21] people do not give up all of their rights to the state. The Lockean state is not the Hobbesian leviathan. Rather, the individual insofar as he is rational only surrenders his right to executive and judiciary power. And he does so only on the condition that the state secure his own natural rights to life, liberty, and property.[22] Moreover, since for Locke the state is simply the *community* formed by the contract, the policy of the state is to be determined by the community, or where unanimous agreement is unobtainable, by a majority vote of the members.[23] Of course, such a majority vote cannot override the basic terms of the social contract—that the individual surrender his right to interpret and enforce the laws of nature and that the state protect his rights to life, liberty, and property within a framework of public law governing everyone equally. The state, then, is the protector of the natural rights of its citizens. For, in Locke's view, it is only to form such a state that it would be rational to leave the state of nature in the first place.

Natural rights, and the state's role in protecting them, are negative in Locke's view. That is, the rights obligate others not to provide essential goods and services but simply to refrain from interfering with each individual's attempt to provide such goods and services for himself. Similarly, the state is not conceived of as a provider of welfare but rather has the negative role of referee. Its job (aside from providing defense against external enemies) is to regulate economic competition by making sure that each competitor respects the rights of others. The Locken state is an umpire making sure that each citizen, in freely pursuing his own welfare, does not infringe on the similar free enterprise of others.

Critique of the Lockean position   A principal objection to the Lockean account of the state is that it permits too unequal a distribution of economic wealth. As we have seen, inequality is introduced into the state of nature through the medium of monetary means of exchange, and is perpetuated into society through the social contract. Indeed, significantly unequal distribution of wealth is characteristic of many Western countries.

Such inequality arises basically from open competition on the free market, at least in an ideal Lockean state. But, in competition for property, children of the previous generation's winners will have far more chance for material success than those of the previous generation's losers. So, in any generation after the first, many competitors will accumulate material goods at least partially because of their advanced starting position rather than because of their own abilities. Although all will have the right to property, they will be unequal in their actual power to amass it. Indeed, the rules of the Lockean free-market competition seem to allow a small group of successful entrepreneurs and their descendants to control an overwhelming amount of property indefinitely. Accordingly, proponents of such economic competition, if they actually favor *fair* competition, must supplement the rules of free-market exchange with some form of income, property, or power redistribution. This amounts to allowing other rights over and above the negative right to liberty and consequently entails abandonment of the referee theory of the minimal state.

It might be objected that if someone *earns* money, they are *entitled* to it.[24] Redistribution is unjust when it involves violation of rights, and persons surely have a right to that which they earned. We will discuss this entitlement theory at length later, but perhaps the following will suffice for now. For people to be entitled to what they acquire in the free market, the initial conditions under which bargaining takes place must be fair. But the initial bargaining positions are not fair if some people are so deprived of basic necessities and education that they cannot develop skills or compete with any real chance of success. Accordingly, the very idea of an entitlement *presupposes* at least a minimal welfare base which guarantees each competitor access to education, health care, and adequate diet and other necessities. Thus, the protest that redistributive measures fail to respect the entitlements of property owners is open to the objection that such entitlements can arise only when redistributive measures guarantee fair access to the competition for property in the first place.

The case that fairness requires more than minimal Lockean rights to liberty also can be based upon Locke's own model of the social contract. The usefulness of the contract model is that it can function as a test for fairness. If we ourselves would agree to a particular social contract under reasonable conditions of choice, the terms of the contract are arguably fair. Conversely, if the terms are such that it would be irrational for us to consent to them, they are arguably unfair. In order to test the fairness of Locke's minimal state, then, we can ask whether contract makers agree to the social contract which creates it.

Locke assumes that the contract makers would build the economic inequality found in the state of nature into the structure of political society. But surely this assumption is questionable. Why would the have-nots in the state of nature enter such an inegalitarian society in the first place? Surely, they would only sign the contract if they realized some gain from doing so. The rule of law, as Locke would argue, is indeed a gain, but it is much more of a gain to those who have property which the law can protect than for those who are poor. It seems plausible, then, that rational contractors would only agree to enter the state if they were guaranteed at least a minimal level of goods and services which would enable them to function as citizens and to want the protection of the law in the first place.

In addition to redistributive arguments based on the requirement of fair competition (arguments which on some interpretations of what fairness requires may have quite strong redistributive implications), we can also argue that the very factors which guarantee Lockean rights to liberty also count in favor of positive rights to necessities. After all, liberty surely is important because it allows us to determine the course of our own lives and to function autonomously. But arguably, medical care, education, food and shelter also are necessary if we are to develop as autonomous agents with plans of life worth living by.

Thus, even if people are entitled to what they earn, it does not follow that such an entitlement is absolute. For persons may also have positive rights to sufficient goods and services to make at least a minimally decent human existence possible. If so, persons may not have an absolute right to everything they earn. Rather, they may be obligated to contribute to efforts designed to satisfy the basic needs of others. Proponents of the entitlement theory, then, cannot simply assume that the only fundamental rights are Lockean negative ones.[25]

Consequently, defenders of the minimal state, which protects only negative rights to liberty, are open to the charges that (1) the economic competition it referees is unfair; (2) the inequalities it sanctions are not likely to be acceptable to all rational individuals under reasonable conditions of choice; and (3) the exclusive emphasis on negative rights is arbitrary.

We conclude that Locke's general account of the principal function of the state is sound. That function should be to protect the natural or human rights of its citizens. However, as our discussion suggests, it does not follow that the state's exclusive concern should be with negative rights to liberty, as exercised in the free market. As we have seen, there is a case for what might be called positive rights, rights to the receipt of basic goods and services, as well.

Positive Rights—The Universal Declaration of Human Rights and the Welfare State

The Universal Declaration of Human Rights was adopted and proclaimed by the General Assembly of the United Nations on December 10, 1948. An examination of this document reveals that many of the rights included go far beyond the negative ones protected by Locke's referee state. For example, consider the following articles:

> *Article 22;* Everyone, as a member of society . . . is entitled to realization . . . in acordance with the organization and resources of each State, of the economic, social, and cultural rights indispensable for his dignity and the free development of his personality.
> *Article 25:* (1) Everyone has the right to a standard of living adequate for the health and well being of himself and his family, including food, clothing, housing and medical care and necessary social services. . . .
> *Article 26:* Everyone has the right to education. Education shall be free, at least in the elementary and fundamental stages.

Unlike Lockean rights, which obligate others not to interfere with personal liberty, the positive rights of The Universal Declaration require more. In addition, they obligate each of us to support or, where they do not exist, work for the creation of institutions that can provide the necessary goods and services. The state, which is presumably the fundamental political unit capable of guaranteeing such rights, becomes responsible for the welfare of its citizens as well as their liberty.

The critique of positive rights   The concept of positive natural or human rights has been criticized on several grounds. We will consider some of the most important here, leaving a fuller account of other significant issues involved for later consideration.

A principal objection to the kind of social and economic rights mentioned in Articles 22, 25, and 26 of The Universal Declaration is that they do not fulfill some of the conceptual requirements for counting as natural rights. The first requirement is that of practicality. As Maurice Cranston points out:

> The traditional "political and civil" rights can . . . be readily secured by fairly simple legislation. Since those rights are for the most part

rights against government interference with a man's activities, a large part of the legislation needed has to do no more than restrain the government's own executive arm. This is no longer the case when we turn to "the right to work," "the right to social security," and so forth. . . . For millions of people who live in those parts of Asia, Africa, and South America where industrialization has hardly begun, such claims are vain and idle.[26]

Moreover, it is held that natural rights must be rights that impose obligations on everyone. Yet such rights as the right to work or to free education seem to be, at best, rights against one's government and not rights against all humankind.[27] Since social and economic rights fail these tests of practicality and universality, they cannot be natural rights to begin with.

Yet another objection rests on an alleged important conceptual difference between the two kinds of rights. Negative rights, by definition, impose obligations to *refrain from acting* in proscribed ways. Positive rights impose obligations *to act* in a required manner. But, so the objection goes, no one is morally required to perform the kinds of acts enjoined. Such acts may be beneficent and altruistic and, as such, should be encouraged. However, they are not morally obligatory. Thus, it may be praiseworthy if a family were to give half its annual income to those less affluent, but they are hardly blameworthy if they fail to do so.

According to the objection, then, there are no positive natural rights. For if there were positive natural rights, people would be obligated not simply to refrain from harming others but to go out of their way to benefit others. And, it is held, there is no such obligation.

Sometimes positive rights are criticized on the ground that their implementation is incompatible with the attainment of other important goods. Thus, it frequently is claimed that the implementation of positive rights would involve drastic and unjustified restrictions on liberty. For in order to appropriate resources needed to honor positive-rights claims, the state would have to limit the individual's right to do with his property what he wills. One cannot spend for oneself that portion of one's income that the government taxes in order to make social security or welfare payments to others. Indeed, some critics have gone so far as to characterize the welfare state as a near slave-master which in effect forces people to work in order to appropriate earnings for the support of others.[28]

To review, positive rights have been criticized on the ground that (a) they are impractical since they cannot be readily secured by fairly simple legislation, (b) they do not impose universal obligations, (c) they impose positive obligations *to* act when there can be no such obligation, and (d) their implementation would require extensive violations of the right to liberty. Are these objections decisive?

A response to the critique   While critics are right to worry that with the addition of positive rights, the idea of natural or human rights may become too bloated, their wholesale dismissal of positive rights is open to question. Indeed, some contemporary philosophers have argued that the whole positive-negative rights distinction is a confused one and that all rights have positive and negative elements.[29] Thus, as Henry Shue argues, if the right to liberty is to be significant, citizens have an obligation *to* provide the resources to support the police and judiciary system.[30] Similarly, all rights may sometimes require us simply to refrain from harming others and at other times to provide positive aid.[31] Before deciding whether the distinction between positive and negative rights makes sense, however, we need to assess points (a)-(d) summarized above.

Now consider the practicality requirement. It surely is true that poor nations will have a harder time satisfying social and economic rights claims than will rich countries. In some cases, they may find it impossible. However, note that exactly the same situation can arise with respect to negative rights. In a technologically underdeveloped country, there may not exist the efficient means of communication and transportation so necessary to prevent acts of violence, the practice of slavery, or even the extermination of one group by another. Here, we should note that Article 22 specifies that each country is obligated to honor social and political rights *in accordance with its available resources.* In other words, each state (and individual too for that matter) is obligated to do what it can in light of its individual situation.[32] This applies to both negative and positive rights alike. Besides, suppose that providing for traditional positive rights does cost more than providing for traditional negative rights. How does that save the distinction? Both kinds of rights need support if they are to be enjoyed.

What about the requirement of universality, which states that natural rights impose obligations on everyone? It supposedly follows from this requirement that positive rights cannot be natural rights. For, in this view, the bearers of positive rights have claims only against their own governments, not on everyone wherever they may be. For example, if you have a negative right to liberty, everyone—even people on the other side of the world—are under an obligation to avoid illegitimate interference with your activities. There seems to be no conceptual difficulties here, for the obligation imposed does not call on anyone to perform any positive act but only calls on them to refrain from acting in certain proscribed ways. Suppose, however, you have the positive right to a free education. Surely, it is implausible to say that inhabitants of China have an obligation equal to anyone else's to provide you with the needed schools. Rather, it is up to your government to provide the needed institutions and so the scope of your positive right is limited.

While we agree that rights claims can become unduly inflated, and acknowledge that individuals should not be reduced to mere means for satisfying the positive rights of others, we suggest nevertheless that this objection to positive rights is overstated. The distinction it attempts to draw does not stand up under examination. True, it is the state's job to implement positive rights but this is often true of negative rights as well. If you have a negative right to liberty, the primary obligation imposed is the negative one of noninterference. But, as in Lockean theory, it may be rational to delegate to the state the authority to enforce laws designed to protect liberty. Of course, it is one thing to say that the state ought to protect citizens from illegitimate interference with their activities and quite another to say the state ought to provide positive goods and opportunities. But, in either case, the conceptual point remains the same. The special responsibilities of the state do not *replace* those of private citizens. Rather, the good state is an instrument through which citizens can most efficiently *discharge* their obligations.

In the case of both negative and positive rights, such obligations are not restricted to one's fellow citizens. Rather, if the rights in question are natural ones, they impose obligations on everyone in both kinds of cases. But it sometimes may be more efficient for each government to concentrate on fulfilling the rights claims of its own citizens. Indeed, it can be argued that if governments were encouraged or even permitted to assume each other's responsibilities in this area, each would spread itself so thin as to lose authority and so satisfy fewer rights claims than would otherwise be the case.

What about claim (c) which maintains that there can be no positive obligations? This claim seems to simply beg the very question at issue. Simply to assume that we can't be obligated to do something (rather than refrain from doing something) is just what is being argued for. One cannot establish that there are no positive obligations as a conclusion by simply asserting that very same point as a premise.

Finally, would recognition of positive rights require extensive violations of the negative right to liberty? There is a danger that positive rights can become so bloated that the individual becomes a mere resource for satisfying the claims of others. There is a genuine problem in specifying just where positive rights claims become so extensive as to violate the liberty of others.

However, this does not mean there are no such claims. After all, as Shue points out, negative rights may also impose positive obligations which can threaten liberty. How much can the state ask you to give up to support the police, who in turn protect others from coercion? The very same problem arises for each kind of right.

Moreover, Shue argues that often the right to a minimum standard of well-being requires no more than protection from the acts of others—just the kind of protection required for a right to liberty.[33] For example, suppose a factory owner moves one of his plants to an even more profitable location. Since the factory to be closed is the chief industry in this small town, a large number of people will simply be unable to support themselves. Hasn't the right to a minimum standard of living been violated by the action of the factory owner in just the same way that a kidnapper violates a person's freedom?

Some who defend the traditional distinction would say, "No." There is a difference between actively harming someone and having the harm result as an unfortunate by-product. That reply might do for a national disaster, e.g., if a tornado had leveled the factory. But moving a factory is *not* like having a factory destroyed. Moving a factory is a purposive human action, and it causes harm just as the acts of a kidnapper cause harm. What presumably distinguishes the factory owner from the kidnapper is the motive for the act. But how does a difference in motive preserve the distinction between negative and positive rights? Perhaps basic rights should be protected against violators with good or neutral motives. Otherwise rights would not be basic moral furniture.

Shue concludes by arguing that there are no fundamental distinctions among basic rights. However, there are distinctions among the duties required to honor rights—specifically duties to avoid depriving, duties to protect from deprivation, and duties to aid the deprived. These duties hold for both the traditional rights—as the chart below indicates:

	DUTIES TO AVOID DEPRIVING	DUTIES TO PROTECT FROM DEPRIVATION	DUTIES TO AID THE DEPRIVED
"Negative" right to freedom	Duties not to eliminate a person's security	Duties to protect people against deprivation of security by other people	Duties to provide for the security of those unable to provide for their own
"Positive" right to subsistence	Duties not to eliminate a person's only available means of subsistence	Duties to protect people against deprivation of the only available means of subsistence	Duties to provide for the subsistence of those unable to provide for their own

Shue's claim that the negative-positive rights distinction is a confused one does have force. Perhaps we should abandon the distinction and conceive of all rights as imposing both positive and negative obligations.

Whether or not the positive-negative distinction should be dispensed with, we conclude that arguments (a)-(d) against positive rights fail. Our discussion does call the wholesale critique of positive rights into question. Thus, either there is as good a case for positive rights as for negative ones or, if Shue is correct, no rights are altogether positive or altogether negative. Rather, each right imposes both negative and positive obligations depending upon context. In either case, the Lockean's exclusive emphasis on the "negative" right to liberty has been misplaced. The case for the minimal state cannot be based on the assertion that the only natural rights the state can protect are purely negative freedoms from interference by others. Claims to at least minimal level of welfare warrant equal protection as well.

If these last arguments have force, the real question is not whether or not we have positive as well as negative rights. Rather, the real question is what fundamental entitlements must be protected if our status as rational and autonomous agents is to be protected. Let us now turn to the issue of whether any claims of natural right can be justified, warranted or adequately supported.

JUSTIFICATION

We can show that people have justified claims of natural right by showing they have fundamental moral entitlements of the kind specified in the first section of this chapter: namely, entitlements that are not due to social, institutional, or legal status or rules, but are general and perhaps inalienable. In this lies the importance of analysis. If we do not have an adequate analysis, we cannot be clear about what conditions must be satisfied if a natural rights claim is to be justified.

But how are we to show that claims of natural right are justified? That is, how can we show that the conditions specified in the first part of the chapter are satisfied? While a full treatment of the issue would require a long digression into ethical and metaethical theory, we believe that at least a plausible case for natural rights can be developed here.

The Egalitarian Argument

When unequal treatment is regarded as unjust, it is often because such discrimination seems to ignore the basic similarity of all affected. Those who receive preferential treatment do not seem to be significantly different from those who are victimized, and so the inequality is held to be arbitrary and unfair.

This type of egalitarian argument is often employed in defense of natural or human rights. The point of the argument is that in view of the factual equalities or similarities between persons, it is arbitrary to distinguish between them with respect to such rights. Since natural rights are entitlements to those goods and opportunities that make a distinctively human sort of life possible, all humans are sufficiently alike to qualify as possessors. As John Locke puts it:

there being nothing more evident than that creatures of the same species and rank . . . born to all the same advantages of nature and the use of the same faculties should also be equal one amongst another without subordination and subjection.[34]

Locke can be read here as maintaining that given human factual equality (similarity), it would be irrational to regard some humans as having a greater claim than others to fundamental rights.

Unfortunately, there are serious difficulties with this type of argument. First, even if all humans are so similar that *if* anyone has natural rights then everybody does, how do we know anyone has such rights in the first place? Second, although it may be conceded that humans are equal or nearly equal in some respects, they are notoriously unequal in others. Locke's argument is that given human similarity, any presumption of superiority would be groundless. It is simply arbitrary, and hence irrational, to treat equals unequally. But are humans equal? Persons are similar in some respects but different in other respects. Hence, the egalitarian must show that it is the similarities and not the differences that are *relevant* to justifying claims of natural right. Persecution of minorities, discrimination against women, slavery, and genocide all have been defended by reference to allegedly relevant differences between victims and oppressors.

The friend of human equality surely will reply that it is the similarities and not the differences that are relevant where possession of natural rights is of concern. Common human qualities that often have been cited as the ground of such rights include rationality, the capacity to feel pain and undergo suffering, the ability to form a rational plan of life, and the need for the affection and companionship of others. But even within these categories, people differ. How is the egalitarian to show that it is the differences that are actually irrelevant?

There are at least two problems, then, with the egalitarian argument. At best, it seems to show only that *if* anyone has natural rights, all relevantly similar beings have the same rights. Second, even if it can be shown that some persons have such rights, it still must be shown that all humans are relevantly similar to the rights bearer(s).

These problems are not necessarily immune to resolution. In what follows, we suggest lines of response that may be satisfactory. While no presently available defense of a fundamental moral outlook is philosophically uncontroversial, this applies as much to utilitarianism as to the natural-rights approach. In moral philosophy, the choice is probably not between strict knock-down, drag-out proof of one's moral position, on the one hand, or irrational whim on the other. We hope that by developing some of the strengths of the natural-rights approach, we can show that there are good theoretical reasons for accepting it. If this theoretical defense is taken together with our critique of such alternate foundations for political philosophy as utilitarianism, and if the implications for action of each framework are considered impartially and objectively, the natural-rights framework, we claim, will most warrant our rational assent.

Natural Rights, Human Dignity, and Respect for Persons

Rights as fundamental moral commodities   Consider as best one can a society whose moral code does not include the concept of a claim of right. People in it may act benevolently most of the time and are not cruel or unfeeling. Indeed, they may be imagined as kinder and more sensitive than the inhabitants of our own planet. What such a culture would lack, however, is the notion of persons as makers of *claims* upon one another, as having basic entitlements which others would be *obligated* to respect. And if occasional improper treatment occurs, there is no cause to complain:

> The masters, judges and teachers don't have to do good things, after all, for anyone. . . . Their hoped for responses, after all, are *gratuities*, and there is no wrong in the omission of what is merely gratuitous. Such is the response of persons who have no concept of rights.[35]

In a society without the concept of rights, we all would be in a position analogous to that of the students at university A or the Southern blacks as viewed through the framework described by Wasserstrom (p. 50). We would lack the conceptual apparatus for asserting that some treatment was owed to us as a matter of right. If we are mistreated, that is a matter between our oppressor and his own conscience.

Rights, we are suggesting, are fundamental moral commodities because they enable us to stand up on our own two feet, "to look others in the eye, and to feel in some fundamental way the equal of anyone. To think of oneself as the holder of rights is not to be unduly but properly proud, to have that minimal self-respect that is necessary to be worthy of the love and esteem of others."[36] Conversely, to lack the concept of oneself as a rights bearer is to be bereft of a significant element of human dignity. Without such a concept, we could not view ourselves as beings entitled to be treated as not simply means but ends as well.

To respect persons as ends, to view them as having basic human dignity, seems to be inextricably bound up with viewing persons as possessors of rights; as beings who are *owed* a vital say in how they are to be treated, and whose interests are not to be overridden simply in order to make others better off. Consequently, to opt for a code of conduct in which rights are absent is to abandon the kind of respect for persons and human dignity at issue. This price, we submit, is simply too high to be worth paying. Our answer to the questions of why people should be regarded as having claims of right at all is simply that a world in which no such claims were ever made or ever regarded as justifiable would be a world that was morally impoverished, and very significantly so at that.[37]

The challenge of elitism   What if members of some special group were to accept the considerations cited above, but maintain that only members of their elite or superior group possessed any rights at all. Others, perhaps blacks, perhaps Jews, perhaps women, perhaps the less intelligent, are held to be inferior or not fully human. In this elitist view, there may well be reasons for recognizing fundamental natural rights. But, the elitists hold, in view of allegedly significant differences between humans, no reason has been given for thinking such rights belong to all humans, i.e., that they are human as well as natural rights.

In evaluating this kind of elitist challenge to equality, one must first get clear exactly what the ground of the proposed discrimination is supposed to be. It is useful to distinguish purportedly empirical grounds from normative ones, so that factual and evaluative issues can be kept apart.

Often proponents of an elitist morality will base their discrimination on alleged empirical differences between their own group and the supposed inferiors they victimize. For example, women have been held to be too emotional or too unaggressive to hold responsible positions. Slaveowners in pre-Civil War America argued that blacks were too simple and childlike to handle freedom, while allegations about differences in the brain size of white ethnics from Eastern Europe were used to justify immigration restrictions against them earlier in this century.

The proper line of defense against such an elitist is to challenge his facts. That blacks are less sensitive than whites, that Jews are conspiring to control economic and political power, that women are unfitted for professional success, and other such elitist generalizations are blatant falsehoods that should have been laid to rest long ago. Moreover, elitism of this sort is often applied inconsistently. Thus, proponents of racial segregation in the South sometimes justified their view by appealing to unequal education attainments of black and white pupils. Leaving aside the point that segregation itself, to say nothing of poverty and deprivation, may have been responsible for what difference there actually was, the most that such an argument justifies is segregation by educational attainment, not by race.

What if the elitist does not appeal to alleged factual differences between his group and those who are oppressed? What if the elitist instead simply asserts that his group, by virtue of its very nature, is superior. Men, by their very nature, should be dominant. The more intelligent should control the less intelligent. Whites (or blacks) just are the superior group? How can such elitist moralities be rationally discredited when they do not rest on empirical claims to begin with?

A particularly plausible response to such assertions is that they are *arbitrary*. They seem to be baseless assertions of purely personal preference rather than expressing a reasoned moral position. As Bernard Williams has pointed out, "The principle that men should be differently treated . . . merely on grounds of their color is not a special sort of moral principle but (if anything) a purely arbitrary assertion of will like that of some Caligulan ruler who decided to execute everyone whose name contained three 'R's'."[38]

But can't the elitist respond that if elitism with respect to rights is arbitrary, so too is the commitment to equal rights arbitrary as well? Why should equality be in a privileged position? If "All persons are not moral equals" is arbitrary, why isn't "All persons are moral equals" arbitrary as well?

However, the egalitarian has a number of effective responses to this move. First, elitism of a fundamental kind may beg the question against its victims. Since all human beings, barring illness or retardation, can function as agents and formulate their own system of values, how can one agent justifiably act on his own value commitments while denying other agents the right to do the same. In acting on his own discriminatory principle, the elitist is assuming his will should take precedence over those of his victims. But how could he justify such an assumption? He cannot appeal to the fact that he differs from his victims in the way specified in his fundamental discriminatory principle, e.g., that they differ racially. The very point at issue is whether he has the right to act on that principle in the first place. Perhaps the victims hold fundamental principles stating that the alleged elitist group is not an elite at all, or even that the alleged elitists are actually *inferiors*. At the very least, isn't the burden of proof on the elitist to explain why he is justified in acting on his elitist principles while his victims lack a similar right to act on their fundamental normative principles? Perhaps part of what justifies us in counting all people as equal members of the moral community, at least in the absence of reasons to the contrary, is the question-begging character of fundamental elitist discriminatory principles.[39]

Second, it is important to note that within the elitist group itself, characteristics that all humans possess are accorded significant recognition. These include the capacity to experience pain and suffering, the desire to be treated with respect and dignity, the sense of oneself as a conscious entity persisting over time with distinctive wants, ideals, and purposes, as well as the ability to view the world from a distinctive, self-conscious point of view. Among themselves, white supremacists, for example, weigh these factors heavily. They do not inflict gratuitous pain on one another, destroy or enslave one another on whim alone, nor do they disregard each other's life plans as of no value whatsoever. Rather, they seem to hold that each member of the elite should be treated just as the egalitarian thinks all human beings should be treated.

But in view of the basic similarities among all humans, discrimination at the fundamental level seems ad hoc. It seems unintelligible that a mere difference in skin color could by itself negate the importance of the factors enumerated above—the factors whose importance is already acknowledged within the elitist community itself. Thus, it hardly seems unreasonable to require the elitist to spell out the *connection* between any proposed ground of discrimination and the worth of individual persons. Indeed, in view of the great plethora of elitist positions, e.g., anti-Semitism, sexism, various forms of racism, it seems far from arbitrary to once again place the burden of proof on the elitist. In practice, elitists themselves give testimony to the arbitrariness of their fundamental discriminatory principles since they themselves generally seek to justify their discrimination by appeal to principles intelligible to everyone. Thus, one is far more likely to hear, "Women should not hold responsible positions because they are emotionally fitted for raising children," than, "Women should not hold responsible positions because they are women."

SUMMARY

Our discussion suggests that natural rights are justified as conditions which must be satisfied if humans are to live and develop as autonomous moral agents. They protect us from being reduced to mere means in the pursuit of the overall social good, or of being victims of oppressive elitist moralities. While the claim that natural rights are fundamental requires more examination than we can give it here, we hope to have made a plausible case for it. While it is doubtful whether claims about natural rights (or any other fundamental basis for morality) can be strictly proved in any mathematical sense, a moral perspective based on rights does seem to capture our firmest intuitions about the foundations of our moral view. Perhaps the ultimate justification of the natural rights perspective, however, is its application in practice; a task to which we will turn in later chapters.

In our view, natural rights are not only the most fundamental of moral commodities; they are also equally the rights of all persons. Attempts to rule out whole classes of competent humans, who clearly are moral agents, on such grounds as race, sex or ethnicity, are open to the charge of arbitrariness. If natural rights are valuable precisely because they protect our status as autonomous agents, all moral agents have a presumptively equal claim to natural rights.

Natural Rights, Justice, and the State

In our view, natural rights are those entitlements whose protection and implementation are needed to safeguard human dignity, autonomy, and respect. In claiming that the natural-rights approach is warranted, we are claiming that it would not be discredited by extended evaluation of its theoretical justification and of its implications for action, and that it would survive such an examination at least as well as any of its competitors.

What are the implications of the natural-rights perspective for political philosophy? Surely, those who believe humans should be regarded as possessors of fundamental rights, whether such rights are regarded as natural ones or as rule utilitarian devices á la Braybrooke (see pp. 40-42), would be sympathetic to the Lockean view of the state. According to Locke, the primary function of the state is to protect the fundamental rights of the individual. States can be ranked according to how well they fulfill their function. Moreover, the Lockean approach provides a framework for *criticizing the excesses of the state.* The state calls its own reason for being into question when it violates the fundamental rights of its citizens.

Unlike Locke, however, we argue for both positive and negative rights. Implementation of positive rights is just as much a prerequisite of promoting human dignity, autonomy, and self-respect as is implementation of negative ones. Accordingly, the proper response to a Lockean defender of exclusive emphasis on negative rights is that there seems to be no way of defending one kind of right without also defending the other. At the very least, perhaps the burden of proof has been shifted so that it is up to the Lockean to show how the distinction is to be made.

We conclude that the primary function of the state is to protect and where necessary implement the positive and negative natural rights of its citizens. Although any attempt to list all natural rights is likely to fail, surely any such list should include the rights to liberty and life, on the one hand, and to the material prerequisites of a minimally decent human life on the other. (The content of these rights will be discussed in Chapters Four and Six.)

However, rights can clash. Perhaps my right to well-being can be secured only by failing to protect your right to liberty. Or in cases of scarcity, it may not be possible to honor everyone's claim of right.

Such conflicts among competing rights claims constitute especially poignant moral dilemmas, for any resolution is imperfect from the moral point of view. Thus, even a satisfactory natural-rights position is only a necessary constituent of an acceptable framework for adjudication of moral disputes. Where conflicts between competing claims arise, appeal is frequently made to *social justice.* Parties to the conflict may request, for example, that the dispute between them be justly settled. Accordingly, if one function of the state is to protect and implement natural rights, it is also plausible to think that it is the state's responsibility to adjudicate the clash of rights justly. In the next chapter, we shall extend the natural rights approach by examining issues that arise where just adjudication of competing claims is at issue.

NOTES

[1]Malcolm X, *The Autobiography of Malcolm X,* with the assistance of Alex Haley (New York: Grove Press, 1965), p. 36.

[2]Joel Feinberg, in "The Nature and Value of Rights," *The Journal of Value Inquiry* 4, no. 4 (1970): 243–57, provides an example of a world without rights. We rely heavily on Feinberg's treatment here, particularly his claim that in a world without rights, good treatment would be regarded as a gratuity.

[3]This has been pointed out by Joel Feinberg in "Wasserstrom on Human Rights," *Journal of Philosophy* 61 (1964): 642–43.

[4]See, for example, John Hospers, *Human Conduct* (New York: Harcourt, Brace and World, 1961), p. 386, and S.I. Benn and R.S. Peters, *The Principles of Political Thought: Social Foundations of the Democratic State* (New York: The Free Press, 1964), p. 102, for discussions of rights and obligations.

[5]Richard Wasserstrom, "Rights, Human Rights and Racial Discrimination," *The Journal of Philosophy* 61 (1964), 640. Our discussion of the nature of natural rights is in great debt to Wasserstrom's, although he is explicitly concerned with rights that *by definition* belong to all humans. Our definition of natural rights leaves it open whether they are possessed by all humans but we argue for such a view in the third section of the present chapter.

[6]Thus, even if, as some philosophers claim, rights are *definable* in terms of obligations, it does not follow that rights talk and obligation talk have the same practical consequences. Rights talk emphasizes the status of persons as active makers of claims, as possessors of entitlements that should be honored rather than as passive recipients of the duties of others. Hence, there are practical reasons for adopting the vocabulary of rights even if the definist claim is correct. We do doubt, however, whether rights can be defined in terms of obligations. Thus, it seems possible that some obligations may not involve correlative rights. Consider, for example, the possibility of obligations that arise from one's station and its duties. For example, the faculty of university A may have professorial obligations to hear student complaints fairly, but the students have no correlative right to such fair treatment.

[7]See A.P. D'Entreves, *Natural Law: An Historical Survey,* (New York: Harper & Row, 1965), p. 17ff. Our historical survey of the natural-rights tradition relies heavily on D'Entreves's excellent study.

[8]Cicero, *Republic,* translated by G.W. Featherstonhaugh, (New York: G.&C. Cavill, 1829), p. 31.

[9]Thomas Aquinas, *Summa Theologica,* 1ae, 2ae, quae 91, articles 1 and 2.

[10]Ibid., 1ae, 2ae, quae 95, art. 2.

[11]Jeremy Bentham, *Anarchical Fallacies,* in John Bowring, ed., *The Collected Papers of Jeremy Bentham* 2 (Edinburgh, 1843), reprinted in A. I. Melden, ed., *Human Rights* (Belmont, Calif.: Wadsworth, 1970), p. 32.

[12]We do not mean to suggest that Nazi genocide or violation of the civil rights of black persons in America could be justified on utilitarian grounds. Clearly, they were not. Rather, our point is that such events may have motivated people to appeal to a moral framework in which the individual was given greater protection than that provided by utilitarianism.

[13]H.L.A. Hart, "Are There Any Natural Rights?" *Philosophical Review* 64, no. 2 (1955): 183.

[14]Ibid.

[15]John Locke, *Second Treatise of Government,* 1690, chap. 2, sect. 6. All quotations are from Thomas P. Peardon's edition of *The Second Treatise* (Indianapolis: Bobbs-Merrill, 1952).

[16]Ibid., chap. 6, sect. 54.

[17]Ibid., chap.5, sect. 27. See also chap. 5, sect. 26.

[18]Ibid., chap 5, sect 46.

[19]Ibid., chap. 5, sect. 50.

[20]Ibid., chap. 3, sect. 21.

21Ibid., chap. 9, sect. 131.

22Ibid., chap 11.

23Ibid., chap. 8, sect. 95–99.

24See Robert Nozick's *Anarchy, State and Utopia,* (New York: Basic Books, 1974).

25See Nozick, *Anarchy, State and Utopia,* for an important defense of the entitlement theory. We will consider his views at some length in Chap. 4 of the present work.

26Maurice Cranston, "Human Rights, Real and Supposed," in D.D. Raphael, ed., *Political Theory and the Rights of Man* (Bloomington: Indiana University Press, 1967), p. 50.

27Ibid., p. 51.

28See Nozick, *Anarchy, State and Utopia,* p. 172.

29Henry Shue, *Basic Rights: Subsistence, Affluence and U.S. Foreign Policy* (Princeton, N.J.: Princeton University Press, 1980), Chapter 2.

30Ibid., pp. 37–40.

31Some philosophers are inclined to argue that the distinction between harming and refraining from helping is of no moral significance, at least in certain contexts. See, for example, Judith Jarvis Thomson, "Rights and Deaths," *Philosophy & Public Affairs* 2, no. 2 (1973): 158–59. See also James Rachels, "Active and Passive Euthanasia," *New England Journal of Medicine* 292, no. 2 (1975): 78–80. Our point is not that the distinction lacks moral significance but that it does not apply here. If starving people have positive rights, we are harming (and not merely refraining from helping) them if we do not take at least some significant steps to alleviate their condition. This is because we, assuming we are well-off ourselves, are keeping from them what is morally theirs, i.e. what they have a right to possess. Of course, our obligations to avoid harming them is a prima facie one that *may* be overridden by the sorts of factor mentioned in the text, but it is a significant obligation nevertheless.

32D.D. Raphael makes a similar point in his paper "Human Rights Old and New," in Raphael, op. cit., pp. 63–64.

33Shue, p. 40.

34Locke, *Second Treatise of Government,* chap. 2, 4.

35Feinberg, "The Nature and Value of Rights," p. 247. See also Wasserstrom. "Rights, Human Rights and Racial Discrimination."

36Feinberg, "The Nature and Value of Rights," p. 252.

37For a different but related line of argument, see Alan Gewirth, *Reason and Morality* (Chicago: University of Chicago Press, 1978).

38Bernard Williams, "The Idea of Equality," in Peter Laslett and W. G. Runciman, eds., *Philosophy, Politics and Society,* 2d series (Oxford: Basil Blackwell, 1962) reprinted in Hugo A Bedau, ed., *Justice and Equality* (Englewood Cliffs, N.J.: Prentice-Hall, 1971), p. 119. For a defense of basic human equality based on appeal to equal human worth, see Gregory Vlastos, "Justice and Equality," in Richard Brandt, ed., *Social Justice* (Englewood Cliffs, N.J.: Prentice-Hall, 1962), pp. 31–72, as well as the argument in Wasserstrom, "Rights, Human Rights and Racial Discrimination."

39For more fully developed versions of this sort of argument, see especially Alan Gewirth, "Categorical Consistency in Ethics," *Philosophical Quarterly* 19, no. 69 (1969), as well as his "The Justification of Egalitarian Justice," *American Philosophical Quarterly* 8, no. 4 (1971) and *Reason and Morality.* See also John Wilson, "Why Should Other People Be Treated as Equals?" *Revue Internationale de Philosophie,* no. 97 (1971).

SUGGESTED READINGS

Becker, Lawrence. *Property Rights: Philosophic Foundations.* Boston: Routledge and Kegan Paul, 1977.
Dworkin, Ronald. *Taking Rights Seriously.* Cambridge: Harvard University Press, 1977.

Gewirth, Alan. *Reason and Morality.* Chicago: The University of Chicago Press, 1978.
Locke, John. *Second Treatise of Government.* 1690. (Widely available in a variety of editions.)
Lyons, David, ed. *Rights.* Belmont, CA: Wadsworth, 1979.
Melden, A. I., ed. *Human Rights.* Belmont, California: Wadsworth, 1970. Contains H. L. A. Hart's "Are There any Natural Rights?" and Richard Wasserstrom's "Rights, Human Rights and Racial Discrimination."
Raphael, D. D., ed. *Political Theory and the Rights of Man.* Bloomington: Indiana University Press, 1967. Contains Maurice Cranston's "Human Rights, Real and Supposed" and Raphael's "Human Rights Old and New."
Schochet, Gordon, ed. *Life, Liberty and Property: Essays on Locke's Political Ideas.* Belmont, California: Wadsworth, 1971.
Shue, Henry. *Basic Rights: Subsistence, Affluence and U.S. Foreign Policy.* Princeton: Princeton University Press, 1980.
Wilson, John. *Equality.* New York: Harcourt Brace Jovanovich, 1966.

Articles

Berlin, Isaiah. "Equality." *Proceedings of the Aristotelian Society,* Vol. 56 (1955–1956). Reprinted in William T. Blackstone, ed., *The Concept of Equality.* Minneapolis: Burgess Publishing Company, 1969.
Ethics, Vol. 92, No. 1, October 1981. This entire issue is devoted to the topic of rights.
Feinberg, Joel. "The Nature and Value of Rights." *The Journal of Value Inquiry,* Vol. IV, No. 4 (1970), pp. 243–57.
_____ "Duties, Rights and Claims." *American Philosophical Quarterly,* Vol. 3, No. 2 (1966), pp. 137–44.
Gewirth, Alan. "The Basis and Content of Human Rights." In J. Roland Pennock and John W. Chapman, eds., *Human Rights: Nomos XXIII.* New York: New York University Press, 1981, pp. 119–47.
_____ "The Justification of Egalitarian Justice." *American Philosophical Quarterly,* Vol. 8, No. 4 (1971), pp. 331–41.
The Monist, Vol. 52, No. 4 (1968). Entire issue is devoted to human rights.
Phillips Griffiths, A. "Ultimate Moral Principles: Their Justification." In Paul Edwards, ed., *The Encyclopedia of Philosophy.* New York: Macmillan, 1967, Vol. 8.
Wasserstrom, Richard. "Rights, Human Rights and Racial Discrimination." *The Journal of Philosophy,* Vol. 61 (1964). Reprinted in Melden, *Human Rights,* cited above.

Four
JUSTICE

When conflicting claims are pressed under conditions of relative scarcity, under which all claims cannot easily be met, problems of justice typically arise. Consider, for example, the problem of distribution of spaces on kidney dialysis machines, a problem we discussed earlier in Chapter One. More patients require spaces on such machines than can be treated. There simply are not enough dialysis machines. Yet many untreated patients surely will die. How are the spaces to be allotted? What is the *just* distribution?

Considerations of justice might not be pressing if there were enough slots for everyone and if provision of sufficient machines would not deplete other contested resources. Then, everyone could easily be treated and no problem would exist. Or, if some patients withdrew their claims to treatment so that all who demanded treatment could be treated, issues of justice would not arise. But when conflicting claims are pressed under conditions where not all claims can be satisfied, we are often called upon to resolve the conflict *justly*.

In the case of the dialysis machines, should spaces be distributed by lottery? Such a procedure would at least count all applicants equally. But is equal treatment always just treatment? People often differ in merit. Perhaps places on the machine should go to the meritorious. Remember the case in which a patient requires treatment only because he disregarded his physician's orders. Is it just to count that patient the same as those who did follow orders, even at the cost of considerable hardship? Is need relevant? Suppose one patient is the sole support of several children while another is responsible only for himself? What if the patient who disregarded orders is the one with four dependents while the patient who obeyed instructions has no dependents? How are need and merit to be balanced off against one another? Indeed, perhaps the strongest argument for a lottery is the difficulty of assessing the weight to be assigned to various other factors that seem significant.

Similar problems arise on a larger scale. Is it just to distribute wealth, honor, or positions on a merit basis? What of those with great need but little merit? Are they to be left to starve in the streets? On the other hand, are all inequalities in wealth arbitrary? After all, who is to say what merit is or who has more of it than another? How are different values to be properly weighed on the scales of justice?

In this chapter, our purpose is to explain and evaluate several theories of the nature of justice. We begin by discussing a number of traditional accounts of justice. We then consider some important contemporary theories of justice, and make some suggestions of our own for improving upon them. We will also apply our analysis to specific problems of economic justice. Later we will extend the analysis to the problem of punishing criminals, to civil disobedience and protest, and to issues of compensatory justice that arise in connection with current controversies over preferential hiring and admissions policies for women and minorities.

TRADITIONAL THEORIES OF JUSTICE

Formal Theories

One major distinction that divides theories of justice is the distinction between *formal* and *material* theories. A formal theory does not provide any content or substance to principles of justice. A material theory does. In the strict sense, a formal theory is one that insists only on the logical criterion of consistency. Any consistent theory of justice satisfies the formal criterion. Consider the following principles of justice:

1. If X is a just result, all situations relevantly similar to X are also just results.
2. If M is our just-making characteristic, let the dispensing of justice be proportionate to the possession of M.
3. Justice is the treating of equals equally and of unequals unequally.

These principles are all formal in the strict sense. They meet the criterion of consistency. However, there is no material content. X and M

are uninterpreted in the formulas. We emphasize that 3 should be understood as a restatement of 1 or 2; be on guard against the philosopher who tries to smuggle some content into 3 by capitalizing on ordinary connotations of "equality." For example, it is easy to say, "Since you should treat equals, equally, there should be equal income for equal work." However, this is a mistake. The consequent is not deducible from the antecedent. One needs the additional premise that the appropriate criterion for pay is work performed. However, such a criterion would not be acceptable to some socialists who insist that equal income for equal need is the appropriate formula. A substantive conclusion cannot be derived from a formal premise.

One must also be careful to distinguish formal theories from general ones. All formal theories are general, but not all general theories are formal. A general theory that is not formal has some content. Something is substituted for the variables X or M. For example, consider the formula, "Justice is giving each person an equal opportunity." This is a general theory but not a formal one. For X, it substitutes content, namely equal opportunity. It is general in that it applies to everyone. For our purposes any consistent justice formula using variables as the justice-making criteria is a formal theory. When norms are substituted for the variables, the theory is a material theory. The distinction should be kept clear. The socialist formula of distributive justice, "From each according to his ability, to each according to his needs" is a material theory, not a formal one.

Aristotle   The classical position on justice that best exemplifies the formalist perspective is that of Aristotle.[1] He maintains that the just is proportionate to the possession of some quality which serves as the just-making characteristic. If A and B are equal with respect to this characteristic M, then their shares should be equal. If they are unequal with respect to M, their shares should be in proportion to M and hence the ratio of their shares to the proportion of M should be equal.

$$\frac{\text{SHARE FOR A}}{\text{A's Possession of M}} = \frac{\text{SHARE FOR B}}{\text{B's Possession of M}}$$

The principle is formal because as Aristotle points out, one can choose any criterion for desert one wishes. The principle is compatible with any criterion. The principle only insists that once the criterion has been established, the ratios should be equal.

The difficulty with formalism is that at most it gives a necessary condition but not a sufficient condition for justice. It is certainly not just that all Jews be put in the gas chamber, even if only Jews are put in the gas chamber and no non-Jews are put there. In other words, consistency is not enough. What the Aristotelian formula needs is some means for specifying what the just-making characteristic, the characteristic M, should be. The formalist theory of justice must be supplemented by material considerations if the theory of justice is to be practicable.

Material Theories

Plato   The earliest fully developed account of justice can be attributed to the Greek philosopher Plato. For Plato, justice involves giving all persons their due.[2] The problem is that of determining a person's due. Plato tries to resolve the problem by providing a functionalist analysis, an approach that in its essentials is shared by Aristotle. This approach is based on a teleological metaphysics in which everything has a purpose or function. Justice is to be analyzed in terms of function. To assert of something that it is performing its function is the same as saying that it is performing justly. A sheep dog is just when it protects the sheep. A race horse is just when it wins races. Human beings are more complicated creatures since they have souls composed of appetite, will, and reason. With respect to human beings, a just person has a harmonious soul. This harmony occurs when each part of the soul performs its appropriate function. Since the rational part of the soul is the higher part, the proper function of reason is to rule appetite and will. When reason rules the soul is harmonious. The individual soul is a microcosm of the state. A just state is a harmonious state where each class performs its appropriate function. The business class is analogous to individual appetite, the class of soldiers is analogous to individual will, and the ruling class is analogous to individual reason. Justice is the harmonious relationship that occurs when the members of the various classes act in accordance with their nature. For Plato, justice occurs when everything is in its proper place.

Plato's philosophy makes a classic case for *meritocracy*. A meritocracy, in the sense in which Plato might defend it, is an organization of society in which one's place in the social hierarchy is determined by one's ability and qualifications for work at that level. ("Meritocracy" also is used to refer to a society in which material rewards as well as positions are distributed according to ability and qualifications.) In the Platonic view, it is unjust and corrupt to place people in jobs they cannot handle well. Some of us are better than others at particular activities. Since ruling is the most difficult and most important human activity, only the best and brightest should rule. To a Platonist, the democratic method of choosing political leaders makes about as much sense as allowing someone who knows virtually nothing of basketball to select the players who make up the team. The just society, to the Platonist, is the one in which everyone gets his or her due. And one gets one's due if one is assigned to one's proper place in the meritocratic structure of society.

This Platonic analysis of justice is inadequate, however. A principal objection is to the elitism of Plato's account. Plato's ideal state is unpalatable even if only wise philosophers were kings and only the unintelligent were slaves. What is objectionable is not the practical difficulty of identifying the best and brightest, great as it is. Rather, Plato's assumption that the best and brightest should have absolute authority is what is most seriously questionable.

Suppose, if only for the sake of argument, that some means existed for determining who is most fitted to rule. Plato's egalitarian critics would respond that it is incorrect to argue from

1. Jones is the best fitted to rule.

to

2. Jones ought to rule.

What is needed is some independent argument to show that those most fitted to rule ought to rule, or that justice requires such a result. Plato just assumes that the best and brightest ought to rule. And he is far from alone in regarding that assumption as virtually self-evident. However, in Chapter Five, we will question the assumption and argue against it.

We need not wait for the account of Chapter Five to call Plato's analysis into question, however. Once we concede that the move from (1) "Jones is most fitted to rule," to (2) "Jones ought to rule," needs support, we can ask what kind of support is needed. Surely, we must consider the claim that those most fitted to rule ought to rule since they deserve to rule on grounds of justice. It is *just* that those with the best qualifications and most merit rule. However, such a move leads to vicious circularity. The circularity is made explicit when we realize what the Platonist has argued.

1. Justice is to be analyzed in terms of giving each person his due.
2. Giving each person his due is to be analyzed in terms of a person's function.
3. The nature of a person's function is to be analyzed in terms of the justice of what he is due.

Plato cannot say both that justice is giving each person his due *and* that what a person is due depends on the justice of the function the person serves.

This criticism at best only refutes one version of what counts as giving a person his or her due. It does not refute the general strategy of analyzing justice in terms of what persons are due. There are numerous other possibilities for analyzing "giving each his due." But that is the problem. No one interpretation of "giving persons their due" will suffice. What a person's due is depends on highly complicated individual circumstances. Whether Jones ought in the name of justice to give Smith ten dollars depends on the circumstances. We can begin the list as follows:

1. Did Smith earn $10 working for Jones?
2. Did Jones promise to pay Smith $10?
3. Is Smith the tax collector?
4. Is Smith holding a gun on Jones?

The reader can expand the list almost indefinitely. In speaking of distributive justice, Nicholas Rescher discusses the canons of equality, need, ability and/or achievement, effort, productivity, social utility, supply and demand, and claims.[3] An informative analysis must acknowledge the various particular circumstances that affect any justice decision. Even if circularity is avoided, to assert that giving each person his or her due is justice is not an adequate analysis. For the formula "Give all persons their due" seems to collapse into arbitrariness if "due" is explicated in terms of only one value, such as ability; but, lacks concrete content if "due" is taken as shorthand for a complex but unspecified process for balancing out a whole series of often conflicting values, such as ability, need, desert, and contribution.

Justice and equality   Another important tradition tries to explicate the link between equality and justice. The nature of this link varies from writer to writer, however. In fact, equality itself is an extremely fuzzy concept and writers in political philosophy tend to blur the various meanings of the term together.

One branch of the tradition emphasizes the formula "treat equals as equals." Justice then is treating equals equally and unequals unequally. However, stated this way, this formula is the formal theory of justice previously discussed. It demands that justice decisions be consistent.

The interesting questions arise when one tries to give some content to the formula, i.e., to specify the characteristics that one is to use in consistent justice decisions. Let us consider briefly some of the characteristics that have been suggested.

At one extreme is the radical egalitarian position.[4] Under such a position it is argued that all people are significantly alike and hence the just society is the strictly egalitarian society. Everyone is treated in exactly the same way. The obvious difficulty with the theory is that the factual premise is false. People are not sufficiently alike to be always treated alike. Their needs, abilities, contributions, physical characteristics, and interests are not identical. To treat them as if they were identical would be to commit great injustice. For example, sex equality in sports such as basketball is taken to require separate competitions for men and women due to innate differences in size, strength, and speed rather than blindness towards sex differences. It is not that extreme equality is impractical, but that it is unjust. Obviously the egalitarian position must be modified.

One modification directs attention away from equal results to equal treatment.[5] In this sense, we treat X and Y equally if our treatment of them shows equal concern and respect for their needs and interests.[6] If we are speaking about police protection, justice is not achieved by giving equal protection to everyone. Some citizens, for example, those threatened by criminals, need more protection than others.[7] Justice is accomplished not by equal police protection but rather by unequal protection based on the principle of equal treatment. Even though $1,000 is spent on the citizen threatened by criminals and only $100 for the average citizen, all citizens are receiving equal treatment. The greater need of the threatened citizen requires the much greater expenditure if all citizens are to be treated equally with respect to police protection, e.g., according to the principle "protect each proportionally to his need for protection." For the remainder of our discussion we will be speaking of equal treatment that may or may not entail equal results, depending on the circumstances.

However, this modification in egalitarian theory is not without its own problems. For one thing, it is *incomplete*. How are we to distribute justly when we lack sufficient resources to make a proportional contribution to all? To this question, the theory of equal treatment provides no answer. Again, it is at least controversial whether equal treatment is always just. Suppose parents have $100 to spend on their two children. Susie requires $90 for music lessons while Pam requires $10 for golf instruction. Is the inequality of result that equal treatment would engender really fair? Is it fair that those with the most expensive interests get the bulk of society's resources? Surely, it is far from clear that the answer always will be affirmative.

Perhaps egalitarians will respond that what is just or fair will be clear in specific contexts. Justice may require one thing in one situation, another thing in a different context. Isn't it clear that the mayor's son should not be excused from paying a speeding fine just because he is the mayor's son but should be excused if he was racing to get a heart attack victim to the hospital?

Such sentiments as these have an attractive ring if one does not examine them too closely. However, our modifications do not eliminate all the problems. Let us consider the practice of licensing drivers of automobiles. In this case, our situation is the driving of automobiles and the characteristic appealed to in the rule is that of being a driver of automobiles. Any person correctly described as a driver is required to have a license. Here is a paradigm case of equal treatment in a particular situation. However, consider the following amended rule. Any person correctly described as an automobile driver and who has blue eyes is required to get a license. Certainly people with identical characteristics, blue-eyed drivers of automobiles, are being treated equally, although this rule, unlike the former one, is clearly unjust. It is not enough that certain identical characteristics be used in specific situations. The identical characteristics being used as differentiating criteria must be relevant to the activity under consideration. If we are charged with dispensing antityphoid vaccine, the relevant characteristic is exposure to typhoid and not the possession of blue eyes. Our egalitarian account must be further amended. Justice in any situation is accomplished when the identical characteristics selected for differentiating criteria are relevant to the activity and when all people with the appropriate characteristic are treated equally.

Even this further modification does not settle all the problems. The typhoid situation might be handled in a straightforward scientific manner. The differentiating condition is obvious since there is a causal relation between being exposed to typhoid, contracting typhoid, and preventing typhoid by vaccination after exposure. Unfortunately, many of the situations where problems of justice arise bear no analogy to our typhoid case. A discussion of voting qualifications illustrates this point clearly. It is unjust to extend the franchise to everyone. Certainly, infants, severely retarded, and perhaps criminals should be excluded. The problem is then before us: What characteristics are necessary if one is to be entitled to vote? Until very recently, literacy was a necessary characteristic. A defense of sorts can be made for the literacy qualifications. One first argues that there is a correlation between literacy and responsible voting. If that correlation can be shown, then there is at least a prima facie reason to make literacy a qualification. The crux of the problem is that in many situations it is not at all clear what the relevant characteristics are. Some are arguing that it is unjust to deny "street people" the right to vote because they lack a permanent address. Even this most recently modified account of equal treatment is incomplete.

Justice and equal rights   Perhaps there is another way out of the difficulty. Situations in which considerations of justice are relevant are of two fundamentally different types. One type is like most of the ones we have been discussing above. Some specific physical characteristic is the relevant one and the decision can be made on fairly straightfoward factual grounds. The dispensation of the antityphoid vaccine is a paradigm case. In the other type of situation physical characteristics are not the prime determinant. Often, in fact, they are hardly relevant at all. People are morally entitled to equal treatment, not on the basis of any specific physical characteristic they possess except that of being rational beings. All men have a right to protection of life, liberty, due process of law, and the pursuit of happiness.

The result is a dual theory of justice based on a dual theory of equality. At the first level, everyone has equal rights. The possession of those rights morally entitles them to equal treatment as rights bearers. At this level we have a moral analogue to the extreme egalitarian theory discussed above. With respect to natural rights, everyone is considered equal; the only relevant characteristic is that the person be a rights bearer. Just what qualifies a person to have natural rights and what the situations are in which he has rights depends on the natural-rights theory in question. A discussion of some of the issues involved is found in Chapter Three. On our own theory every human being has a natural right to liberty and the prerequisites of a minimally decent human life (or well-being) as discussed in Chapter Three.

However, how natural-rights claims are honored and how disputes between rights claims are resolved depends on specific situations. The implementation of rights claims constitutes the lower level. We use the word "lower" because the decisions made at this level implement the rights claims to which we are entitled at the higher level. For example, the dispensation of antityphoid vaccine to those and only to those exposed to typhoid is a working out of the natural right to well-being in specific situations. It is at this second level that differentiation on the basis of physical or societal characteristics is required if justice is to be done. Medicine should go to the sick and not to everyone, food to the hungry and not to everyone, and so on. The differentiating criteria depend on the situation. However, whatever the specific situation, if justice is to be done it must represent an attempt to implement a natural right.

It also is important to note that just inequalities can arise through the free exercise of natural rights. If Jones and Smith open competing bakeries in our town or neighborhood, and if Smith does better because consumers prefer his baked goods to those of Jones, no injustice has been committed. The inequality has arisen simply because of the free choice of the consumers and because of risks voluntarily assumed by both Smith and Jones. Inequality of outcome, therefore, is not to be equated with injustice.

Objections   This account of justice is still inadequate, however. First, the theory is still not complete. Even if a theory of natural rights is accepted, we still have the difficulties of implementation. To provide a minimum standard of living of $12,000 in the United States may be defended as implementation of the natural right to well-being. However, since that program must be paid for by taxing the incomes of those above the standard, those taxed might well argue that their natural right to freedom is being infringed upon.[8] The previously discussed problem of conflicts of rights is with us again. The black struggle for an end to racial discrimination and for equality of opportunity in America was at the outset phrased in the language of rights, specifically the rights to liberty and well-being. Black citizens wanted to use the same public facilities as whites, attend the same public schools, utilize the same transportation facilities (right to liberty), and they wanted their share of America's prosperity (right to well-being). However, the private owners of businesses resisted black demands for integration of their facilities. They did so in the name of property rights (right to liberty). The picture of a future governor protecting his property with an axe handle still comes to mind. In response, a significant segment of public opinion replies with the phrase, "human rights over property rights." Here is a clash of rights that creates what we take to be a paradigm case of a problem of justice. Moreover, it is clear that we have not resolved the problems of relevance with the introduction of the two-level theory.

Second, and more important, as the equality theory of justice is modified, it becomes more and more obvious that the concept of equality can at best provide necessary conditions for justice and not sufficient ones. An analysis of the concept of equality can never provide an exhaustive analysis of the concept of justice. To say, for example, that justice in any situation is accomplished when the identical characteristics selected for differentiating criteria are relevant to the activity and when all people with the appropriate characteristics are treated equally is to make justice depend on more than considerations of equality. We believe it is correct to say that everyone has equal rights to liberty and well-being and that no situation is just if at least one of the rights is not honored. In this respect equality spelled out as a theory of natural rights does provide a necessary condition of justice. However, this equality theory must be supplemented by a theory that enables us to resolve the conflicts that arise between natural rights. Second, it is a necessary condition of justice that whatever principles are accepted for resolving these conflicts and whatever characteristics are accepted as relevant differentiating criteria in particular situations, equals should be treated equally. However, an analysis of equality will neither provide the principles for resolving the conflicts nor determine which characteristics are the relevant ones. When properly understood, equality considerations provide necessary conditions for justice; they do not provide sufficient ones.

Just Procedures and Just Results

A major distinction which might be of great use here is that between just procedures and just results. Ideally one prefers both just procedures and just results. However, sometimes one must be sacrificed for the other. For example, in distributive justice one can achieve a just result, e.g., providing a minimum standard of living for the poor, by unjust procedures, e.g., by a confiscatory tax on producers. Or in retributive justice, a trial by a jury made up of one's peers may well be defended as a just procedure, even though the procedure may lead to an unjust result. An innocent man may be found guilty or a guilty man may be found innocent.

Let us examine the notion of procedural justice by supposing that three friends order a pizza. When the pizza arrives, how should it be divided? Barring special circumstances, the result or outcome which seems most just is that each person receives an equal share. But what procedure should be used to ensure that result? An appropriate procedure for this purpose is to make the person cutting the pizza take the last piece. The pizza example provides an illustration of fairness in both procedures and results. In some cases, however, just procedures alone must be relied upon to determine just results. Consider a lottery as an example. It makes perfect sense to speak of the conditions of a fair lottery. But what makes it fair? Suppose that most entrants are poor, but the winner is an extremely rich man. Can we say that the lottery is unjust? Certainly not. As with horse races, we condemn a lottery which is fixed, but we do not condemn one where the rich are winners. In situations like these, as long as the procedures are just, the results too are just. Many problems of justice that we must handle as a cooperative society are ones of designing a system or set of procedures that provides as much justice as possible. Once we agree on appropriate procedures, then as long as a person is treated according to those procedures, the procedure is just—even if it turns out to produce inequalities that seem by other standards unjust. This point can be illustrated by borrowing an example from Alf Ross, in "The Value of Blood Tests as Evidence in Paternity Cases." The problem is to discover a way to determine whether or not a man is the father of a certain child. Ross considers whether blood tests would be a just criterion to use in this regard:

> If the ultimate end of the rules of evidence is that as many cases as possible be decided correctly, on the basis of assumed facts which are as near the truth as possible, the conclusion will certainly be that in all types of cases in which paternity is an issue blood-test exclusions must be recognized as unconditional and absolute proof. This rule requires that the judge refrain from any attempt to individualize the estimation of the evidence by taking into consideration contrary evidence offered by the mother to show that there are no other sources of paternity possible. If the legal certainty of the decision can be put at 99% and 20 cases arise each year, the judge, if the blood-test evidence is admitted as absolute, will give a right decision in 99 cases out of 100. The aim of an individualizing estimation of the evidence would be to make it possible to find precisely the one case which (every fifth year) can occur, in which despite the blood-test exclusion, the mother is right, and the man, in spite of everything, is indeed the father of her child. However, since the 100 cases do not come up for decision all

together, but successively over 5 years and before different judges, there is no possibility of making a comparison and selecting the most reliable case. The result of an individualizing estimation of the evidence would inevitably be that the blood test would be set aside in more than 1 out of the 100 cases, which means that the average correctness of the legal decisions would decrease. For example, if the blood test were set aside in 10 out of the 100 cases, 9 of the decisions would be wrong, and only 91, not 99, of the 100 cases would be decided correctly.

It is understandable that the judge, concerned intensively with the individual case and guided solely by the desire to give as just a decision as possible in that particular case, may be tempted to take into consideration such evidence as the "virtuous wife" may bring in the defense of her marriage, her child, and her honor, or such as an unmarried mother may bring to win support of her child. But in the interest of the presumed ultimate aim and purpose of evidentiary rules it must nevertheless be insisted that the individualizing estimation be rejected. There is no denying that individualizing would result in a considerable number of incorrect decisions, so that, for fear of committing an injustice against one innocent mother, injustices would be done to a number of alleged fathers.[9]

Here is a superb example of a case where the procedure should be followed even though certain individual cases of unjust results remain. The blood test procedure is the best we can do.

Actually our discussion has distinguished three different types of procedural justice. With perfect procedural justice, the procedure always leads to just consequences, as in the pizza cutting example. With imperfect procedural justice, as with the U.S. trial by jury system or the blood test, the procedure is imperfect because it does not always lead to just consequences. However, the procedure still qualifies as a just procedure because it is the best procedure we have for achieving just results. Later we shall argue that democracy serves as an imperfect procedure for achieving justice in balancing the conflicting rights claims of citizens within a state.

A final example of procedural justice is provided by the lottery example. In this case there are no independent results which serve as a test of the procedure. If the procedure is just, the results produced by the procedure are just as well. Two contemporary philosophers adopt this notion of pure procedural justice to make normative claims about the function of a state. We now turn our attention to John Rawls and Robert Nozick.

JOHN RAWLS'S THEORY OF JUSTICE

Many philosophers would contend that John Rawls's *A Theory of Justice* is the most significant book on the topic of justice in the twentieth century.

Rawls argues that the task of social and political institutions is the preservation and enhancement of individual liberty and well-being. Rawls tries to develop a *procedure* that would yield principles of justice. These principles of justice would then serve as guides in the constuction and evaluation of social and political institutions.

In Rawls's view, questions of justice arise when a society evaluates the institutions and practices under which it lives with an eye toward balancing the legitimate competing interests and conflicting claims which are pressed by the members of that society. If we adopt the language of rights, we can say that Rawls sees problems of justice arising when legitimate rights claims come into conflict. Rawls does not view the citizens of a state as naïve moralists searching for a utopian ideal. Rather, they are sufficiently self-interested to wish to pursue their own individual interests and achieve their own individual goals. Given inevitable competing interests and conflicts, Rawls's task is to attempt to provide a *procedure* that will enable the members of the society to adopt principles for resolving the conflicts and for adopting just practices and institutions. In other words his question is this: By what procedure can self-interested persons with legitimate competing claims adopt principles for just institutions and practices?

Rawls's answer is to appeal to a *contract* process constrained by certain assumptions. Several of the more important assumptions include the following: (1) that human cooperation is both possible and necessary; (2) that the contractees adhere to the principles of rational choice; (3) that all contractees desire certain primary goods that can be broadly characterized as rights and liberties, opportunities and powers, income and wealth—in other words, general goods that are necessary to the attainment of any other individual goods persons may desire; (4) that the contract process be constrained by a *minimal morality* which stipulates that principles adopted by the contractees be general, universal in application, public, and the final court of appeal for ordering the conflicting claims of moral persons; (5) that the parties to the contract are capable of a sense of justice and will adhere to the principles adopted.[10]

The force of these five conditions is to put moral limits on the kind of contract that can be produced. With these five conditions acting as constraints, Rawls's strategy is to ask us to conduct a thought experiment. What principles of justice would we come up with if we were placed behind a veil of ignorance with all other rational agents and instructed to devise a set of principles of organizing society so that justice in the society would be achieved? The key to understanding how the principles of justice are to be selected is the veil of ignorance, or ignorance principle. The ignorance principle states that the contract makers are to act as if they did not know their place in society. Such ignorance guarantees *impartiality* and prevents us from arguing on selfish rather than general grounds. This veil of ignorance would exclude knowledge of one's class position or social status, one's fortune in the distribution of natural assets and abilities, one's intelligence, one's physical **strength**, the nature of one's society, and one's individual conception of the good. Operating in this way, none of the contract makers would have any special interests to defend nor would they have any reasons to form alliances to adopt principles that work to the disadvantage of a minority of other contract makers. In effect, as Rawls applies it, the ignorance principle tells us to act as if our enemy were to assign our place in society. For example, suppose the issue were the distribution of income. Since the veil of ignorance prevents you from knowing how wealthy you are or will be and it prevents you from knowing your occupation and talents, what strategy would it be rational to adopt? Surely, Rawls argues, you would want to protect the position of the least well-off. Similar thought experiments would assure that there would be no racist principles for the organization of social institutions. After all, you cannot be sure that you would not be a member of the race that would be discriminated against. Since the contract makers are like rational egoists operating from behind a veil of ignorance, they would adopt the general principle of seeking to minimize their losses. We can now see how unanimous agreement on the principles of justice is possible. Since everyone agrees that it is rational to reduce one's losses and since no one knows what position they hold in society, the following two principles would be adopted unanimously: (1) Each person is to have an equal right to the most extensive total system of equal basic liberties compatible with a similar system of liberty for all; (2) Social and economic inequalities are to be arranged so that they are both (*a*) to the greatest benefit of the least advantaged, and (*b*) attached to offices and positions open to all under conditions of fair equality of opportunity.[11] These principles which are the result of the contract are just because the procedure which produced them is just. Rawls's hypothetical contract is an example of pure procedural justice.

These are the principles that self-interested persons would choose when constrained by the ignorance condition. Since they do not know particular facts about themselves, they have no specific interests to protect. Rather, the concern is with those goods Rawls calls primary goods—general goods that are necessary to the attainment of any other individual goods persons may desire.

One of the most important of these primary goods is liberty. Since no one will know his or her place, it is in one's interest to adopt principle one, which provides an equal system of liberty for all.

To the question "What are the constituent liberties that comprise the system of liberty?", Rawls provides a list of basic liberties. This list includes:

> political liberty (the right to vote and to be eligible for public office) together with freedom of speech and assembly; liberty of conscience and freedom of thought; freedom of the person along with the right to hold (personal) property; and freedom from arbitrary arrest and seizure as defined by the concept of the rule of law.[12]

The second principle is concerned with the primary goods of opportunities and power, income and wealth. What Rawls does is to consider his principle in contrast to several competing ones and then ask which principles would be chosen by self-interested persons constrained by the ignorance principle. Rawls first considers a system of natural liberty. In such a system, positions are open to those able and willing to strive for them. The principle governing the distribution of wealth in such a system is called the principle of efficiency. In terms of his theory Rawls defines the position as follows:

> Thus we can say that an arrangement of rights and duties in the basic structure is efficient if and only if it is impossible to change the rules, to redefine the scheme of rights and duties so as to raise the expectations of any representative man (at least one) without at the same time lowering the expectations of some (at least one) other representative man.[13]

Rawls argues that this principle of efficiency within a system of natural liberty would be rejected, however. If, after the initial distribution, someone has vastly more wealth than others, nothing could be done to correct the situation that would not run afoul of the efficiency principle. Moreover, the distribution of wealth at any given time has been strongly influenced by the cumulative effect of the natural and social contingencies of past distributions. Accident and good fortune play an important role as to who is wealthy at any given time. Since the veil of ignorance prevents us from knowing our own fortune and since, according to Rawls, it is rational to seek to minimize our losses, the principle of efficiency would not be accepted in the contract. Rational contractors would seek to avoid the risk of turning out to be on the bottom in the efficient society.

Rawls has more positive reactions to the principle of equal opportunity. This principle asserts that people with the same ability, talents, and expenditures of effort should have roughly the same prospects of success in given fields of endeavor. One's family background, race, religion, sex, or social background should not act as impediments to success. To assure equality of opportunity, society imposes heavy inheritance taxes, offers a broad public education, and passes antidiscrimination legislation. To the extent that such societal measures are successful, the distribution of goods and services depends upon ability. talent, and effort.

In Rawls's view the principle of equal opportunity is still not sufficient. Rawls argues that the distribution of talent, ability, and capacity for effort is just as arbitrary from the moral point of view as the distribution of sex, family wealth, and social class. Jones has no more of a right to more money because he is smarter than Smith than he has a right to more money because he is of a certain religion. Distribution is only fair in Rawls's view if human assets are treated as collective social goods. The distribution of goods and services is a cooperative effort on the part of all. Given the cooperative effort, the only fair principle is the one that accepts inequalities only if the inequalities work to the advantage of the least well-off:

> It seems to be one of the fixed points of our considered judgments that no one deserves his place in the distribution of native endowments, any more that one deserves one's initial starting place in society. The assertion that a man deserves the superior character that enables him to make the effort to cultivate his abilities is equally problematic; for his character depends in large part upon fortunate family and social circumstances for which he can claim no credit. The notion of desert seems not to apply to these cases. Thus the more advantaged representative man cannot say that he deserves and therefore has a right to a scheme of cooperation in which he is permitted to acquire benefits in ways that do not contribute to the welfare of others. There is no basis for his making this claim. From the standpoint of common sense, then, the difference principle appears to be acceptable both to the more advantaged and to the less advantaged individual.[14]

Strictly speaking, such considerations do not influence Rawlsian contractors deliberating behind the veil of ignorance. Vicious circularity would be involved if, on one hand, justice was defined in terms of the outcome of such deliberations and, on the other hand, parties to the deliberations voted on the basis of their views on justice. Rather, the people in the original position behind the veil would reject liberal equality of opportunity in order to insure themselves against the possibility of turning out to be a relatively untalented person in a liberal society.

What the quoted passage does show, Rawls would maintain, is that his principles of justice conform to our own considered judgments about justice, those judgments in which we place the most confidence. Perhaps what ultimately justifies the Rawlsian contract procedure is its ability to explain, support, systematize, and provide grounds for reconsideration of our intuitive sentiments about social justice.

When fully spelled out, then, the Rawlsian argument is that the two principles of justice are justified because they and they alone would emerge from a fair procedure of rational choice. The procedure itself is warranted because of its coherence with our most firmly held *considered* judgments about justice and fairness. Finally, Rawls would maintain that were his principles actually applied, then, because of their emphasis on wealth as a product of cooperation, a stable well-ordered society would result.

For much of the remainder of his book, Rawls then applies his theory to the task of creating social institutions in accordance with the two principles of justice. The details of Rawls's analysis takes us beyond the scope of this study, but we should point out that liberty is secured in the writing of a constitution and the implementation of the difference principle is accomplished through the legislature.

To get a better idea of how a pure procedural theory of justice works, let us contrast a libertarian market analysis of economic justice with a more egalitarian view like that of Rawls. We will then evaluate each theory and provide the outline of a procedural theory of our own.

THE MARKET SOLUTION TO ECONOMIC JUSTICE

Classical Laissez-Faire

In classical laissez-faire economics, the problem of distributive justice was to be resolved by the automatic working of the marketplace. Defenders of the marketplace as the procedural mechanism for distributive justice have called upon both utilitarian arguments and arguments based on natural rights to make their defense. The utilitarian arguments are most commonly associated with economists who have developed elaborate models to show that the competitive market is the most efficient way to maximize the production of goods and services. Indeed utilitarian defenses are more common than defenses based on natural rights.

However, a rights based defense is central to the work of the libertarian economists, Milton Friedman and Friedrich von Hayek, and has been passionately argued by the philosopher Robert Nozick.

Milton Friedman argues that the market mechanism enables us to exercise our natural right to liberty in the following ways. First, it guarantees freedom of property including the right to spend our incomes as we see fit. Second, it guarantees freedom of occupation. Each person chooses the occupation he or she most desires consistent with his ability to get hired. Third, it enhances freedom of development. Each person chooses his or her own lifestyle and is free to go as far as possible consistent with one's abilities. Fourth, it enhances freedom of expression. Friedman argues that the competitive market protects the basic freedoms of communication by separating economic and political power and by decentralizing economic power. One's freedom of speech is more meaningful so long as alternative opportunities for employment exist, a condition that cannot exist if the government owns and operates the economy. One's freedom of expression, especially freedom of the press, is also enhanced since ideas inconsistent with those of the government or one's editorial board may still get published. The fear that a competitor may publish the work often overcomes the distaste of certain ideas. For this reason, contemporary libertarians decry the increasing centralization of industry, the growth of government influence, and the establishment of the business-government-university alliance that Galbraith has characterized as the New Industrial State.

Friedman's appeal to our natural right to liberty is also a useful device to combat contemporary critics of the market in general, and of American capitalism in particular. Consider the kinds of criticisms we hear of American life these days. First, many groups believe that their salaries are too low, especially in light of salaries in other professions. In the market, salary depends, at least to a considerable degree, on the extent to which the product or services produced is in demand. Under market conditions, social workers and teachers may get paid less than bartenders and garbage collectors. It does not seem adequate to inform the former group that their lower salaries are justified since their service is less in demand. What about the artist who is ahead of his time and finds that his creations are not in demand? Just how serious should the economic consequences be for those who find the goods and services they have to offer unpopular?

Other critics focus on product quality. They argue that the major corporations do not have adequate concern for the durability or even the safety of their products. The developers of nuclear power plants are criticized for failing to have developed adequate fail-safe safety devices. Nearly every month, another product is added to the growing list of suspected causes of cancer. The aerosol spray can allegedly threatens the earth's protective ozone layer. Surely the market is incapable of policing itself; outside regulation is needed. Or so the critics argue.

Against such critics, Friedman delivers a stern lecture. He thinks the notion of passing judgment on the quality or social desirability of goods is a dangerous one. Who is to decide whether or not a good is socially desirable? Certainly we would not want government officials, or psychologists, or even philosopher kings making that decision. What the marketplace provides is a democratic vote; the supply-and-demand procedure is really a voting procedure for determining quality. What the critic of libertarianism is really attacking is the democratic determination of the marketplace and he is trying to substitute the voices of a few for the voices of all. Such an elitist attitude is (*a*) unjustified because there are no experts on matters of value; and (*b*) dangerous because expert determination of product quality undermines the individual freedom of consumer choice, which the marketplace is designed to protect. The fact that bartenders are paid more than social workers is the price we must pay for our individual freedom. Hence the market solution, which rewards producers on the basis of demand, is the best method of distributing goods and services.

In addition to protecting our natural right to liberty the market enhances our natural right to well-being. Since the workings of the marketplace provide for maximum efficiency, the greatest amount of economic good for the greatest number is produced. To tamper with the market interferes with its efficiency and the end result is a smaller aggregate amount of goods and services. Hence, the unfettered market provides the greatest gross national product from which rights to well-being can be implemented.

The critics of the market mechanism condemn it since it allows distributive patterns that would be intolerable from the moral point of view. On *pure* classical theory, one receives economic reward if and only if (*a*) he has contributed to the productive process; or (*b*) he is voluntarily supported by a producer, either as a member of a family or by gifts through charity. Clearly, to the extent that individuals are unable to contribute to the productive process through no fault of their own and to the extent that voluntary charity is unable to meet their basic needs, the distributive pattern is unjust. It does seem to be a fact that the innocent nonproductive, e.g., the aged, the ill, the mentally defective, receive marginal treatment at best. Exposés regarding these groups in our society are commonplace.

The defenders of the market solution to the problem of distribution are quick to point out the dangers of any other approach, however. The distribution of goods and services is related to and dependent upon the production of them. Any distribution scheme that interferes with the optimal conditions of production is at least inefficient in the sense that fewer goods and services will be produced than could have been produced. If the interference is especially severe, the total number of goods and services will actually decline. There are technical reasons why certain distributive schemes, e.g., taxes, interfere with the optimal conditions for production. Unsophisticated but popular expressions of this argument abound:

"Why should I work so hard if 30 percent of my income is taken up in taxes?"
"Why bother with overtime? Most of the money I make goes to welfare?"
"Hell, why should I work at all? I can do better on welfare."

As sentiments such as these become more and more pervasive, economic growth slows and in severe cases the absolute number of goods and services decline. Well-intentioned guarantees for living standards do more harm than good.

Rather than interfere with incentives, the defender of the market mechanism argues that one should let the rapidly rising living standards that result from an efficient economic system bury the distributive problem in a cornucopia of goods.

A sketch of the argument is as follows:

1. There are certain situations where individuals suffer from an extreme scarcity of goods and services through no fault of their own.
2. However, such situations are inevitable in an economic system where supply and demand play a large part.

3. However, the results of the system as a whole are so beneficial that everyone is better off. For example, a system that produces the means for twenty-four units of happiness and distributes them unequally, twelve, seven, and five, is more just than a system that produces only six units of happiness and distributes them equally two to each.

4. Premise 3 is true even if we feel that the recipient of five units should have received more in that particular system.

5. Hence, problems of distributive justice must be seen in their total context.

6. Therefore, a given instance of an unjust distribution is not an effective counterexample against the theory. The procedure may make everyone better off, including the offended party, than any alternative system.

In fact, the whole argument seems like an elaborate working out of Rawls's principle that "inequalities as defined by the institutional structure or fostered by it are arbitrary unless it is reasonable to expect that they will work out to everyone's advantage and provided that the positions and offices to which they attach or from which they may be gained are open to all."

Here the laissez-faire theorist rests the case. He claims that the theory has the best of all possible worlds—an implementation of both the rights to freedom and well-being—in fact, a maximization of them. These arguments indicate how the adoption of the market mechanism implements both the rights to well-being and freedom. The classical laissez-faire theory of distributive justice is one of the most famous examples of procedural justice. One is not concerned with determining the justice of each individual situation. Rather, one is concerned with a just procedure such that whatever the actual distribution, so long as the procedure is followed, the distribution is ipso facto just. Moreover, this implementation occurs without human moral effort. In fact, such conscious effort would only work to the detriment of the implementation. Instead, the driving force is egoism. As persons try to maximize their own selfish good, the greatest good for all is achieved. In a strange paradox, selfishness produces beneficence: a private vice produces public benefits.[15]

Nozick's Entitlement Theory

Robert Nozick's *Anarchy, State and Utopia* is a valuable contemporary addition to the traditional laissez-faire approach. He agrees with Friedman and others that the free market supports individual freedom. He also believes that the market really does operate as a procedural mechanism of justice but that Rawls's alternative theory is flawed—in part—because it is not a genuine theory of procedural justice.

Nozick wishes to distinguish between historical principles of justice and nonhistorical principles of justice that he calls end-state principles. With respect to distribution, a defender of the historical approach would argue that in assessing the justice of a situation, it is not enough to see how the goods are distributed. We must also look at how the goods were produced and how the distribution came about. ". . . historical principles of justice hold that past circumstances or actions of people can create differential entitlements or differential deserts to things."[16] The historical approach is to be contrasted with those theories that impose on any distribution a fixed end or goal. For example, the utilitarian theory is non-historical. It argues that each distribution should be arranged so as to maximize the greatest good for the greatest number. It is Nozick's point that nonhistorical theories are deficient as theories of justice since they ignore historical circumstances that are ethically relevant. One ought not place people in jail just because total utility would increase if they were jailed. Rather, placing people in jail depends on the historical fact of their being tried and found guilty. We agree with Nozick that historical considerations cannot be ignored. But we do not think that historical considerations are decisive, as Nozick apparently does. We do not think that possession is nine-tenths of the law.

Another distinction Nozick makes is between patterned and nonpatterned principles of justice. A patterned principle selects some characteristic or set of characteristics which specifies how the distribution is to be achieved. Any formula that fills in the blank of "to each according to _____" is a patterned formula.

> Let us call a principle of distribution *patterned* if it specifies that a distribution is to vary along with some natural dimension, weighted sum of natural dimensions, or lexicographic ordering of natural dimensions.[17]

Nozick finds any patterned principle objectionable because the attempt to have the distribution be in accordance with the pattern is an infringement on liberty. Nozick illustrates this point by considering how a famous athlete such as Wilt Chamberlain can upset the pattern. Suppose we achieve our patterned distribution, which in this case is equal. Suppose also that there is such a great demand to see Wilt Chamberlain play basketball that people will pay him twenty-five cents of their ticket price to get him to play. Suppose that during one year one million persons pay him $250,000 to see him play. This gives Wilt Chamberlain far more than he would have received under the equal-distribution formula. What do we do now? To maintain the pattern of equal distribution, we would have to interfere with the transfer of the twenty-five cents by those million persons. As Nozick says:

> The general point illustrated by the Wilt Chamberlain example . . . is that no end-state principle or distributional patterned principle of

justice can be continuously realized without continuous interference with people's lives. Any favored pattern would be transformed into one unfavored by the principle, by people choosing to act in various ways; for example, by people exchanging goods and services with other people, or giving things to other people, things the transferrers are entitled to under the favored distribution pattern. To maintain a pattern one must either continually interfere to stop people from transferring resources as they wish to, or continually (or periodically) interfere to take from some persons resources that others for some reason chose to transfer to them.[18]

Nozick can then magnify these infringements on liberty. Suppose, for example, that we tax people in order to provide others with a better standard of living. What is the difference, Nozick asks, between forcing someone to work five hours for the benefit of the needy and involuntarily taxing someone five hours' worth of work. Nozick claims that there is no difference. "Taxation of earnings from labor is on a par with forced labor." Hence, Nozick has two arguments to show how attempts to achieve patterned distributions result in an infringement of one's right to liberty.

As an alternative, Nozick develops a nonpatterned theory that he calls the theory of entitlements. In Nozick's view a distribution is just if everyone has what he is entitled to. To determine what people are entitled to we must discuss the original acquisition of holdings, the transfer of holdings, and the rectification of holdings. Nozick's theory of acquisition is a variant of Locke's theory of property rights. Any person has a right to any owned thing so long as ownership by that person does not worsen the situation of others. Suppose I farm a plot of land that is neither used nor owned by anyone else. I cultivate the land, plant the seeds, and weed and water the garden plot. Surely, I am entitled to the fruits of the harvest. What Nozick attempts to do is to accommodate all types of legitimate ownership to the case of the garden plot. We are entitled to what we have worked for or freely received by transfer from others.

The scarcity of goods and resources complicates Nozick's account. After all, whenever someone owns something he usually diminishes the opportunity of someone else's owning it. There are not enough resources for a swimming pool and two cars for all. It is the recognition of this problem that accounts for Nozick's addition of the phrase "does not worsen the situation of others."

That phrase needs considerable interpretation, however. For Nozick, someone's situation is not worsened if his opportunities became more limited. At times Nozick speaks as if someone's situation would be worsened if he fell below a certain baseline:

> This excludes his transferring it into an agglomeration that does violate the Lockean proviso and excludes his using it in a way . . . so as to

violate the proviso by making the situation of others worse than their baseline situation.[19]

The reader might be tempted to think that the phrase "baseline situation" means something like "minimum standard of living" or "welfare floor." If this were the case, fairly extensive violations of liberty would be allowed to keep people from falling below the baseline.

However, the examples Nozick chooses for discussion and other more extensive comments that he makes indicate that his view of how one's ownership of something makes another worse off is far more narrow. Nozick seems to indicate that we should compare the situation of the person as it would be with a system of property rights and as it would be without a system of property rights. If Jones acquires something, Smith is not made worse off unless Smith's situation deteriorates to the point where he is worse off than he would be in a system without property rights.

The end result of Nozick's discussion of how one person can be harmed by another's acquisition of property is that nearly everyone is entitled to everything he acquires so long as coercion or fraud is not involved. The theory is rounded out by the contention that what one has justly acquired, one is entitled to transfer to others. One can see why Nozick would adopt the slogan, "from each as they choose, to each as they are chosen." A person is entitled to something if he acquired it without worsening the situation of others or if he received it as a transfer from one who had acquired it without worsening the situation of others.

NOZICK OR RAWLS?

Which theory of procedural justice provides the best account of economic justice—Nozick's or Rawls's.

Nozick's account of acquisition is the key to his theory. In describing how a just acquisition is achieved, he emphasizes liberty at the expense of all other values. His central starting point is the right to liberty. In section one of his book, not discussed here, Nozick shows that the existence of a state does not necessarily violate one's right to liberty. As we have seen, he rejects any principle of distribution that violates the right to liberty. He rejects any interpretation of his own principle that creates such a violation as well. Why should we build a theory of justice in terms of liberty alone? As a consequence of his position, Nozick believes it would be unjust for even a wealthy state to tax individuals in order to provide better food, clothing, or housing for the poor. In Nozick's view we are entitled (have a right) to our legitimate acquisitions but the poor have no right to a minimum standard of living. In Chapter Three, we examined the ground of human rights. If rights claims are justified on the basis of our recognition of the dignity and self-respect of every individual, then the right to a minimum standard of well-being is as firmly justified as our right to liberty. Nozick not only ignores our right to well-being but utterly annihilates it, as it comes into conflict with one's right to liberty. Such an extreme point of view needs considerable defense, which unfortunately is not supplied.

The ideological flavor of Nozick's theory is clearly seen in his discussion of how A's ownership of X can worsen the condition of B. How does Nozick justify his suggestion about how people can be worsened i.e., people are worsened only if they are worse off than they would be in a system without property rights. It is most remarkable that Nozick provides no defense at all. Since Nozick's interpretation is so counterintuitive, surely some justification is called for.

Of course our criticism of Nozick would be less harsh if we could interpret how people's condition could be worsened more broadly. We might say that someone's condition is worsened when it falls below a certain baseline (social-welfare floor). In this way our liberty as expressed through property rights would be checked in the face of extreme need. This interpretation would be clearly inconsistent with most of what Nozick says, however.

Unfortunately, as Nozick himself seems to concede, he does not offer a full-fledged theory of acquisition or indeed of what it means to own anything. With respect to the former there is no discussion of what counts as fraudulent acquisition. Stealing is clearly illegitimate since it violates one's right to liberty. Is advertising legitimate? Even subliminal advertising? Can one prey upon the ignorance of the poor? Must products be proven safe? With respect to the concept of ownership, when does someone own something? Can property owners forbid jet planes to fly over their homes? Do the minerals at the bottom of the ocean or on Mars belong to the person who gets there first? What account can be given of public goods or collective ownership?

Nozick's account of justice is severely limited in scope. By construing "worsening the situation of others" so narrowly he allows nearly any acquisition or transfer to be a just one. By failing to place some constraints on the means of acquisition and by failing to define how someone can be said to own something, many of the important issues are ignored. By taking no account of social institutions and past contributions of others, he ignores the social underpinning of property and overemphasizes the importance and indeed even the rights claims of the isolated individual.

The market model has its difficulties as well. Our chief objection to the market approach to economic justice is that it fails to resolve adequately conflicts between our natural right to liberty and our natural right to well-being. Our first objection is that Friedman's notion of "freedom" is inadequate.

Although we have accepted Friedman's argument that private property is supportive of the traditional freedoms of press, speech, and so on, we do not find all his analysis of "freedom" satisfactory. For example, we believe that this analogy between a democratic voting procedure and consumer purchasing power is inappropriate. In the democratic voting procedure each person has only one vote. In the marketplace voting strength is a function of income strength. Since income is unequal, the analogy between political voting and consumer-purchasing voting breaks down. In fact the analogy is further weakened when one considers the ability of advertising to mold and influence wants.

There are also problems with Friedman's analysis of the market as the enhancer of individualism in matters of taste and expression. Although he has a point when he argues that centralization creates dangers, the market mechanism creates problems as well. Some welfare economists argue that the market itself leads to uniformity and mediocrity. The following is a concise statement of the argument by the economist Tibor Scitovsky:

1. Economic conditions require that most companies operate at a high volume.
2. Since most companies operate at a high volume, it is the tastes of the vast majority which are more important.
3. The tastes of the minority are either omitted or molded into the majority through advertising.
4. In any case, the minority tastes have little influence in the marketplace.
5. The informed and cultivated are in the minority.
6. Therefore the informed and cultivated have little influence in the marketplace.
7. This loss of influence is reflected in substandard products of a uniform nature designed for mass mediocrity.[20]

This argument can be illustrated by a consideration of music. Classical recordings hold only a small percentage of the market. Many symphony orchestras are threatened with extinction and even the major symphonies are in the throes of financial difficulties. However, certain rock stars command over $1,000,000 for a single performance.

Moreover, the marketplace does not adequately protect freedom of employment. In the classical model there are no unions to protect the individual employee against his employers. Even with unions in the picture, constraints of other types work against employee mobility. Training, family ties, and social affiliations make it difficult, and in some cases impossible, for employees to leave present occupations for better conditions elsewhere. In these respects the marketplace fails to provide conditions for genuine job alternatives. Also, there is no protection against recession and plant closings.

Finally, it is frequently rational to choose to be coerced. It is not uncommon for people to choose to impose deadlines upon themselves in order to provide the necessary discipline to reach their goals. Modern game theory provides many illustrations of instances where it is rational to be coerced. Consider a landlord in a decaying neighborhood trying to decide whether he should repair his property. Suppose his position with respect to any other landlord can be represented in the following game matrix:[21] (In the matrix, the payoffs to the individual owners have been identified.)

| | | OWNER A | | |
		Column 1 Invest		Column 2 Do Not Invest	
OWNER B	Row 1 Invest	B .07	A .07	B .03	A .10
	Row 2 Do Not Invest	B .10	A .03	B .04	A .04

Clearly the best joint result is that they both invest (Column 1, row 1). However, to achieve this result both Owner A and Owner B must be coerced to cooperate. Otherwise, so long as Owner A and Owner B act independently, Owner A will choose Column 2 no matter what Owner B does and Owner B will choose Row 2 no matter what Owner A does. If Owner B chose Row 1 Column 1, B would receive only .07 or less than the .10 B could receive in Row 2. B should not invest. If B were in Column 2 Row 1, B would receive only .03 when B could receive .04 in Row 2, so B should not invest. Since A would only receive .07 in Column 1 Row 1, A should be in Column 2 Row 1 where A would receive .10. A should not invest. If A were in Column 1 Row 2, A would receive .03, when A could receive .04 in Column 2 Row 2. A should not invest. The square which satisfies A should not invest and B should not invest is Column 2 Row 2. That result is in the best interest of neither. Since both Owners want the best result, they will agree to coercion. On this occasion, agreement to coercion is an expression of freedom.

In general our point is this: Although laissez-faire capitalism supports the value of freedom in many instances, it also ignores or even inhibits that value in many other instances. Freedom from external constraints is not always enough. A just society must frequently provide genuine alternatives, e.g., something more than a choice among ten rock music stations. Moreover, we indicated that not all coercion is bad; indeed certain types of coercion may be supportive of freedom itself.

Capitalism and well-being The classical response to the egalitarian critique of the marketplace is to bury the objection in a cornucopia of economic goods. The long-range growth of the economic system makes everyone better off in the long run. The moral problem centers around the expression "long run." As John Maynard Keynes so cheerfully reminded us, "In the long run we are all dead." It may be just to distribute eight units of economic welfare to one person and two units to another in order that tomorrow we can distribute twenty units to the one and fifteen to the other. However, it seems unjust to distribute eight units to one person and two units to another so that their great-grandchildren may receive twenty and fifteen units respectively. The philosophical point is a simple one. It is simply not true that all unjust distributions can be rectified in the long run. Certain basic economic necessities ought to be provided now, not later. Thus, the future can only justify the past if the individuals are the same in both cases. For certain groups in our society, particularly blacks, the long run has become very long indeed.

We now consider the Rawlsian alternative.

Evaluation of Rawls's theory   Since its publication, Rawls's book has been subjected to intensive analysis by philosophers, political scientists, and economists. Indeed, graduate seminars on Rawls can be as technical and detailed as seminars on topics that have been with us for some time. All the arguments that have been advanced against Rawls's theory cannot be considered here.

Moreover, his three-tiered relationship makes Rawls's theory a very complex one. One might accept his two principles without accepting the notion of the hypothetical contract from which they were derived. Alternatively one might approve of the conception of the original position with its hypothetical contract and veil of ignorance but disagree with Rawls as to what principles of justice would ultimately be adopted. It is also possible to agree with much of what Rawls says about particular institutions without accepting his more general theory, and conversely. Our criticisms of Rawls focus on three main areas:

1. Rawls's statement of the contract conditions either begs or leaves open important moral questions.
2. In his analysis of the contract conditions, Rawls fails to provide an adequate account of individual rights.
3. Rawls's statement of the two principles and his lexical ordering of them is incomplete and unclear and hence it is hard to evaluate his theory in practical situations.

With respect to the first type of objection, many critics have charged that in specifying what facts we are in ignorance of, Rawls is "stacking the deck." That is, his only reason for specifying the contract conditions as he does is that his principles of justice are then the only ones that could be chosen. This can be most clearly seen in his discussion of the adoption of the second principle. It is difficult to see why rational egoists would unanimously adopt it. Wouldn't some be willing to take risks on getting the larger shares as an alternative to the difference principle? Surely some would gamble on a society where 90 percent of the people lived in affluence and the other 10 percent at a bare minimum over a society where 100 percent of the people lived in poverty although above the bare minimum. To avoid this contingency, Rawls stipulates that in the original condition one of the facts we must be ignorant of is our propensity to take risks.[22] But surely this looks like an ad hoc stipulation designed to rule out a competing alternative.[23]

Other critics argue that Rawls's account is biased in favor of individualistic theories.[24] This contention is based on Rawls's account of the nature of the good. In the original condition, Rawls rules out any knowledge of what each of us considers to be the good life. Rather, our knowledge of our desires is limited to what Rawls calls the primary goods. Primary goods are goods like rights and liberties, powers and opportunities, income and wealth, which every rational person should want since these goods are necessary for achieving any other goods. By limiting our knowledge of the good in this way, Rawls can argue that no one would choose a society where the pursuit of one good at the expense of all others prevailed. For example, no one would choose a society where religious persecution was practiced, since behind the veil one does not know if one would be in the majority religion or not. But again, isn't this stipulation biased against individuals who hold alternative theories of justice in which one value, such as predominance of a religion, or a limited set of values are given preeminence? As several critics have indicated, Rawls's refusal to rank particular conceptions of the good implies a very marked tolerance for individual inclination.

In other words being neutral with respect to various theories of the good is not a neutral decision. It reflects a built-in liberal, individualistic assumption that is undefended within the theory. In recent discussion, Rawls himself seems to acknowledge that his assumptions are not neutral but goes on to maintain that they are morally favored. They stipulate conditions under which we can choose as free and equal beings. If Rawls makes such a move, however, it is hard to see what advantage his theory has over a traditional natural rights appeal to human equality. The contract situation, with the veil of ignorance, is no longer seen as a justification for fundamental human rights but rather is seen to presuppose them. However, to assess the merits of this criticism fully would take us far afield. Our remaining two criticisms of Rawls focus on issues central to the concerns discussed in this book.

One such criticism contends that the contract procedure provides an inadequate justification for individual rights. We think that Rawls's account of the original position is incomplete. In addition to a procedure for formulating adequate principles, he must provide an analysis of who should be entitled to participate in the procedure. In other words, Rawls must say something about who is to be a contract maker. However, Rawls's comments on this problem are vague and indecisive. As you recall one of Rawls's principles for evaluating institutions is that everyone participating in a practice or affected by it, has an equal right to the most extensive liberty compatible with a like liberty for all. Sometimes it seems as if Rawls is using this principle to determine who shall be a contract maker.[25] If Rawls is indeed making this move, he is guilty of a logical error. Since the contract procedure is designed to produce principles—indeed, the contract procedure *defines* what are to count as acceptable procedures, one cannot use one of the principles so derived to determine who shall participate in the procedure. If Rawls is to speak of an equal right to participation, this is not to be equated with the principle of equal liberty, against which we measure the social institutions and practices.

At other times Rawls argues that one is to be a participant if and only if one has the capacity for a sense of justice:

> The capacity for a sense of justice is then necessary and sufficient for the duty of justice to be owed to a person—that is, for a person to be regarded as holding an initial position of equal liberty.[26]

In *A Theory of Justice* Rawls elaborates this position more fully. He argues that the required capacity for a sense of justice be minimal and that it is incorrect to conclude that the greater one's capacity for a sense of justice, the greater weight one's opinions should have in the contract process. He also assumes that for all practical purposes this minimal capacity for a sense of justice is possessed by the overwhelming majority of humanity. He believes this assumption insures that everyone has equal rights.[27]

Our own view is that moral psychology provides an insecure foundation for one's equal right to be a contract maker. Rawls argues that a sense of justice evolves according to psychological laws. More specifically it develops from the morality of authority and the morality of association. These moralities themselves require certain psychological background conditions for development, namely, that one is raised by loving parents and that one matures in a socially cooperative society characterized by just institutions and bonds of friendship and mutual trust.[28] However, these conditions obviously do not hold in a great many cases. Hence if Rawls's psychology is correct, his assumption that nearly everyone has the minimal capacity for a sense of justice may well be incorrect.

Once this question is raised, we see no advantage for Rawls's view over our normative theory of equal rights.[29] Whereas the rights theory begins with a normative claim, Rawls must find a way to bridge the gap between the factual assertion that a person has a certain psychological capacity and the normative claim that such a person has a right to be a contract maker.

Moreover, our rights theory does not depend upon the success of one's family and society in providing the appropriate psychological background so that one might be a rights bearer.

The final objection concerns the lack of clarity in Rawls's statement of the two principles of justice and his lexical ordering of them. With respect to the first principle, the principle of equal liberty, Rawls's discussion is inadequate on several grounds. First, objections can be made to his list of basic liberties. That list includes "political liberty (the right to vote and to be eligible for public office) together with freedom of speech and assembly; liberty of conscience and freedom of thought; freedom of the person along with the right to hold (personal) property; and freedom from arbitrary arrest and seizure as defined by the concept of the rule of law."[30] Rawls provides no theory that indicates which liberties should be on the list and which liberties should not be on it. For example, Rawls does not include the freedom to choose what Rawls refers to as one's own life plan. Also, he has not included the freedom to select one's own lifestyle among the basic liberties. There is no reference to freedom to use drugs or to select one's own sexual partner.[31] Yet no *grounds* are provided for such exclusion.

Second, Rawls's account of how liberty is constrained is too narrow. Rawls argues that liberties can only be constrained by allowing for the exercise of other liberties. Consider the damages done by libel or slander. Consider the harms of pollution. What basic liberty can be involved to curtail these types of harms?[32]

Finally, Rawls has no effective mechanism for balancing off the competing liberty claims so that the most extensive total system of equal basic liberties is achieved. Note that Rawls believes that the liberty principle would be unanimously adopted in the original condition and can be used as a measure for determining the justice of a society's institutions. However, we contend that it would only be selected if we know in advance how conflicts of liberty are to be resolved.

Rawls admits that the assignment of priorities to the various basic liberties is a difficult undertaking:

> Different opinions about the value of the liberties will, of course, affect how different persons think the full scheme of freedom should be arranged. Those who place a higher worth on the principle of participation will be prepared to take greater risks with the freedoms of the person, say, in order to give political liberty a large place.[33]

So long as people know that their value rankings of the various liberties are likely to differ, it seems rational to believe that they would insist on determining a procedure for bringing about compatibility of all individual's liberty packages. Only in this way could an individual lessen the chance of his or her having a total system of freedom inconsistent with the value ordering of freedom that he or she turns out to have.

The likelihood of obtaining a unanimous vote on such a procedure seems remote. Rawls's liberty principle would be accepted unanimously only if its full meaning is not carefully spelled out. Attempts to provide the principle with some content greatly reduce the chances of the principle being accepted unanimously.

We also question the plausibility of the second principle and Rawls's lexical ordering of the two principles. As you recall Rawls's justification for the difference principle was that it treated talents and abilities as collective assets. Given this perspective, Rawls argued that the difference principle is the principle which would be adopted by those behind the veil of ignorance. Rawls's analysis has been seriously challenged by Robert Nozick and David Gauthier.[34] Nozick's point is that the most able and talented would not agree to the difference principle since they made all the sacrifices and have little to gain. After all, who has the most to gain from social cooperation? Surely it is the least able and talented. Hence the less able should be willing to agree not only to an equal distribution of the fruits of social cooperation but to something considerably less than equality. For example, why wouldn't it be rational for those behind the veil of ignorance to argue that everyone should reach a welfare floor, which in affluent societies would be quite high, but after this floor has been reached everyone should receive in proportion to one's contribution. If such a proposal is irrational, we have not been shown why.

Another serious objection arises when we consider the relations between the two principles. By ordering them lexically, Rawls is saying that the conditions of the first principle must be completely satisfied before one tries to satisfy the second condition. Rawls's ordering of the principles in this way has received universal criticism. Surely such a lexical ordering would not be accepted by a unanimous vote of the contract makers and surely such a priority rule would be unjust. In underdeveloped countries, it may be rational, at least sometimes, to sacrifice basic liberties for improved economic well being. Although all too often, such an argument is used by a powerful elite to deny others their rights, it need not always be without force. For example, sometimes it may be justifiable to restrict free choice of occupation in order to place key workers in crucial positions, if severe economic deprivation can be prevented by such a policy. Rawls himself seems to recognize the force of this point since he is careful to limit the range of applicability of the priority of liberty.

> The supposition is that if persons in the original position assume that their basic liberties can be effectively exercised, they will not exchange a lesser liberty for an improvement in their economic well-being, *at least not once a certain level of wealth has been maintained.*

It is only when social conditions do not allow the effective establishment of these rights that one can acknowledge their restriction. The denial of equal liberty can be accepted only if it is necessary to enhance the quality of civilization so that in due course the equal freedoms can be enjoyed by all. The lexical ordering of the two principles is the long-run tendency of the general conception of justice consistently pursued under reasonably favorable circumstances.[35]

Once the lexical ordering rule is compromised, however, Rawls must provide some indication of the principles for determining the guidelines of compromise. Under what conditions should the lexical ordering be given up? The necessity for some guidelines will become more evident if we can show that exceptions to the priority rule are not isolated and unusual but rather are pervasive and quite normal. To what extent would rational egoists in the original condition compromise liberty for economic betterment? Speculations here would surely be highly abstract, but evidence abounds that currently economic betterment is valued more highly than Rawls thinks. Indeed, tradeoffs are not limited to so-called underdeveloped countries but exist in even the most affluent societies. Even the most casual observer of the United States cannot help but be impressed by the apparent dominance of pocketbook issues over issues of liberty. When such attitudes prevail in the most affluent society, the long-run tendency of society to develop to the point where the lexical ordering will prevail is very long indeed. If we look toward actual societies, the compromise of the liberty principle is very extensive indeed.

Of course Rawls might well argue that current societal practices do not mirror what reflections would be made by persons operating in the original condition operating under a veil of ignorance. This point would be well taken but then it is incumbent upon Rawls to indicate the point where the lexical ordering of the two principles is in fact legitimate. Vague comments about "due course" and "a certain level of wealth" are not adequate.

Finally, Rawls's view that our talents, capacities, and even our character are the arbitrary results of a natural environmental-genetic lottery, and so are social assets, is vulnerable to the charge of being disrespectful to persons. For example, why should our liberty be so valued if how we use it depends on such contingencies as our tastes, our inclination, and skills? Why shouldn't our kidneys be viewed as social assets since the luck of the draw determines who has and who lacks healthy kidneys? What is left of the individual once skills, capacities, and character are stripped away? Perhaps Rawls is just as guilty as the utilitarian of not taking the differences between persons seriously. At least on the intuitive level, it often seems just, as in competitive athletics, to let outcomes be determined by individual skills, effort, and character, so long as such practices do not undermine the rights of others, positive and negative alike. Perhaps that is all Rawls means to say, but his remarks about the natural lottery and the reduction of individual characteristics to social assets suggest a de-individualized view of the person that seems morally unattractive.

Despite these difficulties, Rawls's achievement surely is such that subsequent normative political theorizing must at least wrestle with his views. His theory of justice, as we hope we have shown, is a thoughtful, penetrating, and sophisticated approach to political theory, one which succeeds in systematizing many people's considered judgments about justice. We suggest, however, that it be viewed not as a completed edifice but rather as a foundation upon which more adequate theories of justice can be constructed.

In particular, three areas of Rawlsian theory seem especially defensible. First, Rawls seems correct in arguing that political institutions must buttress rather than destroy self respect. Second, his criticisms of utilitarianism have force. We agree that the plight of the least well off deserves special attention. Finally, Rawls's emphasis on procedural justice is well taken. It is upon this Rawlsian foundation that an alternative view can be grounded.

Our own suggestion for resolving problems of distributive justice as well as for many other justice issues is to consider a suggestion made by Rawls that he himself abandons. Perhaps a solution may be found if we take the perspective of procedural justice but extend it from application to hypothetical deliberations behind a veil of ignorance to actual democratic procedures in the real world. If Rawls's critics are right, his version of hypothetical or ideal contractualism does not adequately resolve many significant moral and political issues. Perhaps democracy, suitably constrained, is a procedure which can resolve such controversies fairly.

JUSTICE AND DEMOCRACY

We can best illustrate our own theory by comparing and contrasting it with some of the positions dissected in this chapter. We agree that it is very difficult if not impossible to determine specifically what is just for each and every situation. Considerations of justice are simply too complicated for that to be done. We do not follow others, however, in abandoning the concept of justice. Rather, we think Rawls is right in emphasizing procedural justice for, only in this way, can the argument be met.

We are careful, however, to put constraints on what kind of procedures will qualify. Questions of justice arise because the rights claims of individuals come into conflict. The right to liberty frequently clashes with other rights, such as that to a minimally decent standard of living. However, our view of rights is much broader than that of Robert Nozick, since he limits rights claims to the right of individual liberty.

Given that legitimate rights claims frequently conflict, we have argued that it is the function of the state to provide morally acceptable procedures for adjudicating these conflicts. Since the adjudicating of rights claims is what justice is all about, we can conclude that a function of the state is to provide justice.

Since we will take a procedural approach to the problem of justice, we share a fundamental assumption with Rawls. However, we reject the hypothetical contract/veil-of-ignorance approach. As the previous discussion indicates, that approach does not yield a determinate outcome. In the next chapter, we will argue that a form of democratic voting as well as other traditional democratic institutions provide the best means for settling conflicts of rights and, hence, for approximating justice. For Rawls's hypothetical contract, we substitute a form of democratic government.

We wish to emphasize, however, that the framework of individual rights puts considerable constraint on the types of issues that can be subject to democratic vote. The proper objects of state action are the implementation of individual rights and the resolution of rights conflicts. Moreover, an individual's right can only be denied on the basis of providing for another individual right. Appeals to such abstractions as the maximization of utility or the greater glory of the nation are out of place. Hence, we agree with Nozick that people have a right to form associations, acquire possessions, and develop individual lifestyles. However, since we have a broader concept of individual rights, we will allow more constraints on our individual right to liberty.

Finally, although we agree with Rawls that individual liberty is important and that the plight of the least well-off deserves special attention, we reject the specific wording of Rawls's two principles and their lexical ordering. We suggest that the historical circumstances of a people are relevant in determining appropriate principles of justice. The existence of goods and resources and the state of technological advance are important determinants of the principles that should be adopted for implementing our right to well being and for protecting our rights to liberty and privacy.

In summary our theory of justice is the following:

1. Problems of justice arise as individuals attempt to implement their rights.
2. The function of the state is to provide a mechanism for adjudicating the conflicts of individual rights claims and for implementing them.
3. Suitably constrained, a form of democracy is the appropriate procedure for providing justice.
4. Our individual rights framework provides some limitations on the kinds of questions that can be submitted to the democratic mechanism.
5. Other moral principles place constraints on the democratic mechanism but these principles can only be discovered by analyzing particular problems in particular historical circumstances. We do not believe a set of principles lex-

ically ordered can be derived independent of such particular historical circumstance.

Our next chapter provides the required arguments for points 3 and 4. The remaining chapters of the book give some examples of how our analysis is to be extended to particular problems in differing historical circumstances.

NOTES

[1]Aristotle, *Nicomachean Ethics*, Book Five.

[2]Plato's theory of justice is fully developed in his *Republic*.

[3]Nicholas Rescher, *Distributive Justice* (Indianapolis: Bobbs-Merrill, 1966).

[4]This tradition is represented by the French egalitarian Gracchus Babeuf (1760–1797).

[5]One of the most sophisticated contemporary discussions of equal treatment is by Ronald Dworkin, "What is Equality?" Part I, *Philosophy & Public Affairs* Vol. 10, No. 3, Summer 1981, Part II, *Philosophy & Public Affairs* Vol. 10, No. 4, Fall 1981.

[6]There is considerable contemporary discussion as to what preferences and/or interests should be legitimately considered. One discussion occurs in Ibid.

[7]This example is taken from Gregory Vlasto's important article, "Justice and Equality" in Richard B Brandt, ed. *Social Justice*, (Englewood Cliffs, N.J.: Prentice-Hall, 1962), pp. 31–72.

[8]This criticism is developed by Norman Bowie, "Equality and Distributive Justice," *Philosophy*, vol. 45 (1970): 140–48.

[9]Alf Ross, "The Value of Blood Tests as Evidence in Paternity Cases," *Harvard Law Review* 71 (1958):482. © 1958 by the Harvard Law Review Association.

[10]John Rawls, *A Theory of Justice* (Cambridge, Mass.: Harvard University Press, 1971), pp. 126, 416–33, 93, 411, 130–36, 496–503, 567–77.

[11]*Ibid.*, p. 302. Rawls provides more complicated formulations throughout his book.

[12]*Ibid.*, p. 61.

[13]*Ibid.*, p. 70.

[14]*Ibid.*, p. 104.

[15]For a delightful discussion of this paradox, see Bernard Mandeville, *Fable of the Bees* (Oxford: Clarendon Press, 1924).

[16]From Robert Nozick, *Anarchy, State and Utopia* (New York: Basic Books, 1974), p. 155.

[17]*Ibid.*, p. 156.

[18]*Ibid.*, p. 163.

[19]*Ibid.*, p. 180.

[20]Tibor Scitovsky, "A Critique of Present and Proposed Standards" and "On the Principle of Consumer's Sovereignty" in *Papers on Welfare and Growth* (Stanford: Stanford University Press, 1964), pp. 232–40, 241–49.

[21]The example here is taken from Otto A. Davis and Andrew B. Whinston, "Economic Problems in Urban Renewal" in Edmund S. Phelps, ed., *Private Wants and Public Needs* (New York: W. W. Norton & Co., 1965), pp. 140–53.

[22]John Rawls, *A Theory of Justice*, p. 172.

[23]This point has been made by a number of philosophers, including Brian Barry, *The Liberal Theory of Justice* (Oxford: Clarendon Press, 1973), pp. 96, 230; R. M. Hare, "Critical Study: Rawls's Theory of Justice II," *Philosophical Quarterly*, 23 (1973): 247–51; Russell Keat and David Miller, "Understanding Justice," *Political Theory* 2 (1974): 25–27; Thomas Nagel,

"Rawls on Justice," *Philosophical Review* 82 (1973): 229-30; and David Lewis Schaefer, "A Critique of Rawls's Contract Doctrine," *Review of Metaphysics* 28 (1974): 100.

[24]Critics who develop this point include Brian Barry, *The Liberal Theory of Justice*, pp. 228-29; Maurice Mandelbaum, in his review essay in *History and Theory* 2 (1973): 240-50; and Thomas Nagel, "Rawls on Justice," p. 228. Rawls has attempted to answer this objection. See John Rawls, "Fairness to Goodness" *Philosophical Review* 84 (1975): 536–54.

[25]See, for example, John Rawls, "Constitutional Liberty and the Concept of Justice," in Carl Friedrich and John Chapman, eds., *Nomos 6 Justice* (New York: Atherton Press, 1962), pp. 99, 101, 103.

[26]John Rawls, "The Sense of Justice," *Philosophical Review* 72 (1963): 281–305.

[27]John Rawls, *A Theory of Justice*, pp. 505–7, 510.

[28]*Ibid.*, pp. 462–79.

[29]We omit here a discussion of the practical problems raised by children and the severely retarded.

[30]John Rawls, *A Theory of Justice*, p. 61.

[31]Critics who make this point include H. L. A. Hart, "Rawls on Liberty and Its Priority," *University of Chicago Law Review* 40 (1973): 534–55; and Robert F. Ladenson, "Rawls's Principle of Equal Liberty" (unpublished paper).

[32]This point has been made by H. L. A. Hart, "Rawls on Liberty and Its Priority," p. 547.

[33]John Rawls, *A Theory of Justice*, p. 230.

[34]Robert Nozick, *Anarchy, State and Utopia*, pp. 183–97; and David Gauthier, "Justice and Natural Endowment: Toward a Critique of Rawls's Ideological Framework," *Social Theory and Practice* 3 (1974): 3–26.

[35]John Rawls, *A Theory of Justice*, p. 542 (emphasis ours).

SUGGESTED READINGS

Ackerman, Bruce A. *Social Justice in the Liberal State.* New Haven: Yale University Press, 1980.
Aristotle. *Nicomachean Ethics.* Martin Ostwald, trans. Indianapolis: Bobbs-Merrill, 1962.
Blocker, H. Gene and Smith, Elizabeth H., eds. *John Rawls's Theory of Social Justice.* Athens, Ohio: Ohio University Press, 1980. A collection of essays.
Brandt, Richard, ed. *Social Justice.* Englewood Cliffs, N.J.: Prentice-Hall, 1962.
Daniels, Norman, ed. *Reading Rawls: Critical Studies of A Theory of Justice.* New York: Basic Books, 1975. A Collection of essays.
Feinberg, Joel. *Social Philosophy.* Englewood Cliffs, N.J.: Prentice-Hall, 1973. Chapter Seven.
Friedman, Milton. *Capitalism and Freedom.* Chicago: University of Chicago Press, 1962.
Friedrich, C. J. and Chapman, J., eds. *Nomos VI: Justice.* New York: Aldine-Atherton, 1963.
Nozick, Robert. *Anarchy, State and Utopia.* New York: Basic Books, 1974.
Perelman, Charles. *Justice* New York: Random House, 1967.
Pettit, Philip. *Judging Justice.* Boston: Routledge & Kegan Paul, 1980.
Plato. *The Republic.* Francis MacDonald Cornford, trans. New York: Oxford University Press, 1967.
Rawls, John. *A Theory of Justice.* Cambridge, MA: Harvard University Press, 1971.
Rescher, Nicholas. *Distributive Justice.* New York: Bobbs-Merrill, 1966.
Wilson, John. *Equality.* New York: Harcourt, Brace Jovanovich, 1966.

Articles
Berlin, Isaiah. "Equality." *Proceedings of The Aristotelian Society.* Vol. LVI (1955–1956), pp. 301–26.
Dick, James C. "How to Justify a Distribution of Earnings." *Philosophy and Public Affairs,* Vol. 4 (1975), pp.248–72.
Katzner, Louis. "Presumptivist and Nonpresumptivist Principles of Formal Justice." *Ethics* LXXXI (1971), pp. 253–58.

Kaufmann, Walter. "Doubts About Justice." *Ethics and Social Justice,* Howard E. Kieter and Milton K. Munitz eds. Albany: State University of New York Press, 1968.

Keat, Russell and Miller, David. "Understanding Justice." *Political Theory,* Vol. 2 (1974), pp. 3–31.

Rae, Douglas W. "A Principle of Simple Justice." *Philisophy, Politics, and Society,* 5th Series, Peter Laslett and James Fishkin, eds. New Haven: Yale University Press, 1979.

Schaefer, David Lewis. "A Critique of Rawls's Contract Doctrine." *Review of Metaphysics,* Vol. XXVIII (1974), pp. 89–115.

Wood, Allen W. "The Marxian Critique of Justice" *Philosophy and Public Affairs,* Vol. I (1972), pp. 244–82.

Five
DEMOCRACY
AND POLITICAL
OBLIGATION

"Democracy" is an honorific term. Normally, to call people democrats is to praise them, while to call people undemocratic is normally to suggest that their political morality is questionable. So powerful have the honorific connotations of "democracy" become that even totalitarian states have taken to calling themselves "true" or "people's" democracies.

But if the meaning of "democracy" is stretched so wide that virtually any government counts as one, the word is trivialized. In calling a state democratic, we would not be ruling out any particular way it deals with its citizens. So if any examination of the purported justifications of democracy is to prove fruitful, it is important to be clear about what is and what is not to count as a democracy.

Such clarity is especially important because of the prominent place given democracy in the writings of such theorists as Locke, Madison, Rousseau, and Rawls. Moreover, we have argued that states or governments are to be evaluated according to the degree to which they satisfy two fundamental criteria. First, they should protect and, where appropriate, implement the natural or human rights of their citizens. Second, they must institute just procedures for the adjudication of conflicting claims of right. We maintain that, at least in countries whose population exists significantly above the subsistence level, democracy is the principal procedure for such adjudication. Hence, there is need to ascertain how democracies are to be distinguished from other forms of governments.

Any account that purports to provide necessary and sufficient conditions of democracy is likely to be controversial. To avoid such lengthy controversy, it seems useful to provide, not an exhaustive list of defining conditions, but rather an admittedly incomplete list of paradigm features of democracy. By a paradigm feature of democracy is meant a feature so characteristic of democracy that (1) one would point to it in teaching a child the meaning of the word "democracy" and (2) to the extent that any government fails fully to exemplify the feature, then to that extent does it become less clear that the government in question is a democracy. Thus, a paradigm feature of baseball is that it is played by two teams of nine players each. However, if we were to witness a sandlot game in which each team had eight players, we would still call it baseball. Presumably, if there were only two on a side, we would be quite reluctant to call what was going on a game of baseball. Perhaps we would say the players were only practicing. Similarly, a government may still be a democracy even if it does not fully exemplify a paradigm feature of democracy. However, any government that fails to exemplify one or more features to a significant extent is no democracy at all. As with the baseball example, borderline cases are also possible.

Three characteristics that seem to be paradigm features of democracy are (*a*) the holding of regular elections, the results of which can genuinely alter policy and the people who make it; (*b*) the existence of universal suffrage; and (*c*) the provision of civil liberties essential to the election process itself. Let us consider each of these characteristics in turn.

The first, *a*, excludes from the category of democracy those states whose rulers claim to follow the will of the people but never allow that will to be expressed in genuine, periodic elections. In particular, genuine elections must be a contest between different points of view, such that the election results can alter policy and the people who make it. One-party "elections" are not genuine ones in this sense.

The second condition, *b*, rules out a state where a significant number of persons are denied the franchise for morally unacceptable reasons. Thus, a state in which women are denied the vote is an elitist state, not a democracy. Paradigm cases of justified exclusion include disenfranchisement of young children, the psychotic, and the severely retarded. Exclusion of criminals might well constitute an arguable borderline case. In view of the arguments of Chapter Three, factors such as race, religion, sex, or ethnic or social background cannot justify exclusion.[1]

The third requirement, *c*, distinguishes the democratic from the majoritarian state. Majoritarianism is the view that all political issues ought to be settled by a majority vote, or by those elected officials who have received majority support.[2] Historically, however, democracy has been thought of as containing built-in safeguards for individual rights. The United States Constitution's Bill of Rights is an example. Such checks are justified as safeguards against the dictatorship of the majority, a group that can be as tyrannical as any individual despot.[3] At the very least, a democracy must protect those procedural rights, such as the right to vote and the right to free speech, without which elections become a mockery.[4]

This is what makes such unfortunate features of recent American democracy as excessive government secrecy and illegal domestic spying by intelligence agencies so reprehensible. By depriving the citizenry of information needed for intelligent voting or by intimidating or harassing those who dissent from official policies, such abuses undermine the democratic process itself. And, as we will see, where the democratic process is significantly undermined, whether there is any obligation to abide by the dictates of "democratic" decisions becomes questionable. Exactly where the point of vanishing obligation is to be located is controversial. Surely, however, there is a special obligation of the officials of a reasonably democratic government to keep it that way and not undermine the very process they have sworn to uphold.

Each of these features, regular genuine elections, universal suffrage, and protection of individual rights is a paradigm feature of democracy in the sense already explicated. The dispute over whether or not a given state is democratic is not merely verbal. As will be argued later, the extent to which a state is democratic determines the extent to which we ought to support it and perhaps even whether we are under any special political obligation to respect its authority. Let us now consider what, if anything, might justify allegiance to democracy.

THE JUSTIFICATION OF DEMOCRACY

Utilitarian Arguments (Individualistic)

Utilitarian arguments for democracy are those that argue from the good consequences promoted by democracy to the desirability of democracy as a form of government. Note, that in this context, the utilitarian is concerned with the consequences promoted by the workings of an *institution* and not with those of any one action. The utilitarian is evaluating the *system* of democracy rather than any individual act performed within the system. The utilitarian arguments considered below are termed individualistic, because, like those of Bentham and Mill, the good consequences to which they appeal are individual goods for individual persons. In the next section, we will consider the arguments of collectivist or holist utilitarians who appeal to a group or the general good.

Here, as elsewhere in this book, it is understood that the utilitarian cannot appeal to considerations of justice or natural right as last resorts in political argument. Rather, the utilitarian must ground natural rights and justice—if they are appealed to at all—on their utility.

The weakest of the utilitarian defenses of democracy appeals to the material benefits enjoyed by citizens of the Western democracies. It is true that at present most or at least a great many citizens of such states enjoy a higher standard of living than that of most citizens of most other countries. So, in political argument, the democratic form of government is sometimes defended by appeal to the material benefits that accrue to those who live under it.

That argument is quite weak, however. It is unclear, for one thing, whether the standard of living in a democracy is a result of its being a democracy, of its economic system, of its exploitation of other countries, of its plentiful natural resources, or of a host of other possible explanatory factors. Thus, in the absence of detailed support, the inference that a country's wealth is due, or even largely due, to its political system is extraordinarily weak.

Moreover, proponents of such an argument, by their own logic, would be forced to admit that *if* a totalitarian country did come to enjoy a higher standard of living than a democracy, there is a stronger reason for preferring the former to the latter. This is unacceptable, however, because no *moral* basis for democracy is provided. As subsequent arguments will show, there are good moral reasons for preferring democracy to other forms of government, even at a significant cost in material wealth. This is not to deny the importance of relative affluence, since severe deprivation may cause democratic values to be lost in the struggle for mere survival. It is to distinguish relative affluence as a *causal prerequisite* of democracy from relative affluence as a *justification* of democracy. Affluence may well be the former but it is doubtful if it counts as the latter.

A second utilitarian argument maintains that a democracy, by *distributing* power among the people, is most likely to avoid the abuses of power that result from its concentration in too few hands. If any group of leaders does misuse its power, in a democracy there are regular procedures that the people may use to separate such leaders from their power.

This is indeed a strong argument for democracy. In a great many contexts, the abuses of power may be avoided by distributing it to the people. Although the growth of power of the President in the United States and the use of such power in Vietnam and in the Watergate affair may lead one to wonder just how much of a check is provided, the utilitarian point still seems sound. *Generally,* but not always, distribution of power may prevent its abuse. Even in the case of Vietnam, the American people had the right to remove their leaders from office if they so wished.

We should point out, however, that this argument is two-edged. The totalitarian can reply that the very success of democracy in curbing the abuse of power, or at least acting as a check to abuse, may also be its

Achilles' heel. For when quick, effective use of power is needed, democracy may not be able to supply it.

Although we agree with the utilitarian that the misuse of power is generally more to be feared than failure to use it, this conflict cannot be fully resolved if we remain within a utilitarian framework. Both sides are appealing to consequences—the issues being the empirical ones of whether the misuse of power is worse than failure to use it in various contexts, or whether one is more likely to occur than the other. In a later section of this chapter, we will argue that power ought to be distributed among the people, not simply to maximize want satisfaction and minimize want frustration, but because the people have a *right* to such a distribution. Thus, we will maintain that democracy is best justified from the point of view of equality, justice, and rights rather than that of utility and efficiency.

Moreover, although democracy may provide for some checks on power by protecting certain rights and perhaps by creating constitutional checks and balances on the branches of government, democracy may be compatible with other kinds of inequality of power. Economic and social inequalities may give some individuals or groups more leverage over the democratic process than others. Such inequalities, if sufficiently great, can undermine the significance of democracy itself. (We will return to this point in our discussion of pluralism in the section on "Nonindividualistic Defense of Democracy," (p. 120-27) as well as in our discussion of democracy and equality in the section on "Democracy as a Requirement of Equality" (p. 127-33).

Perhaps the most effective defense of democracy in terms of its consequences was provided by John Stuart Mill. In his *Considerations on Representative Government,* Mill argued that participation in the democratic process developed the intellectual and moral capacities of citizens, while under other forms of governments, the citizens, or more accurately, the subjects, remained passive and inert.[5] In a democracy, according to Mill, people are encouraged to understand issues, develop and express points of view, and implement desires through political involvement. In a despotism, however, citizens are passive receptors for the will of the elite. Therefore, Mill maintains, those who value individual development are committed to valuing the form of government that best fosters it—democracy.

While we are very sympathetic to Mill's approach here, some qualifications must be made. First, as the last paragraph suggests, it is not clear that Mill's position is genuinely utilitarian. In emphasizing the development of each individual's intellectual and moral capacities, and in de-emphasizing such quantitative factors as production of pleasure, Mill has moved a great distance from classical utilitarianism.[6] Instead, Mill seems to have shifted to a self-realizationist perspective where the goal is to promote the rational development of persons. The problem with such a view is that of determining how any one ideal of human nature or development can be shown to be better than any other. However, in defense of Mill, it can be argued along lines suggested earlier that one can never be justified in abandoning rational discourse itself. Since justification requires the giving of reasons, the claim that one is justified in abandoning reasoned discourse is incoherent. It amounts to the claim that one has reasons for not having reasons. In this interpretation, Mill's self-realizationist ethic can be grounded on the same foundation that supports one of our arguments for natural rights. It, like part of our own view, rests on the imperative to be rational, an imperative that can be rejected, but only by those who are willing to lead the unexamined and therefore unjustifiable life.

Mill's argument is that participation in the democratic process promotes rational development. However, actual democracies may not have as much of an effect on individual development as Mill expected. Mill's empirical claims about how individuals develop in a democracy may not hold when politicians market themselves as products (much as corn flakes are presented to the public), and rational discussion in the media and among the citizenry is notable largely for its absence. For this reason, a democrat might be wary of basing too much of his case on Mill's argument. People may not react to the actual democratic process as Mill thought they would to an ideal one. Mill could reply with force, however, that if any form of government is to develop human capacities for rational thought and action, democracy is the most likely to succeed. If democracies in practice encourage mindlessness, that is a reason for getting them to more fully live up to democratic ideals, not for abandoning democracy altogether.

Accordingly, some of the utilitarian arguments for democracy have considerable merit. In some if not all cases, democratic checks on power function effectively. Moreover, democracy may have some effect, and perhaps a large one under certain conditions, in developing the rational capacities of many citizens. Surely, democracy fares better then totalitarianism in promoting such an end.

However, utilitarian arguments for democracy do not tell the whole story. By the very logic of utilitarianism, *if* a totalitarian state were to produce the greatest good, that state is to be rated best. If the utilitarian were to reply, following Mill, that dictatorships do not contribute to the rational development of citizens, and so *cannot* produce the greatest good, then it would seem that a new nonutilitarian value has been introduced into the argument. What counts, in this view, is the development of the *individual*, not extrinsic goods, that the static individual can enjoy. Accordingly, this defense of democracy rests on the assumption that the individual person is *morally significant*. This indeed is an important claim, but there is nothing distinctively utilitarian about it. As we shall see, the assertion of the importance of the individual is central to the egalitarian defense of democracy—a defense that is distinctively nonutilitarian in character.

Insofar as utilitarian defenses of democracy are utilitarian, they provide only a contingent defense of democracy. Where other political systems provide good results, those systems pass the utilitarian test as well. On the other hand, insofar as utilitarian defenses of democracy are fully successful, it is doubtful to what extent they remain utilitarian. It is evident then, that other defenses of democracy merit serious consideration.

Nonindividualistic Defenses of Democracy

So far, democracy has been evaluated by an individualist standard, namely, according to the benefits democracy provides for individual citizens. Even Mill, who emphasized the socializing and humanizing effects of democracy as a collective process, was basically part of the individualistic utilitarian tradition. What such an approach may ignore is the role of the group in human life. To bring out such a role, two nonindividualist approaches to democracy will be considered, that of the pluralists, on the one hand, and that of the eighteenth-century French philosopher Jean Jacques Rousseau on the other.

Pluralism   Pluralism can be conceived of as a descriptive account of democracy advanced by analytical social scientists *and* as a justification of democracy as well. It has its roots in the *Federalist Paper #10* of James Madison. Madison accepted the basic Hobbesian account of human nature. Persons are basically selfish and take any opportunity to dominate their fellows. In order to prevent dominant individuals or groups from controlling the political power, Madison thought it necessary to distribute power widely. Democracy was the form of government that best accomplished this end.

Madison's approach is called pluralism because of his advocacy of multiple centers of power. Wide distribution of power, rather than consitutional checks and balances, was, he believed, the best protection against tyranny. It is the pluralistic society that prevents despotism. Democracy, by allowing for the give and take of bargaining between competing centers of power, promotes pluralism.

So far, Madisonian pluralism resembles the utilitarian argument for the wide distribution of power that was considered earlier. Indeed, Madison is perhaps the finest articulator of that argument. What is of interest here is the union of this pluralistic approach with an emphasis on the role and value of group life in a democracy.

What contemporary pluralists add to the Madisonian account are an emphasis on the importance of interaction between *groups* and an emphasis on *extraconstitutional checks* on the accumulation of power. The two additions are related in that it is the competition and compromise between groups that constitute the extraconstitutional checks on government, such as the decision of a legislator from Maine to support a program from

Alabama on the understanding that the representatives from Alabama will support a project which benefits the citizens of Maine.

Individualists tend to view persons as egoistic utility maximizers. Recall Hobbes's view of human nature and Bentham's claim that pleasure and pain dictate what persons will do as well as what they ought to do. Critics of individualism, however, would question how successfully people can function as autonomous, isolated, atomic individuals. Indeed, as sociologist Emile Durkheim argued, isolation and rootlessness themselves are the source of many psychological and social problems.[7] Moreover, it is doubtful empirically if people do frequently function as isolated utility maximizers. Rather, it is as members of groups, coming out of traditions, embedded in a social structure, that we actually find individuals. By raising the ethnic and religious group to the center of attention, the pluralist theorists have provided the framework within which a theory of democracy based on group interaction can be constructed.[8]

In the pluralist view, the democratic process is a set of ground rules within which different groups can each pursue their interest. Ground rules are necessary, for without them we would revert to a Hobbesian state of nature, a war of every group against every other group. Within the ground rules, the plurality of groups provides a check on the power of any one element in society. What we have is a shifting majority, made up of many minorities temporarily voting alike in the pursuit of their share of the pie. "Constitutional rules are mainly significant because they help to determine what particular groups are to be given advantages or handicaps in the political struggle." It is the competitive extraconstitutional balance of power among groups that protects us from despotism. "Thus the making of governmental decisions is not a majestic march of great majorities united upon certain matters of basic policy. It is the steady appeasement of relatively small groups."[9]

Such a view has several advantages. In particular, it incorporates the importance of tradition, identification with a group, and social structure in the life of individuals. A significant loyalty of many individuals is to the group with which they identify. Moreover, pluralism incorporates this emphasis on the value of group life, on community rather than possessive individualism, into a traditional defense of democracy as a check upon tyranny. However, regardless of its merits as a *descriptive* theory about how democracy *does* work, pluralism has serious weakness as a *normative* theory about how democracy *ought* to work.

In particular, critics have emphasized that whether the pluralist intended to promote such an end, pluralism has conservative implications. As one critic, Robert Paul Wolff, argues:

> the application of the theory of pluralism always favors the groups in existence against those in the process of formation. . . . The theory of

pluralism does not espouse the interests of the unionized against the non-unionized, or of the large against small business; but by presenting a picture of the American economy in which those disadvantaged elements do not appear, it tends to perpetuate the inequality by ignoring rather than justifying it."[10]

As a theory, pluralism views democratic society as a common ground where groups pursue their interests within an agreed-upon procedural framework. In practice, however, critics charge that pluralism counts some groups as more equal than others. "The very passivity of government as 'referee' suggests that the 'game' is likely to be dominated by the oldest and strongest players."[11]

The pluralists themselves are not unaware of this difficulty. Robert Dahl acknowledges, for example, that "if a group is inactive, whether by free choice, violence, intimidation, or law, the normal American system does not necessarily provide it with a checkpoint anywhere in the process."[12] While the system often has expanded to include previously unrepresented groups, it need not do so, nor need it provide opportunities for new groups to be heard or recognized. Accordingly, a major disadvantage of a normative defense of democracy based on pluralism is that pluralism contains no built-in protections for emerging or less powerful groups. Democracy should encompass more than simple power relationships, whether it is relationships between individuals or between groups that are at issue.

A second difficulty with pluralism arises from the competitive picture painted of the democratic process. With each group struggling to attain its own interest, there is no incentive for any group to defend the common or public interest. Each party to the political struggle can hope that the common good will be taken care of by others and concentrate its energy on securing its own private benefit:

America is growing uglier, more dangerous, and less pleasant to live in, as its citizens grow richer. The reason is that natural beauty, public order, the cultivation of the arts, are not the special interest of any identifiable social group. . . . To deal with such problems, there must be some way of constituting society as a genuine group with a group purpose and a conception of the common good.[13]

The pluralists have certainly made a major contribution to the theory of democracy. As political scientists, they have presented an interesting hypothesis about how democracy does work, one that surely warrants extensive consideration. However, pluralism is at best incomplete as a theory of how democracy ought to work. Group life is too often ignored by the individualist, and yet it is of the highest value to many persons. But even if we accept that the group is the proper unit of analysis here, pluralism contains no account of the fair or just apportionment of power among groups. Moreover, it seems to replace the individualist picture of society as composed of isolated, competing atomic individuals with the hardly more edifying picture of isolated, competing groups. In each case, the common values that are essential to all are left out of the picture. It is precisely these problems that the philosopher Rousseau hoped to avoid.

Democracy and the general will Perhaps the difficulties noted above arise because the assumption on which they are based—that democracy involves conflict between different interest groups—is itself faulty. An alternative account of democracy can be based on the views of the French philosopher Jean Jacques Rousseau (1712-1778). In his book *The Social Contract*, Rousseau formulates the problem of justifying the state's claim to authority over the individual as follows. The problem is to determine if there is

> a form of association which will defend and protect with the whole common force the person and property of each associate and by which each person, while uniting himself with all, shall obey only himself and remain as free as before.[14]

How can the individual retain autonomy while acknowledging political authority? (See the first section of Chapter One.)

Rousseau's solution is in the social-contract tradition that we have already encountered in the work of Locke, Hobbes, and, in contemporary form, Rawls. But while Hobbesian contractees give all their power up to a sovereign to enhance security and Lockean contractees give up some rights to better protect others, Rousseau's associates give up all their rights to enhance *personal autonomy*. They do this by ceding their rights to the *association* or *community*. Since each is an equal member, none is disadvantaged more than any other. Each is to have the same voice in group decision making.

Rousseau is making the important point that equality is a fair compromise between parties contracting to create a collective-decision procedure. If no party has any threat advantage over any other and if principles are not arbitrarily tailored to favor any particular group, then equality—one person, one vote—seems to be the favored result. (Rousseau seems to have anticipated the kind of contractual argument employed by Rawls. Rawls himself has acknowledged a great debt to Rousseau.)

But how is Rousseau to deal with the problems plaguing pluralism? The answer lies in Rousseau's conception of the political community. For Rousseau, the community is not simply an aggregate of individuals, to be swayed by majority vote, as in Locke. On the contrary, the parties to the contract could not retain their autonomy, Rousseau argues, if they were to accept the Lockean conception of majority rule. Majority rule, in its usual sense, implies that the minority should abide by the policies supported by the majority even when they, the minority, oppose such policies. Submission to majority rule involves abandonment of autonomy since one suspends one's individual judgment when it is not in accord with majority view. Rousseau's contractees surrender *all* their rights to the community, but only because it is the function of the community to pursue *the common good*. Hence, each individual remains "as free as before" since, unlike what happens in the case of majority rule, no individual's or group's good is to be subordinated to any other's. The community, guided by its *general will*, is to pursue the general or common good, which is as much any one citizen's good as any other.

Rousseau, like Hobbes, Locke, and Rawls, should not be read as offering a historical account of a social contract. Rather, Rousseau is exploring the *rational* basis of the state by asking under what conditions reasonable persons could accept the political order. His answer is that it is rational to acknowledge the authority of the state only if the state is a political *community*, not an *aggregation*. In the latter, each individual or group selfishly pursues its own interests, leading to the kind of problems facing pluralism. A community, on the other hand, is not simply an aggregation of egoists. Rather, it is a group with a common goal—the securing of the common good for its members.

But how is the common good to be discerned? Rousseau believed that the *general will* of the community could discern the common good. This general will is to be distinguished from particular wills, even when the particular wills of each citizen agree:

> There is often a great difference between the will of all and the general will; the general will studies the common interest while the will of all studies private interest, and is indeed no more than the sum of individual desires.[15]

Individuals express their particular will when they vote their own personal preferences and desires. The general will is expressed only when citizens assume an impersonal standpoint and vote to secure the common good. One votes the general will when one abandons one's own selfish perspective and attempts to see things from a point of view common to oneself and others.

It is the merit of Rousseau's approach that he focuses our attention on the common good and the public interest; on what unites a collection into a community rather than an aggregation of competing individuals or interest groups. In such a state, no individual or group can be dominated by another, for the only interests the state can legitimately pursue are the interests of all. Rousseau's political philosophy serves as a counterweight to competitive individualism and pluralism alike—to a world where some affluent egoists or groups live in private splendor while such public goods as parks, clean air and water, and a beautiful and healthy environment vanish. But while Rousseau's emphasis on the common good is valuable, his approach is open to serious criticism on a number of points.

Evaluation of Rousseau's position   Rousseau's argument, as presented above, can be stated as follows:

1. A political association has authority only if it preserves the autonomy of the associates, i.e., keeps them "as free as before."
2. It preserves the autonomy of any given associate only if it does not subordinate the pursuit of his or her interests to the pursuit of those of others, for he or she could not rationally consent to such a system.
3. Such subordination can be avoided only if the association is restricted to pursuing only the common interests of the associates.
4. Therefore, a political association has authority only if it restricts itself to pursuit of the common interests of the members.
5. The general will and only the general will discerns the common interest.
6. Therefore, a political association has authority only if it allows for expression of the general will, i.e., for democratic voting in which each votes from the point of view of all.

How is this argument to be evaluated?

One problem is presented by premise 5. Is it really true that if voters try to discern what is in the common interest they will succeed in doing so? On the contrary, it can be argued that there is little reason to think that the majority will usually perceive the common good, or wherein it lies, let alone that it will always do so.

Indeed, critics contend that Rousseau's apparent assumption of the infallibility of the general will is actually dangerous to civil liberties. Rousseau has argued that those who oppose the general will must be "forced to be free."[16] Since only the general will expresses the common good, and each rational citizen has consented to pursue the common good, each rational citizen has consented to obey the general will. Hence, in forcing the citizen to abide by its dictates, we really are carrying out the dictates of the citizen's rational self, and so are not really coercing him after all.

As critics have pointed out (see the first section of Chapter Six, of this book), this argument confuses satisfaction of rational wants with freedom. Coercion in people's interest, even coercion designed to get them what they would want under certain conditions, is still coercion. It is hardly forcing people to be *free*.

Rousseau assumes that the general will is infallible, or at least likely to be correctly expressed on any given occasion. Hence, there is no need to protect individual rights, for such rights are not needed as checks against a strong-willed but mistaken majority. But since the assumption of infallibility surely is mistaken, individual rights need to be protected against the tyranny of the majority. Indeed, if the considerations presented in favor of natural rights have force, claims of natural rights ought to be honored *even if the majority is infallible.* If a physician knows that informing a patient of a diagnosis of cancer will make that patient severely depressed, it does not follow that the patient ought not to be told. The patient's right to control his or her own life may be paramount. Indeed, if Y has a natural right to liberty, such paternalistic interference may be in violation of it.

If individual rights are honored, then a sphere of individual, private entitlement is protected. Within that sphere, individuals may follow their own possibly selfish judgments. It seems that we can eliminate such pursuit of private ends only by ignoring claims of individual right as well. Accordingly, Rousseau's view of the state is open to the criticism that pursuit of the common good is allowed unduly to dominate the pursuit of individual interest:

> Political problems very often demand a choice between conflicting interests. And though there may be good reasons for a given choice, it can rarely be one in which all interests are harmonized. Again, even where the objective is of general benefit, a truly "common good," it does not follow that it should therefore override all other claims; yet this is precisely what Rousseau felt about the common good.[17]

This is not to deny the importance of the common good or the public interest.[18] However, the common good or public interest does not automatically take precedence over all other values in all other contexts. Surely, a healthy environment is in the public interest if anything at all is. But suppose that we could prevent a two percent increase in cancer caused by pollution only by suspending basic civil liberties for an extended period of time. Or suppose we could prevent the increase in cancer only by severely limiting each individual's pursuit of private interest. Whether the gain is worth the loss is at least controversial. Rousseau's emphasis on the common good remedies a serious deficiency in pluralist theory but at the price of going too far in the opposite direction. In accepting premise 3, that the state avoids subordination of some citizens to others only by pursuing the common good, Rousseau opens himself to the objection that the common good should not always take precedence over the pursuit of private satisfactions. Rousseau thinks he has eliminated subordination but actually subordinates private interests to those that everyone has in common. By insisting that the general will represents the real will of each individual, he overlooks the private wants of the concrete individual. Conflicting interests seem to be a central feature of political life. Rousseau obscures this conflict and so provides no mechanism for dealing with it.

A second problem with Rousseau's argument arises in connection with premise 2. This premise states that any citizen's autonomy is preserved only if the political association never subordinates the individual's interests to those of others, i.e., if it only pursues the common good. However, while a majoritarian democracy often pursues some people's interests at the expense of others, it may well be in the rational interest of everyone to consent to a decision procedure that allows just that to happen. Rousseau may not have given adequate weight to the distinction between (*a*) adoption of a decision procedure being in everyone's interest and (*b*) the actual decisions resulting from its application being in everyone's interest. Where *a* holds, it may be rational to consent to the procedure in spite of the fact that its application may not work to everyone's benefit. Imagine, for example, two children, who constantly quarrel over who is to make the first move in a board game. Rather than constantly fight, it may be rational for them to agree to a rule determining who goes first. Perhaps the rule is, "Each participant shall roll a die and the one with the highest number on the face of the die shall move first. In case of ties, the procedure is to be repeated until a winner emerges." On any given occasion, one child will lose if the rule is followed. Nevertheless, it may be rational for them both to adopt the rule and avoid interminable quarrels. Accordingly, premise 2's identification of an autonomous decision with one that never leads to the subordination of interests confuses the rationale for consenting to a *decision procedure* with that for evaluating the outcome of *individual decisions*. As in the case of the children, it may be rational to allow for some subordination of interests in the application of a procedure when it is significantly in everyone's interest to adopt such a procedure in the first place. (See Chapter One, our section on Reconciling Authority and Autonomy, for a discussion of this point.)

In spite of these criticisms, Rousseau has called our attention to the importance of common interests and the value of community. Moreover, Rousseau leaves democrats with some perplexing questions. If each group is to pursue its own interests, as the pluralists suggest, how are permanent minorities—groups that can always be outvoted by the others—to be protected? And how are egoistic individuals or groups to protect public interests as well as private ones? Even if the criticisms of Rousseau's approach are decisive, the problems he set out to solve still remain.

Democracy as a Requirement of Equality

Our own approach is in the egalitarian tradition of contractarians such as Locke and Rawls. Social-contract theorists begin with the model of equal parties arriving at an agreement rationally acceptable to all. We too begin with the assumption that each individual counts equally as a possessor of fundamental rights. Now suppose that such individuals have need of a decision procedure for resolving conflicts that arise among them. Since it is impractical to handle each case on a purely individual basis, what they need is a system of generating rules, laws, and judicial institutions. It is these rules, laws, and institutions that will be applied to particular cases. But how are they to be arrived at?

Since all citizens possess equal rights, no citizen has any moral authority that others lack. Since each is a possessor of equal rights, none starts out under the authority of any other. But since all are equal, and equal cases should be treated equally, it is plausible to think that each citizen should count for one and only one in the process of generating rules, laws, and institutions for conflict resolution. According to this view, democracy is justified as a *fair compromise* between equals for sharing of decision-making power.[19]

A similar conclusion would be reached by Rawlsian deliberators behind the veil of ignorance. For Rawls, "the constitutional process should preserve the equal representation of the original position to the degree that this is feasible."[20] In ignorance of who they are, what they value, and to what society they belong, persons are left with no rational basis on which to discriminate. Accordingly, the rational vote is for equality in the decision-making process.

Many critics of democracy will find this sort of equality to be its greatest weakness. Plato was able to dismiss democracy as "a charming form of government, full of variety and disorder, and dispensing a sort of equality to equals and unequals alike."[21] In this sort of elitist view, ideal government is government by the best and brightest. The attributes of a good leader include wisdom, sensitivity, integrity, and the ability to inspire others. But democracy, so the argument goes, counts everyone equally and so reduces leadership to the lowest common denominator. To avoid this, Plato, in his *Republic,* advocated the formation of a guardian class, which was to include those citizens best equipped to lead the state. The guardians were to be trained especially for leadership while members of the other classes, e.g., warriors and artisans, were to be trained to carry out the tasks they performed best. In the ideal state, each component would perform the function for which it was best fitted.

Democrats and their elitist critics alike can agree that not everyone is equally suited for political *leadership.* After all, one can be committed to democracy without believing that all people are likely to be equally good Presidents of the United States. What democrats will want to stress, however, is the *value* of counting people equally for purposes of political decision making. Pluralists, for example, will deny that just because some people may make better leaders than others, the *selection* of leaders ought to be removed from the populace. The pluralists will argue that any self-perpetuating governing class is likely to rule mainly in its own interest.

Hence, there is a need for a plurality of centers of power, either at the individual or group level, as a check against just the sort of tyranny to which Plato's system can lead.

But still, critics may object, isn't democracy just forced on us by practical difficulties? If we could produce wise and benevolent leaders, shouldn't all power be turned over to them? Democracy, in this view, is not the best form of government, all things considered. Rather, it is the best we can do, given our limitations.

Even if the critics were right here, the case for democracy would still be strong. After all, it is the real and not the ideal world we are worried about. But ideals are important, if only as guides to improvement, as signals indicating in which direction we should move. Therefore, we should face squarely the elitist claim that *if* we could select the wisest and most benevolent among us, then they and they alone should rule.

There seem to be three key assumptions underlying the elitist case. These are that (1) the value of a form of government is determined by the wisdom of the political decisions to which it is likely to lead; (2) wise and benevolent political leaders are likely to make wise political decisions without being accountable to the people; and (3) when the first two assumptions hold, all power should be given to the wise and benevolent.

The democrat will argue against each assumption. In reply to the first assumption, Mill's case for the effect of democracy upon participants can be emphasized. On this view, the value of democracy lies as much on the development of the best that is within each particular person as it does on the outcome of the decision-making process. A benevolent dictatorship is at best likely to reduce the citizenry to the status of satisfied pigs. Democracy at least aims at turning people into dissatisfied Socrateses.

Against the second assumption, democrats will deny that the good of the people can be identified independently of the expression by the people of their preferences through the democratic process. As one theorist recently maintained:

> in order to know which members of the community have the greatest capacities to contribute to the common good, we must know with some concreteness the forms that the common good will take. But what these forms will be cannot be known prior to the expression of the interests, needs and desires of the members generally. . . . In sum, the well being of a body politic cannot be ascertained in advance of the directive decisions made by its members, and therefore contributions to such well being, or the capacity so to contribute, cannot be used to determine who shall have a right to participate in those fundamental decisions.[22]

Indeed, even if a common good or public interest can be discerned independently of the expression of preference by the citizenry, it need not take precedence over the pursuit of private interest. And while in any individual case, a wise and benevolent observer may know one's interest better than one does oneself, the democrat will argue that it is extremely unlikely that this would be true in any great number of cases. The dispute over assumption 2 turns into an empirical one between the democrat and the elitist. The former holds that, in general, the interests of the people cannot be discerned independently of their binding expression of those interests. The latter holds that wise and benevolent rulers can know what is good for the people better than do the people themselves. In the elitist's view, the people in effect are to be treated as children.

Suppose, for the sake of argument, that assumptions (1) and (2) of the elitist are granted. Often, what is not noticed is the invalidity of the inference that therefore all power should be given to the wise and benevolent. Thus, if X is selling *his house*, even if an outside observer Y could get a better price for it, it does not follow that X must turn over the selling to Y. For it is X's house and he has the *right* to sell it, even if he does not get the best price available. Similarly, if X were to place his life in Y's hands and follow Y's directives, X might have a happier life than would otherwise be the case. However, X has the *right* to run his own life.

As we just argued, the inference from "Y can make better decisions about X's life than can X" to "Y has the right to make decisions about X's life and X does not" is fallacious. Greater wisdom does not entail the right to rule. Indeed, if each citizen is a possessor of fundamental individual rights, each is equally entitled to rule. The strongest moral foundation for democracy lies in the importance of the individual. Whether one starts out with a theory of natural rights as developed earlier, or regards individual rights as rule-utilitarian devices,[23] it is the moral equality of individuals that justifies the democratic process. Accordingly, the elitist has not justified assumption 3. Rather, democracy is justifiable on grounds of fairness. Even if it does not always yield the best decisions, it is a procedure for collective decision making that counts equals as equals and respects individual rights. Hence, we are entitled to reject the elitist case, even under those ideal (if unattainable) circumstances in which the wisest and most benevolent among us can be identified and brought forth.

Nevertherless, a number of problems remain. Suppose, for example, that in a democracy all procedural rights are implemented, yet one group is continually outvoted. Its interests are continually ignored over a long period of time and it becomes a permanent minority. Second, suppose voters continually ignore the common good and the public interest, choosing only to satisfy their own personal wants instead. Can the democratic theorist deal adequately with the problems of oppressed minorities and the common or public interest?

Oppressed minorities in a democracy Critics of democracy sometimes point to the fact that under such a political system, majority interest groups can unite at the ballot box to repress permanently the interests of minorities. Many would argue that in the United States, blacks and the poor have constituted just such a permanent minority group on election day. When such charges are true, they constitute a serious objection to democracy. Although everyone's vote counts for one under such circumstances, some people, because of the groups to which they belong, lack significant protection for their interests. Their votes are not important enough for politicians to worry about.

Now, there is nothing about democracy that rules out such unjust repression of a minority by the majority. A just procedure does not always yield substantively just results.

However, when we reflect on the *justification* of democracy, a reply to the critic can be formulated. On the natural-rights–egalitarian view, democracy imposes *moral limits* on the majority. As each citizen of a democracy is counted as a moral equal, on this justificatory approach, no citizen's rights should be overridden on the basis of mere power. Democratic government

> is not a matter of . . . mere will—even if by the majority. It proceeds in an atmosphere of criticism, on the presumption that a sufficient justification cannot be given for a decision by appeal to someone's will . . . simply because it is that will. . . . the whole (democratic) process presumes the give and take of criticism and justification, conducted within the framework of moral criteria.[24]

Although democracy can degenerate into the kind of interest-group egoism critics describe, such egoism contradicts the very point of having a democracy in the first place. Equals should not be treated as mere means for the fulfillment of others' wishes—regardless of the balance of power between the parties. As the very point of having democratic procedures is to acknowledge the moral equality of others, it is surely self-frustrating, from a justificatory point of view, to use those very procedures to violate or ignore the rights of others. Of course, anyone is likely to be in a minority on some occasions. The concern here, however, is with a group whose interests have been ignored again and again. Any democrat should be prepared to lose on occasion but no one should be a loser virtually all the time on a wide variety of issues. Hence, to the extent that a given democracy allows for the oppression of permanent minorities, then to that extent are the reasons for abiding by the democratic process seriously weakened. (See the third section in this chapter, "Political Obligation," for further discussion of this point.)

Democracy and the common good There is no easy solution to the problem of how to interest rational individuals in sacrificing for the common good. Since the good in question is common, it is always rational to contribute less than one's share in the hope that others will pick up the extra. Since everyone reasons in the same way, public goods receive inadeqate support. Hence the paradox of public squalor amidst private affluence. Where private goods are concerned, everyone will bid what he thinks the product is worth, for the highest bidder wins and everyone else loses. But where public goods are concerned, it is rational to try to be a "freeloader," which is exactly why labor unions favor closed rather than open shops.

On the other hand, if persons always functioned only as Hobbesian rational egoists, the political order would be impossible. (See the discussion of Hobbes in the section of Chapter One entitled "Evaluating the Political Order.") Indeed, if persons were incapable of valuing anything but their own good, human life as we know it might well be impossible. Relationships such as love and friendship, as well as traits such as intellectual honesty, require the taking of an impersonal point of view other than a narrow egoistic one. Perhaps understanding of the foundations of the democratic process itself can provide *moral* motivation for concern with the public interest. And, as Rawls has argued, since the moral society is likely to win the loyalty of fair-minded citizens, and indeed to promote fair-mindedness, it is likely to be the *stable* society as well.

More practically, we have seen, as in the case of Hobbesian theory, that it can be rational for people to impose sanctions collectively on themselves in order to make previously irrational behavior rational. It is sometimes in our self-interest to create institutions that discourage us from directly following our self-interest. Since all of us are hurt by significant injury to the environment, to the educational system, or to facilities for cultural and aesthetic expression, perhaps we can agree upon incentives that make it rational for us to help protect such public goods. Thus, automatic payroll deductions for Social Security protect us from our own economic irrationality. To circumvent our own inability to save, we vote for forced saving. Public-interest lobbies, institutional devices such as that of the ombudsman, and judicious use of tax benefits perform a similar function. The trick is to design *institutions* we have some rational incentive to support, which automatically perform functions it would not be in our interest to perform as individuals.

Although this may not *insure* protection of the public interest, it is surely less unsatisfactory than Rousseau's method of forcing us to be free. People need not always function as rational egoists and, even when they do, it may be possible for them of their own volition to channel their egoism in a constructive direction. Whether institutional incentives strong enough to protect the public interest and weak enough to leave room for individual liberty can be provided remains a serious problem facing democratic theorists.

Democracy and equality   In the egalitarian view, democracy is a political procedure that counts equals as equals. But in what specific ways should democracy manifest such equality?

The most obvious answer is to count everyone alike for purposes of voting. Each person gets one and only one vote. Given that individual rights necessary to the democratic process are respected, each person is an equal in terms of democratic procedures themselves.

However, it is often charged, with reason, that such procedural equalities can be negated by extrasystematic inequalities of wealth and power. Thus, socialists, democratic Marxists, and egalitarian liberals will maintain that democracy can flourish only when gross economic inequalities have been eliminated throughout society. Such inequality is undemocratic, it is held, because it permits the concentration of vast amounts of power in an allegedly private realm free from democratic control. Yet this power can be used to influence or mold public opinion and so significantly affect the democratic process. As R. H. Tawney has maintained:

> In so far as an economic system grades mankind into groups, of which some can wield, if unconsciously, the force of economic duress for their own profit or convenience while others must submit to it, its effect is that freedom itself is similarly graded. . . . a society, or a large part of it, may be both politically free and economically the opposite. . . . It may possess the political institutions of an advanced democracy, and lack the will and ability to control the conduct of those powerful in its economic affairs, which is the economic analogy of political freedom.[25]

Thus, vast concentrations of economic power can provide special advantage in purchasing time on mass media (as well as *ownership* of the media itself), can have an undue effect on politicians desirous of financial support, and can provide the wielders of such power with world-wide contacts and communications systems that can be operated to their advantage. The strongest case for a regulated or publicly controlled economy may well be based on the claim that such regulation is required to implement democratic values.

Many friends of democracy will reply that such regulation infringes upon individual liberty. Indeed many argue that a free enterprise system is necessary if democratic institutions are to thrive. Chapter Four presented arguments for and against that point of view. We also argued in that chapter that economic institutions ought to be bound by certain moral constraints. To the extent that an actual economic system is bound by those constraints, the degree of inequality would be lessened. Hence, the threat to democratic institutions presented by inequality would be lessened as well. Moreover, some inequality is a necessary consequence of free people making individual choices in an open democratic society.

REVIEW

In Chapter One, it was asked under what conditions a state had political authority. As an aid to answering such a question, it was suggested that the proper function(s) or purpose(s) of the state should first be identified. Our investigation so far indicates that the proper function of the state is to (1) protect and, where appropriate, implement the natural or human rights of its citizens; and (2) provide for the just adjudication of competing claims (including claims of right) among citizens. Function 2 is a procedural requirement. In the view developed here, procedures for adjudicating conflicting claims may fail to honor a claim of right only in order to protect or implement other claims of right. It is the argument of this chapter that democracy is a paradigm procedure for conflict adjudication. Of course, not all societies can reasonably be expected to be democratic. They may be so poverty stricken, for example, that efficiency takes precedence over democracy. Or they may have a traditionally accepted hierarchical power structure that cannot be altered without great disruption and harm. But while such excuses may sometimes be valid, they too often function as ideological subterfuges protecting the abuse of power by an elite.

Even at its best, however, democracy constitutes only a just *procedure* for adjudicating conflicts. Just procedures may lead to unjust results. Depending upon the seriousness of the injustice, various forms of protest, from civil disobedience to (in cases of gross, outrageous, and systematic injustice) revolution, may be called for. We will discuss the valuable role of protest *within* the democratic process in Chapter Eight. Now, we turn to political obligation in a democracy.

POLITICAL OBLIGATION

If a state satisfies the criteria stated above, it is doing what the political order is supposed to do. Consequently, there are good reasons for supporting it. However, it does not follow that it has *authority* over us and that we are *obligated* to obey its edicts. Similarly, there may be good reasons for following a low-cholesterol diet but we need not be under any obligation to do so. What is good to do is one thing. What we are obligated to do need not be what is good to do.

Robert Paul Wolff, in his *Defense of Anarchy* (see the first section of Chapter One, "Authority vs. Autonomy and Conscience"), was perfectly consistent in holding that while there might be good reasons for obeying the edicts of certain states, no one is under any obligation to do so.

Even if Professor Wolff is correct in holding that no state has political authority and therefore no one has a political obligation to obey, it is still important to distinguish good states from bad ones. Our criteria 1 and 2 are designed to do just that. Accordingly, if they are defensible, they tell us which states we have good reason to support. However, are there any states we are *obligated* to obey? Are there any that have authority over us? If so, how do they come to have such authority? Let us consider the issue of political authority and obligation, keeping in mind (as argued in Chapter One) that such obligations need not be absolute and that respect for legitimate authority need not entail blind subservience to its dictates.

The Theory of Social Contract

The theory of social contract, particularly as developed in the writings of such classical contract theorists as Hobbes, Locke, and Rousseau, contains an account of political obligation. In the contract view, obligations arise from special acts of commitment by agents. Thus, X becomes obligated to pay Y five dollars by promising to do so. Likewise, citizens acquire political obligations by contracting to acknowledge the state's authority. Political authority arises from the *consent* of the governed. Consent is expressed through the social contract.

However, well-known difficulties face the contract approach. If the act of signing the contract is viewed as a historical one, when did it occur? And since the current generation surely never signed, from whence does their obligation, if any, arise? These questions appear unanswerable if social-contract theory is interpreted literally.

Locke attempted to modify the literal historical interpretation by relying on the notion of 'tacit consent:'

> every man that has any possessions or enjoyment of any part of the dominions of any government does thereby give his tacit consent and is as far forth obliged to the laws of that government during such enjoyment, as anyone under it; whether . . . his possession be of land . . . or a lodging only for a week, or whether it be barely traveling freely on the highway . . . .[26]

But surely this is unsatisfactory. If even use of public highways is construed as tacitly consenting, it is far from clear what would count as *withholding consent*. By Locke's criterion, even revolutionaries plotting to overthrow a government have tacitly consented to obey it merely by their use of public roads. Surely, this Lockean account of tacit consent is too broad.

However, it is far from clear that narrower criteria of tacit consent are any more satisfactory. For example, suppose it is maintained that voting is a necessary and sufficient condition of tacitly consenting. Unfortunately, this criterion seems to be too narrow. Voting can hardly be a necessary condition of consenting for we surely would want to say that many of those who fail to vote nevertheless (tacitly) consent. If a person who would have voted fails to do so because of illness on election day it is surely plausible to think that such a person consents to political authority. (Indeed, if we take this condition seriously, it follows that since only about half the electorate vote in United States elections, only about half are under the moral authority of the government.) Moreover, it is doubtful if voting is a sufficient condition of consent. It is at least controversial whether those who vote simply out of habit, or because a boss-dominated political machine tells them to, are consenting to the political order.

Perhaps some criterion of tacit consent can be formulated which is neither too broad nor too narrow.[27] At this point, however, other approaches seem more promising.

Suppose we consider *hypothetical* versions of the social-contract approach. At first glance, it would seem that such an approach is unhelpful. Even if there were an ideal contract that all rational persons *would* sign under appropriate conditions, these conditions are only hypothetical. How can persons be obligated by a contract they *would have* but never *did* actually sign?

This question seems unanswerable if we appeal only to contract theory. However, if we are allowed to appeal in addition to a principle philosophers have called the principle of fairness, perhaps a plausible answer can be constructed.

Fairness and Obligation

John Rawls has stated the principle of fairness as follows:

> this principle holds that a person is under an obligation to do his part as specified by the rules of an institution whenever he has voluntarily accepted the benefits of the scheme or has taken advantage of the opportunities it offers to advance his interests, provided that this institution is just or fair. . . .[28]

The intuitive idea here is that if a person voluntarily accepts the benefits of a cooperative arrangement, he has indicated to others his intention of playing a role in upholding the arrangement. Without this indication, he could not accrue the benefits, for others would not cooperate without the assurance that everyone will bear their share of any burdens involved. Hence, it is illegitimate—a form of cheating—for anyone to act as a free rider without some special justification.

According to Rawls, the institution must be fair or just if obligations are to arise from participation in it. "It is generally agreed that extorted promises are void *ab initio*. But similarly, unjust social arrangements are themselves a kind of extortion, even violence, and consent to them does not bind."[29] Rawls's theory of obligation has two parts, then. First, just or fair institutions are to be identified by appeal to an ideal hypothetical contract. Second, we become obligated to follow the rules of any particular institution by voluntarily taking advantage of the benefits or opportunities it offers. It is at this second stage that the principle of fairness applies.

Unfortunately, the principle of fairness is itself open to strong objection. That is, Rawls's theory, which relies upon that principle, lacks just what Locke's approach emphasizes, namely *consent*. As Robert Nozick points out, "the principle . . . would not serve to obviate the need for other person's consenting to cooperate and limit their own activities."[30] Without a consent requirement, the principle of fairness obliges us to uphold any just or fair institution from which we benefit, even if we would not choose to participate in it.

Obligation and Rights

Nozick's criticism of Rawls could be answered if we could distinguish between institutions we have a *duty* to support and those that we need support only if we so desire. Consent would not be required where institutions of the first sort are concerned. Rather, we would have a prepolitical obligation to support or enhance (and where they do not exist to help create) institutions of the required sort. Then, once we actually reap the advantages provided by such institutions, we are *politically* obliged, by application of the principle of fairness, to carry our share of the burdens the institutions impose.

Rawls adopts just such a strategy by appealing to our *natural* duties, i.e., duties that hold independently of any voluntary act of commitment to a particular institution or person. Thus, we have a natural duty not to be cruel. If one were to be discovered dipping helpless babies in jam and then feeding them to army ants, one could not excuse oneself by declaring, "I have never consented to the institution of avoiding cruelty." So, according to Rawls, we have a natural duty to support just institutions. As a contractarian, Rawls holds that we have this duty because such a conclusion would be accepted by rational persons deliberating behind the veil of ignorance.[31]

Given the lack of agreement over just which principles would be accepted behind the veil, let alone over whether the contract approach is warranted, it would be helpful if conclusions similar to Rawls's can be derived from a natural-rights framework. We believe they can. Natural rights impose obligations on others. These obligations require us not only to refrain from interfering with others but also to do our share in supporting institutions that provide social and material prerequisites of an at least minimally decent human existence. Now, it is the function of the state to protect and implement claims of natural right. Since we are obligated to respect such claims, and since the state is the most efficient means of so doing, we thereby are obligated to support the state. (This is so, of course, only if the particular state in question is fulfilling its proper function to a reasonable extent—or at least not oppressing its citizens, thus undermining its very *raison d'être*.).

On both the Rawlsian and the natural rights view, we have a natural duty to support the good state. Once we are part of such an institution, we have a special duty, based on the principle of fairness, to carry our share of the burdens, e.g., by obeying the laws such institutions impose. Natural duties bind us to support a legitimate political order. The principle of fairness creates the political obligation to acknowledge the authority of *some particular* political framework.

Although such obligations are genuine, they need not be *absolute*. A procedurally just political-decision procedure may yield grossly unjust decisions. In such cases, decent persons may find themselves with conflicting obligations. There is no a priori reason to believe that the obligation to follow the dictates of political authority will always take precedence. However, if the argument of this section has force, there is a prima facie obligation to obey. If political obligation does not imply blind subservience, it is not a myth either. Rather, it arises ultimately from our obligation to respect others as rights bearers equal to ourselves.

AN OVERVIEW

In Chapter One, we asked the following questions:

1. Under what conditions should the state's claim to authority be accepted?
2. How wide should that authority extend?
3. What are the obligations of a citizen to the state and its laws? What is the proper response of political authority to lawbreaking, on the one hand, and social injustice, on the other?

We have approached question 1 by attempting to identify the function(s) of the state. In our view, it is the function of the state to protect, enhance, and implement the natural or human rights of its citizens and to provide for just adjudication of conflicting claims that may arise among the citizenry. Given this account, question 1 might be answered as follows: A state has authority over its citizens and they a prima facie obligation to respect that authority if and only if the state is not in serious violation of the above criteria and the citizens benefit by the advantages provided by the state, i.e., by having their rights protected or implemented, or through the use of adjudication procedures.

Most of the remaining chapters discuss the implications and consequences of our theory. In Chapter Six our concern will be with the nature and scope of individual liberty. We will examine how the right to liberty constrains the democratic process. Chapter Seven is directed to our legal institutions. In that chapter we consider various justifications of punishment and the question of whether civil disobedience is ever morally justifiable. The issue of oppressed minorities in a democracy receives extended analysis in Chapter Eight where we discuss preferential treatment and reverse discrimination. Our final chapter focuses on the moral obligations, if any, which arise as the result of relations among states.

NOTES

[1] See the exchange between Felix E. Oppenheim and Virginia Held in *Political Theory* 1, no. 1 (1973): 54–78 for a discussion of whether value-laden or value-free definitions of terms like "democracy" are more valuable.

[2] See Brian Barry, *Political Argument* (New York: Humanities Press, 1967), pp. 58–66 for a discussion of majoritarianism.

[3] See, for example, Felix E. Oppenheim, "Democracy: Characteristics Included and Excluded," *Monist* 55, no. 1 (1971): 29–50 for a *narrower* account of democracy. Oppenheim would claim that *c* is a characteristic of a *liberal* society, not a democratic one.

[4] However some theorists such as Professor Herbert Marcuse and others who argue that democratic rights are of little or no significance in an inegalitarian "one-dimensional" society because they serve to make the established order appear just when it isn't.

[5] John Stuart Mill, *Considerations on Representative Government* (1861) in Marshall Cohen, ed., *The Philosophy of John Stuart Mill* (New York: Modern Library, 1961), particularly pp. 401–6.

[6] See our discussion of Mill's utilitarianism in the section on Mill in Chapter Two.

[7] Emile Durkheim, *Suicide,* in many editions.

[8] See David B. Truman, *The Governmental Process* (New York: Knopf, 1951); Robert Dahl, *A Preface to Democratic Theory* (Chicago: University of Chicago Press, 1956) and *Who Governs? Democracy and Power in an American City* (New Haven: Yale University Press, 1961).

[9] Dahl, *A Preface to Democratic Theory,* p. 137 and p. 146.

[10] Robert Paul Wolff, *The Poverty of Liberalism* (Boston: Beacon Press, 1968), pp. 152–53.

[11] Eugene Lewis, *The Urban Political System* (Hinsdale, Illinois: Dryden Press, 1973), p. 147.

[12] Dahl, *A Preface to Democratic Theory,* p. 138.

[13] Wolff, *The Poverty of Liberalism,* p. 159.

[14] Jean Jacques Rousseau, *The Social Contract* (1762), book 1, chap. 6, trans. Maurice Cranston (Baltimore: Penguin Books, 1968), p. 60.

[15] Ibid., book 2, chap. 3 (p. 72 in Cranston).

[16] Ibid., book 2, chap. 7 (p. 64 in Cranston).

[17] S. I. Benn and R. S. Peters, *The Principles of Political Thought* (New York: The Free Press, 1965), p. 319.

[18] See Brian Barry. *Political Argument;* and Virginia Held, *The Public Interest and Individual Interests* (New York: Basic Books, 1970).

[19] This position is argued for in an excellent book by Peter Singer entitled *Democracy and Disobedience* (New York: Oxford University Press, 1974).

[20] John Rawls, *A Theory of Justice* (Cambridge, Mass.: Harvard University Press, 1971), pp. 221–22.

[21] Plato, *Republic*, book 8, 558, quoted from the translation by Benjamin Jowett (New York: Modern Library 1941), p. 312.

[22]Carl Cohen, "The Justification of Democracy," *Monist* 55, no. 1 (1971): 22.

[23]See the discussion of rule utilitarianism, especially that of David Braybrooke, in Chap. 2 of the present work.

[24]S. I. Benn and R. S. Peters, *The Principles of Political Thought*, p. 417.

[25]R. H. Tawney, *Equality* (New York: Harcourt, Brace and Company, 1931), pp. 224–25, and George Allen and Unwin, Ld., quoted by kind permission of George Allen and Unwin, Ltd., London, © 1964.

[26]John Locke, *Second Treatise of Government* (1690), ed. Thomas P. Peardon (Indianapolis: Bobbs-Merrill, 1952). chap. 8., sect. 119.

[27]See D. A. J. Richard's discussion in *A Theory of Reasons for Action* (Oxford: Oxford University Press, 1971), pp. 148ff.

[28]Rawls, *A Theory of Justice*, pp. 342–43.

[29]Ibid., p. 343.

[30]Robert Nozick, *Anarchy, State and Utopia* (New York: Basic Books, 1974), p. 95.

[31]Rawls, *A Theory of Justice*, p. 333 ff.

SUGGESTED READINGS

Braybrooke, David. *Three Tests for Democracy: Personal Rights, Human Welfare, Collective Preference.* New York: Random House, 1968.

Cohen, Carl. *Democracy.* Athens: University of Georgia Press, 1971.

Flathman, Richard E. *Political Obligation.* New York: Atheneum, 1972.

Levine, Andrew. *Liberal Democracy: A Critique of Its Theory.* New York: Columbia University Press, 1981.

Locke, John. *Second Treatise of Government.* 1690. (Widely available in a variety of editions.)

MacPherson, C. D. *Democratic Theory: Essays in Retrieval.* New York: Oxford University Press, 1973.

Mill, John Stuart. *Considerations on Representative Government.* 1861. (Widely available in a variety of editions.)

Nelson, William. *On Justifying Democracy.* Boston: Routledge & Kegan Paul, 1980.

Pennock, Roland and Chapman, John W., eds. *Liberal Democracy Nomos XXV.* New York: New York University Press, 1983.

Pennock, Roland. *Democratic Political Theory.* Princeton: Princeton University Press, 1979.

Rawls, John. *A Theory of Justice.* Cambridge, Mass.: Harvard University Press, 1971. Chapters IV and VI.

Rousseau, Jean Jacques. *The Social Contract.* 1762. (Widely available in a variety of editions.)

Simmons, A. John. *Moral Principles and Political Obligation.* Princeton: Princeton University Press, 1979.

Singer, Peter. *Democracy and Disobedience.* New York: Oxford University Press, 1974.

Tussman, Joseph. *Obligation and the Body Politic.* New York: Oxford University Press, 1960.

Articles

Barry, Brian. "Is Democracy Special?" *Philosophy, Politics and Society,* 5th Series, Peter Laslett and James Fishkin, eds. New Haven: Yale University Press, 1979.

Dahl, Robert A. "Procedural Democracy." *Philosophy, Politics, and Society.* 5th Series, Peter Laslett and James Fishkin, eds. New Haven: Yale University Press, 1979.

Fishkin, James. "Symposium on the Theory and Practice of Representation." *Ethics,* Vol. 91, No, 3 (April 1981). The entire issue is devoted to representation.

Hook, Sidney. "The Philosophical Presuppositions of Democracy." *Ethics,* Vol. 32 (1941–1942), pp. 275–96.

The Monist, Vol. 55, No. 1 (1971). Entire issue is devoted to the topic, "Foundations of Democracy."

Six
LIBERTY

Although virtually everyone claims to be a friend of liberty in the abstract, many turn out to be only fair-weather friends in the concrete. Although most Americans willingly pledge allegiance to their flag and to the liberty and justice for which it stands, all too frequently the very values the flag supposedly symbolizes are lost sight of in the heat of controversy. This is especially true of liberty. Liberty enables people to act in ways others cannot control. People are left free to act in ways that some might find repulsive, immoral, and subversive. Too often, those affronted react by trying to limit liberty itself.

Thus, fundamentalist religious groups have tried, with some success, to eliminate from the public schools those textbooks that do not support certain religious and political values. Similarly, guardians of the public's virtue have tried and continue to try, again with some success, to remove controversial books from library shelves. Throughout our history, those who have dissented from official policy often have been faced with economic and even physical retaliation.

Other problems concerning liberty arise, even if those involving its infringement are ignored. Thus, even the staunchest friends of liberty disagree over its scope and limits. Your liberty to swing your arm may end where your neighbor's nose begins. But should you be free to take high risks? Even if the only reason for doing so is to show off to friends? Should attempts at suicide be prevented? Or should people be free to end their own lives if they wish? Are there limits to free speech? If so, what are they? If not, does it follow that viciously racist or anti-Semitic speeches are protected by law? Can behavior be prohibited simply because it is offensive to others? If so, how offensive must it be. If not, does it follow that anything goes in public, even if what goes on deeply disgusts virtually all who witness it?

In Chapter Five, it was argued that democracy constitutes a fair process for adjudication of conflicting rights claims. Our concern here is to delineate the scope of one kind of such claim, the claim to individual liberty, and also to indicate how the right to liberty can act as a needed constraint on the democratic process. Consideration of the scope and limits of individual liberty will also enable us to deal with the second principal question on political philosophy posed in Chapter One; namely, that of ascertaining the proper limits of the state's authority over the individual. It is to such questions concerning liberty that we now turn.

THE CONCEPT OF POLITICAL LIBERTY

Our concern is with *political* liberty. Thus, some disputes over liberty of other kinds need not concern us. For example, there has been some dispute over whether the laws of nature are restrictions on human liberty. Are humans unfree to jump over the moon or do they simply lack the ability to do so? No stand need be taken on this issue since if there is any constraint on liberty here, it surely is not political liberty that is constrained. Political liberty seems to be associated with the absence of constraints imposed by *persons*. Thus, a mountain range may render inhabitants of a valley unfree to leave, but it is not their political liberty that is restricted.

There is some temptation to identify liberty with the ability to satisfy one's wants and desires. Suppose that Jones is locked in a room but wants nothing more than to remain there. Is Jones free? Are the citizens of a ruthless dictatorship, where criticism of the despot is not permitted, free so long as they actually support the government and do not want to criticize the dictator?

One difficulty with the view that one is free if one does as one wants is that wants themselves can be coercively imposed. John Stuart Mill, in his essay "On the Subjection of Women," suggests that even if women behave as they want, they are not free if what they want to do is itself the result of coercion:

> All causes, social and natural, combine to make it unlikely that women should be collectively rebellious to the power of men. . . . Men do not

want solely the obedience of women, they want their sentiments. . . .
They have therefore put everything in practice to enslave their
minds. . . . When we put together three things—first, the natural
attraction between opposite sexes; secondly, the wife's entire depen-
dence on the husband, every privilege or pleasure . . . depending
entirely on his will; and lastly, that the principal object of human
pursuit . . . and all objects of social ambition, can in general be sought
or obtained by her only through him, it would be a miracle if the
object of being attractive to men had not become the polar star of
feminine education and formation of character. . . . Can it be
doubted that any of the other yokes which mankind have succeeded
in breaking, would have subsisted till now if the same means had
existed, and had been so sedulously used, to bow their minds to it?[1]

If Mill is correct in claiming that the wants of many women have been
formed coercively, then surely such women are not free even if they are
doing what they want to do. One might as well say that we can liberate
prisoners simply by getting them to want to remain in prison.[2] On the
other hand, we must be careful of dismissing others as "brainwashed" or
"socialized" just because we reject their views. Thus, the tendency of some
feminists to dismiss the criticism of more traditional women as the result of
social indoctrination too often functions as a device for avoiding the need
to deal with objections and for taking opponents seriously as persons.

    A second unacceptable consequence of the view that one is free if
what one does is what one wants to do has been pointed out by Joel Feinberg. Consider, Feinberg asks us:

the case in which Doe can do one thousand things *including* what he
most wants to do, whereas Roe can do only the thing he most wants to
do. On the (freedom as the ability to do as one wants) model, Doe and
Roe do not differ at all in respect to freedom.[3]

Surely such a consequence is absurd. So too, then, is the theory that implies
it.

    Accordingly, liberty ought not to be confused with being able to do as
one wants. The willing slaves of a dictator may be happy but they are not
free! But what is liberty? Discussion of political liberty profitably can begin
with Sir Isaiah Berlin's important paper "Two Concepts of Liberty."

Berlin's "Two Concepts of Liberty"

    In "Two Concepts of Liberty," Berlin attempts to distinguish *negative*
from *positive* liberty. The first

is involved in the answer to the question "What is the area within which the subject . . . is or should be left to do or be what he is able to do or be, without interference by other persons?" The second . . . is involved in the answer to the question "What, or who, is the source of control or interference that can determine someone to do, or be, this rather than that."[4]

Negative liberty concerns the absence of external constraints imposed by others. Positive liberty concerns self-mastery, or control over one's own fate. Let us examine negative and positive liberty more closely.

Negative liberty   According to Berlin, one lacks negative liberty "only if you are prevented from attaining a goal by human beings."[5] Negative freedom is the absence of coercion. Coercion "implies the deliberate interference of other human beings."[6] Such interference prevents action that the agent otherwise could have performed.

Is Berlin correct in maintaining that for negative liberty to be violated, constraints must be deliberately imposed? This identification of constraint with coercion or deliberate interference seems unfortunate. If Bradley accidentally locks Adler in his room, Adler is just as unfree to leave as he would be if Bradley's behavior were deliberate. Similarly, if through a series of actions whose consequences were unforeseen, our economic system develops in a way that closes significant options for most people, surely their liberty has been restricted. Lack of intention may well mitigate personal responsibility. But freedom can surely be restricted unintentionally. Hence, constraints on negative liberty need not be deliberately imposed.[7]

Negative liberty is the absence of constraint imposed by others. Such liberty is embodied in the notion of civil liberties, which are barriers against interference by the state. Lockean natural rights, as we have seen, were concerned primarily with negative liberty. What then is positive liberty?

Positive liberty   Berlin tells us that

The "positive" sense of the word "liberty" derives from the wish on the part of the individual to be his own master. I wish my life and decisions to depend on myself, not on external forces. . . .[8]

Positive freedom, according to this account, is self-mastery. One might be subject to no constraints imposed on others yet lack positive freedom. For example, if one is neurotically indecisive, then even if no one else prevents one from attending a movie, one may be unfree to go because of inability to make up one's mind. Likewise, compulsive desires, overwhelming depression, and perhaps even ignorance can restrict positive liberty.

Berlin believes that the concept of positive liberty is dangerous. Demagogues might claim that just as the neurotic is in the grip of irrational desires that prevent free choice, so too might the citizenry need to be forced to be free of their "irrational" desires for democracy. Once demagogues take this position, they may ignore the actual desires of the citizenry in order to "bully, oppress, torture (the citizens) in the name . . . of their 'real' selves."[9] Berlin is quite right to point out the fallacy here: namely, that of equating what we might want if we were not what we are with what we do want, and then assuming that if we are forced to promote the former, we are being liberated. This fallacy may lie behind the claim of some totalitarians that the citizens of a dictatorship have true freedom in spite of their protests to the contrary.

Berlin's essay is a warning against the appeal to positive liberty, with all the abuses to which such appeal may lead. Indeed, positive liberty can and has been perverted in just the way Berlin points out. However, the fault may lie more in the misuse of positive liberty than in the logic of the concept. Surely, there is nothing absurd in the claim that mental illness, exhaustion, or even lack of knowledge constrain one's decision-making ability and obstruct autonomous deliberation. The danger lies in the additional step that the subject must be coerced in order to be freed. This additional step is the one that should be criticized, although sometimes, as in the treatment of the psychotic, we may be warranted in taking it. Be that as it may, the fault seems not to lie in the claim that there are constraints on self-mastery but rather with the further claim that the victim should be forced to be free.[10]

It is doubtful, then, if the concept of positive liberty is *inherently* dangerous. However, it is also doubtful if it can be sharply distinguished from the concept of negative liberty. After all, compulsive desires, neuroses, ignorance, and the like normally arise from the action or inaction of others. If so, it is perhaps more useful to distinguish between *internal* and *external* constraints on liberty than between two kinds of liberty.[11] This suggests that ultimately there is only one concept of liberty. This alternate suggestion, that there is only one concept of liberty, will now be explored.

Liberty as a Triadic Relation

Perhaps the clearest account of a unitary concept of liberty is that advanced by Gerald C. MacCallum, Jr. He argues that liberty claims are best understood as expressing triadic relations:

> whenever the freedom of some agent or agents is in question, it is always freedom from some constraint or restriction on, interference with or barrier to doing, not doing, becoming or not becoming something.[12]

Liberty claims accordingly are to be analyzed according to the following schema:

X is (or ought to be) free from Y to do or become (or refrain from doing or becoming) Z.

According to this account, the simple claim to be free must always be understood as elliptical for a more complex claim that specifies whose freedom is at stake, what it is from, and what it is for. For example, both advocates and critics of open housing legislation claim to be for liberty. But the advocates are for the liberty of buyers from bigoted homeowners, which is to be used for purchasing homes or renting apartments. Critics are for the freedom of owners from legislation in order to sell to whomever such owners wish. Rhetorical appeals to freedom simply disguise what is at stake unless their structure is made fully clear.

The difference between negative and positive liberty turns out to be not a difference between two kinds or concepts of liberty at all. Rather, it is between two different ways of filling in the "Y" variable in the above triadic schema. Negative freedom can best be understood as freedom from external constraints, while positive freedom concerns freedom from internal ones.

What might "X," "Y," and "Z" stand for? "X" is to be understood as ranging over not only individuals but groups, corporations, states, and other kinds of institutions. "Z" ranges not only over actions but deliberations as well. Thus, as a result of imposed psychological blocks, a member of a group that has been subject to systematic discrimination may be unable to conceive of becoming a physician or attorney. In such cases, it seems correct to say that such a person is unfree even to *consider* certain alternatives.

Much controversy arises over the range of the "Y" variable. Many theorists, anxious to extend the scope of liberty, view poverty, ignorance, lack of opportunity, and lack of health as constraints on liberty. They are then able to justify the efforts of the welfare state at correcting such conditions as required by concern for liberty. Other theorists argue, however, that liberty ought to be distinguished from the conditions under which liberty is significant or valuable. Suppose, for example, that Smith will not be admitted to college because he does not realize that certain college-preparatory courses must be taken in secondary school. In the first view, Smith may be considered unfree to attend college. His ignorance is a constraint on his freedom. In the second view, he is perfectly free to go. No one is stopping him from taking the appropriate courses. Unfortunately, because of his ignorance, his freedom is not of much value. But he is free, nevertheless. Proponents of the second interpretation often criticize the activities of the welfare state as actually limiting liberty through excessive regulation. In this view, the welfare state spends so much time trying to improve the conditions of liberty that liberty itself gets lost in the shuffle.

This dispute seems largely verbal, however. While our sympathies lie with exponents of the broader interpretation, because they correctly point out that such "conditions" of liberty as ignorance and poverty often result from human action, the truth of their point does not depend on the language used to describe it. Certainly, if we consider poverty a constraint on liberty, then if we value liberty, we will want to eliminate poverty. But equally, if we believe that poverty diminishes the value or significance of liberty, then, if we value liberty, we will still want to eliminate poverty. Someone who distinguishes between liberty and the conditions of liberty need not be a defender of a laissez-faire free-market economy. Similarly, one can adopt the broad interpretation of liberty while defending laissez-faire. One would simply maintain that liberty from centralized government regulation is more important than liberty from poverty, ignorance, or lack of opportunity. Accordingly, whether or not one adopts the broad or narrow interpretation, the verbal issue of what is a constraint on liberty and what is a condition of liberty should be distinguished from the substantive issue of what conditions must be altered if liberty is to be extended (made more valuable).

This is not to deny that the choice of conceptual frameworks may have important consequences. Given the favorable connotations of "liberty," it is probably easier to muster political support for elimination of what are termed constraints on liberty than for efforts to increase the value of liberty one is already believed to possess. On the other hand, in some contexts, the blurring of the distinction between liberty and conditions under which liberty is of value may result in concern for negative rights being unduly subordinated to concern for implementation of positive ones. Hence, the intelligent choice of conceptual schemes requires thorough investigation and evaluation of the consequences of adoption in particular contexts.

The following conclusions emerge from this discussion of the concept of political liberty.

1. Liberty claims are often elliptical and need to be filled in as indicated by the triadic schema.
2. Liberty should not be confused with other values, such as want satisfaction, with which it can conflict.
3. Restrictions on liberty need not be deliberately imposed.
4. Conditions such as poverty and ignorance can restrict liberty or (depending upon one's choice of vocabulary) decrease the value or significance of liberty.

With these points in mind, some of the political and social issues concerning the scope and limits of individual liberty will now be considered.

LIBERTY: ITS SCOPE AND ITS LIMITS

Liberty is of great value because of its intimate connection with human dignity and self-respect, with autonomy and individuality, with free inquiry, and a host of other values.[13] To be always at another's beck and call, to be always dependent on other's permission for action is incompatible with the development of self-respect and retention of human dignity and autonomy. It also precludes the kind of growth and exploration that inquiry requires.

However, other values can conflict with liberty. One individual's liberty can conflict with another's welfare. Moreover, individual liberty may be threatened by the state. It is not surprising, then, that those in the liberal democratic tradition have been concerned to demarcate the proper scope or range of individual liberty. The problem is that of deciding just when it is justifiable for individuals, groups, and institutions to impose barriers on choice or action. For example, should someone be free to watch pornographic movies at home? At a movie theater? In a kindergarten classroom? Should free speech be extended to those who support racist and totalitarian ideologies? Does freedom include the freedom to advocate the elimination of freedom?

What is wanted is a criterion for distinguishing those areas in which restraint on others is permissible from those in which such restraint is illegitimate. Perhaps the most important criterion of demarcation was proposed by John Stuart Mill in his eloquent defense of individual freedom *On Liberty*.

In *On Liberty*, Mill declares that:

> the sole end for which mankind are warranted individually or collectively in interfering with the liberty of action of any of their number is self-protection. That the only purpose for which power can be rightfully exercised over any member of a civilized community, against his will, is to prevent harm to others. His own good, either physical or mental, is not a sufficient warrant.[14]

This passage has long been cited in defense of civil liberties and individual freedom. Each person, it asserts, is to be granted a sphere of inviolability in which to do as he or she wishes. The sphere is limited only by the like sphere of others. Paternalistic coercion for the good of the agent is ruled out. Interference with one person is justifiable only when necessary to protect others from harm. Self-regarding actions—those that affect only the agent—may not be interfered with. Other regarding actions—those that may lead to harm to others—are fair game for regulation in the interests of public safety.

Mill defends his harm principle, as it is called, by appeal to utility. Before considering its justification, however, it will be profitable first to consider more closely just what it states. In particular, how are we to understand "harm"? If we do not know what is to count as harm to others, we cannot apply the harm principle.

Perhaps physically hurting or causing someone pain is the criterion of harming. However, one can hurt or cause someone pain without harming them, so this proposal fails. For example, a dentist may hurt someone when filling a cavity, but the dentist is helping and not harming the patient. Likewise, someone may be harmed without being physically hurt or being caused to experience a painful sensation, e.g., by having valuable possessions stolen.

Harm seems to be a broader notion than that of physical hurt or pain. We will assume here that *interests* delimit harm. To harm X is to damage X's interests.[15] Since it normally is not in one's interest to be physically hurt or caused to experience pain, physically hurting or causing pain normally are ways of harming. But they are not the only ways. Insulting, excluding, discriminating against, and degrading are other ways of harming that need not involve physical hurt or pain. While the concept of an interest is far from clear, an interest at least seems to be something necessary for carrying out our actual or potential desires, or for securing our good. Understood in this way, the harm principle states that interference with anyone's action is justifiable only when necessary to prevent damage to the interests of others.

But is the distinction Mill attempts to draw between self- and other-regarding actions viable? Aren't all acts really other-regarding? Even the reading of a book in the privacy of one's own home can change one's character in a way ultimately detrimental to others. Thus, Mill's contemporary, James Fitzjames Stephen, maintained that:

> the attempt to distinguish between self-regarding acts and acts which regard others is like an attempt to distinguish between acts which happen in time and acts which happen in space. Every act happens at some time and in some place, and in like manner every act that we do either does or may affect both ourselves and others.[16]

Mill is not without reply to this objection. He acknowledges, for example, that acts performed in the privacy of one's home might constitute a bad example for others who learned of them. He rejoins that if the example is truly a bad one, others, seeing the harm brought about to the agent, will not follow it.[17] Likewise, Mill denies that long-range, indirect consequences of an act, render it other-regarding. He distinguishes harmful consequences of neglect of a *duty* from remote long-range consequence of ordinary human actions. If we were to interfere with the latter, no sphere of liberty would exist at all. Hence, "No person ought to be punished simply for being drunk: but a soldier or policeman should be punished for being drunk on duty."[18] It is only the immediate, direct risk of harmful consequences that can justify interference. However, even if these replies are satisfactory, the harm principle still faces many serious objections. We will consider attempts to override it in three areas, namely, those concerning offensive acts and the enforcement of morality, paternalistic interference, and interference with freedom of thought and discussion.

Offensive Acts and the Enforcement of Morality

Offensive acts   The self/other-regarding distinction has been attacked by appeal to the idea of an offensive act. On this argument, since any act, e.g., demonstrating for peace, interracial handholding, public dancing, might offend *someone*, all acts are other-regarding.

To avoid such a consequence, it is sometimes suggested that we distinguish offending from harming. For, if we were to count the giving of offense as harm, the harm principle would be vacuous. Since any act might be offensive to some, any act might be harmful to some. Thus, it is claimed, it is important to draw a sharp distinction between offending and harming.

But surely it is implausible to think that the giving of offense is never harmful to the offended party. People may be deeply offended at witnessing what they regard as immoral or obscene acts and behavior. A deeply religious person may be significantly pained by seeing or hearing about what he regards as a sacrilegious speech or play. Virtually anyone in contemporary Western societies would be disgusted by public defecation. In at least some such cases, the offense given can be not only upsetting but can induce rage, affect health, and perhaps even alter the course of a person's life, e.g., as when someone makes it her or his life work to stamp out pornography.

Can the claim to liberty be reconciled with the claim to be safe from constant offense? A first step at reconciliation would involve distinguishing easily avoidable from unavoidable offensive acts. If the act or behavior that is regarded as offensive can be avoided with a minimum of effort, it is not unreasonable to expect those who object to make the minimal effort required. Surely, liberty is of great enough value to outweigh the minimal effort required to avoid offense. Thus, having sexual relations on the subway during rush hour may be legally prohibited. Sex between the proverbial consenting adults in private should be beyond the scope of the law. Anyone should be free to watch a pornographic movie if they so wish but such freedom should not extend to lurid billboard advertisements that passers-by cannot help but witness.

How exactly is the boundary between the avoidable and the unavoidable to be drawn. It is doubtful if any precise formula can be constructed that then can be applied to cases in a mechanical fashion. In practice, the boundary should be established by democratically enacted statute, as applied by the judiciary. However, there are limits on how far democracy may go here. These limits are set by the value of liberty itself. In view of the importance of individual liberty, the burden of proof is on those who would limit it to show at least: (*a*) that the allegedly offensive behavior cannot be easily avoided; (*b*) that it is not feasible to provide a restricted area where the behavior in question need not be witnessed by the general public; (*c*) that the behavior is widely regarded as deeply offensive in the community as a whole; and (*d*) that the allegedly offensive behavior is not the expression of an ideology or ideal that ought to be protected under the heading of free speech. We also should remember that since *any* act may offend someone, we cannot prohibit all offensive behavior without surrendering liberty entirely.

In practice, the courts often have appealed to the standard of what the community in general finds offensive, obscene, or revolting. The trick, which has not yet been performed satisfactorily, is to characterize the relevant community properly. Presumably, one should not define the community so narrowly that the showing of the very same movie is allowed in one and prohibited in the other of two neighboring suburbs. Yet one might not want to define the community so broadly that what is permissible on 42nd Street in New York City must also be permissible in an Amish community.

It is reasonable to conclude that the guidelines sketched above should be interpreted as placing a heavy burden of proof on those who would restrict liberty to minimize offense. This is a moral judgment concerning the importance of liberty that we hope is warranted in view of the arguments for liberty in Chapter Three, as developed in later sections of this chapter.

The enforcement of morality   In 1957, in Great Britain, the Wolfenden Report concluded that homosexual behavior between consenting adults in private should not be subject to criminal sanction. In the spirit of Mill's harm principle, the report argued that the law should not favor particular patterns of behavior or ways of life unless necessary to protect others. The Wolfenden Report reflects the view of those liberals who follow Mill in maintaining that the widespread belief that a practice is immoral, even if true, is not itself a reason for imposing criminal penalties. In this view, crime and sin are not coextensive categories.

This liberal view was attacked in Mill's time by James Fitzjames Stephen and in our own by the distinguished British jurist Lord Patrick Devlin. Let us consider Devlin's case for the enforcement of morality.

Devlin's Argument. The foundation of Lord Devlin's position lies in the claim that society has a right to protect its own existence. He then maintains that a common public morality is one necessary condition of a society's survival. But certain acts, even though they may not harm other individuals in Mill's direct sense, undermine the public morality.[19] Accordingly, society has the right to regulate such acts in self-defense. ". . . society may use the law to preserve morality in the same way as it uses it to safeguard anything else that is essential to its existence."[20]

Devlin does not maintain that every act widely believed to be immoral should be legally prohibited. In fact, he favors maximal tolerance, consistent with the security of society.[21] The position Lord Devlin takes, then, is that "without shared ideas on politics, morals and ethics no society can exist."[22] This central core of the public morality, which is essential to society's very existence can and should be protected by the criminal sanction. Contrary to some critics, Devlin does not view morality as a "seamless web," every strand of which is to be protected.[23] All he need be committed to is that *some* elements of the public morality are so essential to society's existence that sins against them are to be counted as crimes as well.

Hart's and Dworkin's Counterattack. There is a serious problem for Devlin, however, which critics have not hesitated to exploit. The problem is this: How are those elements of the public morality essential for society's survival to be distinguished from those elements unessential for society's survival?

Devlin would respond that the proper test is the reaction of the "reasonable man." The reasonable man or woman should not be confused with the rational one:

> He is not expected to reason about anything, and his judgment may be largely a matter of feeling. . . . For my purpose, I should like to call him the man in the jury box, for the moral judgment of society must be something about which any twelve men or women drawn at random might after discussion be expected to be unanimous.[24]

It is this feature of Devlin's position that has drawn fire from H.L.A. Hart and Ronald Dworkin. Hart and Dworkin raise the banner of objective morality against Devlin. Thus, Hart maintains that if all Devlin means by "morality" is widely shared feelings of indignation, intolerance, and disgust, there is no justification for giving such prejudices the status of law. Rather, Hart asserts that "the legislator should ask whether the general morality is based on ignorance, superstition, or misunderstanding . . . and whether the misery to many parties, the blackmail and the other evil consequences, especially for sexual offenses, are well understood."[25] In a similar vein, Ronald Dworkin maintains that Lord Devlin has not distinguished moral convictions from personal prejudices. At the very least, moral convictions must be based on reasons rather than emotion, must be arrived at autonomously, and must pass minimal standards of evidence and argumentation. The trouble with Devlin's position, Dworkin tells us, "is not his idea that the community's morality counts, but his idea of what counts as the community's morality."[26]

Reflections on the Debate. This last criticism of Devlin surely has force. Devlin, for example, seems committed to prohibiting interracial handholding if a randomly selected jury in a segregated society would find such behavior intolerable. Surely, Devlin's critics are right in contending that the "reasonable man" is not the proper source of wisdom on the nature of the public morality. But then, Devlin is left without means of distinguishing essential from unessential elements of the public morality. He relied on the "reasonable man" to make the distinction but that reliance is unwarranted.

However, Devlin and his critics do seem to agree on one point, namely, that *if* essential aspects of the public morality could be identified, they should be protected by law. But surely there are enormous problems about identifying the essential aspects. Social scientists might tell us what people *believe* are essential but this would not show if such beliefs are *correct*. Who is to be the final arbiter? Do we want physicians making the decision? Philosophers? Captains of industry? Labor leaders? Professional golfers? No answer of this kind seems convincing.

Perhaps we ought to appeal to the democratic process, the decision of the majority of all the people. But this would bring us right back to Devlin's "reasonable man" standard, one that has already been rejected as inadequate.

What we suggest is that the whole issue can be avoided. Devlin and his critics each make an assumption that can be rejected, namely, the assumption that a society is entitled to protect itself from any kind of assault on the essential elements of common public morality through use of the criminal sanction. We suggest that even if the essential elements could be identified, society has no such right. That is, it is always an open moral question whether any society *ought* to survive, where "survival" is understood merely in terms of "survival of an essential public morality." Perhaps the shared morality ought to be changed, even if this means bringing a new society into existence. Devlin, and apparently Hart and Dworkin, do not clearly distinguish between *legitimate* and *illegitimate* methods for bringing about change. Respect for others forbids forcing change down their throats. Society surely has the right to protect its members against coercion. On the other hand, as Joel Feinberg points out:

> a citizen works *legitimately* to change public moral beliefs when he openly and forthrightly expresses his own dissent, when he attempts to argue, persuade and offer reasons and when he lives according to his own convictions with persuasive quiet and dignity, neither harming others nor offering counterpersuasive offense to tender sensibilities.[27]

What this passage suggests is that if one is really committed to democratic change along lines developed in Chapter Five, one must be prepared for public debate and decision on whether the public morality ought to be

revised. But how else is change to be promoted except through consideration of argument and example. As indicated in Chapter Three, *action* can
be a contribution to moral inquiry. Hence, the ruling out of experiments in
living is not permissible. For example, new living arrangements between
men and women, communal child-raising practices, or demands for equal
rights for homosexuals may be attacked as subversive of the social order.
But what could be better evidence of whether the social order ought or
ought not to change than an examination of the lives of those who choose
alternate ways of living? Devlin has not adequately distinguished majoritarianism, i.e., the standard of the reasonable man, from democracy and
the safeguard for rational inquiry that democracy presupposes.

We suggest, then, that legal prohibition of offensive or immoral acts
be confined to those cases where the objectionable behavior is difficult to
avoid. In other cases, the value of liberty itself, as well as the requirements
of the democratic process, properly understood, restrict the scope of the
state's authority over us.

Paternalistic Interference

Paternalistic interference is interference for the benefit of the agent
whose liberty is infringed upon. Its aim is the good of the person coerced,
not the prevention of harm to others. According to the harm principle,
paternalistic interference is unjustified, at least where adults are involved.
But is such a view acceptable?

Examples of allegedly paternalistic interference range from suicide
prevention and involuntary confinement of mentally ill but not dangerous
patients to passage of statutes requiring motorcycle riders to wear helmets
and automobile occupants to wear seat belts. To be sure, such interference
need not always be paternalistic. Accident victims may have to be cared for
at the public expense, for example, so the statutes requiring helmets and
seat belts can be viewed as protecting the public from undue medical costs.
For the moment, however, let us consider if such statutes, and other similar
kinds of interference, are justifiable *when* they are paternalistic in character. Perhaps this issue can best be explored by considering in detail a kind
of intervention that is often regarded as both paternalistic and justified,
namely, intervention in order to prevent suicide.

Paternalism and suicide prevention   Suicides are not always or even usually self-regarding. Loved ones, dependents, and associates of the victim
frequently are liable to harm. Accordingly, in a number of cases intervention may be justified on other-regarding grounds. However, even here, it is
doubtful if extensive, lengthy interference with freedom is justifiable on
other-regarding grounds alone. The loss of liberty may outweigh the benefits received. (In any case, a person who is constantly suicidal is unlikely to

be helpful to family, friends, and associates.) So, while remembering that suicide prevention often can be justified on other-regarding grounds, it is also well to remember the costs of ruling that a person's life is really not his or her own, but is under the control of others. The case that is of interest here, however, is that of suicide that does *not* harm others. Is *purely paternalistic* interference with a potential suicide justifiable?

Most of us will be moved in two apparently conflicting ways on the issue of the legitimacy of suicide prevention. On the one hand, at least in cases where either there are no dependents or dependents are unlikely to be seriously harmed, we are inclined to say that a person's life is that person's own business. At least in cases where suicide is unlikely to involve harm to others, interference seems to imply that the agent in question is really like a child, unable or unwilling to make responsible decisions. On the other hand, it does seem callous simply to stand by, allowing other humans to take their lives. It looks as if our compassion is at war with our libertarianism here. Is there any way to reconcile the two?

One strategy of reconciliation is to restrict the applicability of the harm principle so that it allows at least some kinds of suicide prevention. Mill himself suggests one such approach when he declares that:

> It is, perhaps, hardly necessary to say that this doctrine is meant to apply only to human beings in the maturity of their faculties . . . . Liberty, as a principle, has no application to any state of things anterior to the time when mankind have become capable of being improved by free and equal discussion.[28]

This passage suggests a position according to which intervention with another's action in order to prevent suicide is justifiable where there is reason to believe the agent in question has not made a rational, responsible decision.

How might one fail to make such a decision? For one thing, a person might be in the grip of an abnormal, highly emotional mental state, e.g., extreme anxiety or depression. While in such a state, suicide might seem a desirable alternative. However, if the person were to return to normal, suicide would no longer seem acceptable. Surely it is justifiable to intervene in such cases in order to make sure that a person's decision to commit suicide is one that has been given sufficient consideration and examination. To allow a fleeting desire or an unusual emotional state to bring about such an irrevocable decision is to ignore the agent's own rational plan of life that might be adhered to given further opportunity for reflection. As one suicidologist has declared of the proverbial businessman on the ledge of a tall building, "He is on the ledge rather than in his office because he wants to jump. But he is on the ledge rather than in the air because he wants to live."[29] Intervention, at least for the purpose of allowing due consideration and time for cessation of abnormal and/or fleeting moods and impulses, seems fully acceptable.

And, of course, the potential suicide might not just be in the grip of a fleeting depression or an abnormal mood. Such a person may be highly neurotic, mentally ill, or under the grip of a recurring compulsive desire. In such cases, it may be doubted whether the person involved has *decided* to commit suicide at all. Suicide becomes more like something that happens to one rather than something one does.

It is true, however, that psychiatrists such as Dr. Thomas Szaz have raised suspicions about the legitimacy of the very category of mental illness.[30] And, as we have seen, Sir Isaiah Berlin has warned us of the dangers of forcing people to be free. But surely it is sometimes the case that people are not in control of themselves and so cannot make rational, responsible decisions. At the very least, we can conclude that if the responsible (rational)/nonresponsible (nonrational) distinction can sometimes be applied, it provides a justification for intervention for the sake of suicide prevention.

Care must be exercised, however, in avoiding two kinds of mistakes. First, it should not be concluded that simply because a person is a potential suicide, that person *necessarily* fails to be rational or responsible. This would be to rule out the possibility of a rational, responsible suicide *by definition*. Such a move is trivial for it can alter only what we call the facts, not the facts themselves. We would simply have to invent a new word to refer to rational, responsible agents who take or attempt to take their own lives. The claim that no suicides are rational or responsible would be true, but only tautologically so because of linguistic fiat. The danger here is that of mistaking linguistic legislation for fact, and on the basis of such a confusion, interfering with the freedom of autonomous agents. Second, one must be wary of too extensive interference in the lives of potential suicides. Thus, it seems incompatible to say both that a patient's mental state is fleeting or abnormal *and* that the patient must be confined for long periods of time. Intervention of some preliminary sort may be justified in *all* cases of potential suicide as a fail-safe device, designed to allow the agent to think his or her situation through or to provide counseling. But the assumption that an agent is not rational or responsible can be overridden in particular cases. Indeed, when the person in question is suffering from a painful terminal disease, failure to allow suicide may not only unreasonably infringe on liberty, but may be just plain cruel as well.[31]

Does this reasoning imply that a person should be allowed to contract into slavery? It might seem as if such an act should be permitted under some circumstances. Interference might be justified to insure that the agent is rational and autonomous. But once such a conclusion is established, there would seem to be no grounds for interference.

We suggest, however, that while such reasoning may be cogent in the case of suicide prevention, it is not cogent in the case of contracting into slavery. The decision to commit suicide, especially when motivated by a desire to escape the ravages and indignities of a painful terminal illness, can itself be an expression of autonomy and dignity. Suicide may be contemplated because illness or some other evil would rob the subject of autonomy and dignity. Without these, the subject believes, life is not worth living. To contract into slavery, however, is to *choose* a life without autonomy or dignity. While suicide can be committed out of respect for such values, the decision to become a slave represents their abandonment. Hence, we suggest that the harm principle is overriden in cases where the agent would choose such extreme degradation that the very values of human dignity and respect for persons, which lie at the foundation of the harm principle itself, are irrevocably abandoned.

Extension to other cases   This discussion of suicide prevention suggests that the following are acceptable principles of paternalistic interference.

1.   One may paternalistically interfere with another in order to insure that that person's behavior is autonomous.
2.   One may paternalistically interfere with the behavior of nonresponsible persons, e.g., children, the severely depressed and disturbed.
3.   One may paternalistically interfere with another's behavior in order to prevent an act the consequences of which are final in that (*a*) they irrevocably commit the agent to an act or way of life which is likely to be extremely harmful to him; *and* (*b*) which constitute an abandonment of the very values of rationality, human dignity, and self-respect that justify concern for individual liberty itself.

These principles are at best only prima facie justified. In any given case, they may be outweighed by the value of liberty. However, they do constitute guidelines that indicate the sort of considerations *relevant* to justification of paternalistic interference. Each, we suggest, is compatible with the harm principle. Principle 2 states the limits of applicability of the harm principle while 1 allows interference for purposes of checking that the limits have not been exceeded. Principle 3 indicates that the harm principle is limited by the very same values that justify it itself.

How might these principles apply in practice? Mountain climbing, for example, although risky for the participants, could not be interfered with justifiably. Normally, mountain climbers are autonomous rational agents. Although the decision to climb may be momentous, in the sense of 3*a*, it surely does not represent an abandonment of autonomy and rationality or self-respect. The decision to participate in an activity which, although dangerous, requires great skill, gives participants a sense of achievement and exposes them to the beauty and majesty of our world. It is not only an intelligible decision but often may be an admirable one as well. On the other hand, a more plausible, if not fully satisfactory, case can be made for legislation that requires that seat belts be worn in motor vehicles. The failure to wear such belts is more often a matter of lack of proper habits than conscious choice. Finally, 3 does seem to sanction interference with activities that will lead to drug addiction. Heroin addicts, for example, certainly seem to run afoul of both 3*a* and 3*b*

In *On Liberty*, Mill maintained that

> the human faculties of perception, judgment, discrimination, feeling, mental activity and even moral preference are exercised only in making a choice . . . . The mental and the moral, like the muscular powers, are improved only by being used. . . . He who lets the world, or his own portion of it, choose his plan of life for him, has no need of any other faculty than the ape like one of imitation.[32]

Those who find a society of apelike mimics abhorrent have good reason to be skeptical of paternalistic intervention. However, such skepticism admits of justified exceptions where paternalism is designed to protect the autonomy of the agent in the long run.[33]

Freedom of Thought and Discussion

The second chapter of *On Liberty* is entitled "Of the Liberty of Thought and Discussion." It is perhaps the most eloquent and moving defense of such freedom available. In that chapter, Mill sets himself the task of applying the harm principle to freedom of thought and its natural extension, freedom of speech. Exactly how he thought the harm principle would apply in this area, however, is unclear.

Perhaps Mill believed no harm to others could arise from absolute freedom of thought and discussion. Such a view is most implausible, however. All he need establish is that any harm arising from such freedom is always outweighed by the benefits. As a utilitarian, Mill needs to establish the usefulness of such freedom apart from any appeal to abstract rights or justice. It is this relatively modest conclusion—that the benefits of absolute freedom of thought and discussion always outweigh the costs (in some utilitarian sense of "outweigh")—that will be of immediate concern here.

Mill is insisting on absolute freedom in this context. Interference with thought or discussion in itself is never warranted. "If all mankind minus one were of one opinion, mankind would be no more justified in silencing that one person than he, if he had the power, would be justified in silencing mankind."[34] We will now consider Mill's argument for this thesis.

Mill's defense of liberty of thought and discussion   Mill believed that freedom of thought and discussion are valuable because of their intimate connection with *rationality*. To be rational is at least in part to use procedures that enable us to detect our errors and arrive at more warranted belief. Mill held that thought and open discussion are the principal procedures that allow us to attain such a goal:

> the particular evil of silencing the expression of an opinion is that it is robbing the human race, posterity as well as the existing generation—those who dissent from the opinion still more than those who hold it. If the opinion is right, they are deprived of the opportunity of exchanging error for truth: if wrong, they lose what is almost as great a benefit, the clearer perception and livelier impression of truth produced by its collision with error.[35]

Without freedom of discussion, and the open exchange and criticism such discussion involves, we are deprived of the chance of having our errors corrected and condemned to hold the views we do hold as prejudices, without rational foundation. Thus, it can be plausibly argued that eventually criticism of the American involvement in Vietnam was able to bring about a perceivable shift in public sentiment about the correctness of the war. Free discussion is the mechanism for detecting and correcting error.

Mill considers the objection that we must often act on information that might be false, not having the time to check or even consider all available evidence. Why then should we not suppress an opinion if we have good reason for believing it to be false and dangerous? Mill replies that it is one thing to reject an opinion after arguments for it have been considered but quite another to ban it without even a hearing. "Complete liberty of contradicting and disproving our opinion is the very condition which justifies us in assuming its truth for purposes of action."[36]

Mill's first premise of his defense of freedom of thought and discussion is that such freedom is necessary for the correction of error and appreciation of truth. As a utilitarian, Mill also must establish a second premise; namely, that correction of error and appreciation of truth are *useful* in some utilitarian sense of that term. Presumably, Mill would argue that the process of inquiry would allow society to avoid serious error by exposing mistaken reasoning or dubious assumptions. Hence, it is more likely that a free society will choose optimal policies than it is that an unfree society will make such choices. Moreover, Mill also argues forcefully that freedom of thought and discussion leads to a diversity of points of view, which in turn produces inventiveness and independence among the citizenry. New ideas produced by an inventive and independent people lead to social, technological, scientific, and intellectual *progress*, which in turn benefits the society as a whole.

However, it is at least unclear whether such a classical utilitarian defense of free thought and discussion can succeed. Since what best promotes utility may vary from context to context, how can an *absolute* prohibition on interference be justified by appeal to utility? Thus, James Fitzjames Stephen argued that

> the question whether liberty is a good or bad thing appears as irrational as the question whether fire is a good or bad thing. It is both good and bad according to time, place and circumstances. . . . We must confine ourselves to such remarks as experience suggests about the advantages and disadvantages of compulsion and liberty in particular cases.[37]

Utilitarians might try to meet such an objection by appeal to the utility of *rules* rather than acts. Rule utilitarians, such as those discussed in Chapter Two, could maintain that even if interference promotes utility in particular cases, the rule that has the most utilitarian support is the one enjoining noninterference. Stephen, however, would probably challenge the empirical premise on which the rule utilitarian case rests; namely, that the rule of noninterference with liberty of thought and discussion best promotes utility. Stephen might rejoin that an open, free society promotes the kind of anxiety and rootlessness that are avoided by traditional, closed societies. Thus, it would appear that even if the classical utilitarian defenses of liberty, whether of the act or rule variety, do go through, it is only by relying on controversial empirical claims.

However, we suggest that Mill's best argument is not in the mainstream utilitarian tradition at all. Rather, although he often equivocates, Mill regards the development of critical, autonomous individuals as the intrinsic good to be produced. For Mill, "The worth of a state in the long run is the worth of the individuals composing it."[38] Social institutions are to be judged according to the kind of individuals they develop. Although the relationship between free discussion and promotion of a favorable ratio of want satisfaction to want frustration is unclear, the relationship between free discussion and the creation of critical, autonomous individuals is not. The latter are produced, Mill believed, through participation in the former. Since the goal is development of an atmosphere where such individuals can grow and flourish, Mill held that an absolute prohibition on interference was justified.

Whether Mill ever unequivocally adopted such a position is unclear, although he surely was attracted by it. In any case, we suggest that a stronger defense of liberty of thought and discussion can be made along such lines rather than through appeal to quantitative considerations of utility.

Our discussion suggests, then, that the right to individual liberty is best justified by showing it to be a precondition for the promotion and protection of personal autonomy. Whether or not liberty best promotes the overall general happiness, without it individuals cannot determine the course of their own lives. Freedom of thought and discussion are particularly important aspects of human liberty. The exchange of ideas it protects provides the frame work within which we can make informed and intelligent choices, influence the views of others by appealing to their own rational capacities and function as autonomous moral agents within a community of equals.

Liberty, Pornography, and Censorship

Before concluding our discussion of liberty, it will be helpful to consider a controversy to which many of the strands of our discussion apply. Debate over the morality and censorship of pornography raises the kinds of questions about personal liberty and its limits which have been of concern in our examination of liberty. While all the ramifications of this debate cannot be explored here, perhaps the bearing of the principles we have discussed can be clarified and examined.

It is exceedingly difficult to provide a widely acceptable definition of such terms as "pornography" and "obscenity" since different groups will try to build their own conclusions into the analysis, as when pornography is defined in terms of reduction of women to sex objects. Keeping that in mind, we will characterize "pornography" as material, such as film or literature, which depicts sexual activity or arousal in graphic and explicit ways, which has little if any literary or artistic merit, and which is designed primarily to elicit sexual arousal in the audience. This definition is relatively neutral in that it leaves open whether pornography, as so defined, is or is not to be morally condemned. It also leaves open the question of whether pornography is obscene.[39] If obscenity is understood as that which is grossly offensive to general community standards, it is debatable whether pornography is obscene. The many users of pornography obviously do not find it grossly offensive. To merely stipulate that "pornography" refers to what is obscene seems arbitrary. More important, such linguistic stipulation does not settle the substantive issue of whether pornographic material, as we define it, actually is obscene, regardless of what such material is called.

Should the use of pornography be censored? If so, on what grounds? Isn't what goes on between consenting adults their own business, not that of the law? Since censorship is a restriction on the liberty of individuals, it requires special justification. Can such a justification be provided?

It sometimes is argued that censorship of pornography can be justified through application of the harm principle. On this view, while the use of pornography appears to be a private matter between consenting individuals, appearances are deceiving. Arguably, the use of pornography has serious other-regarding implications which place it within the proper realm of public regulation.

On one version of this view, pornography, by frequently picturing women as objects of sexual domination by men, perpetuates and reinforces stereotypes of women as the sexual property of males. This, in turn, increases the likelihood of sex abuse and sexual violence directed at women.

Such a view rests on empirical assumptions about the effects of pornography. These are not the only assumptions it is possible to make, however. One could also argue that pornography, at least of the sort that appeals primarily to males, allows men to discharge sexual frustration in a harmless way, thereby *preventing* the kind of sexual abuse and crime which might otherwise take place.

Which set of assumptions is correct? Unfortunately, we are not now in a good position to tell, as different studies tend to point in different directions. In Denmark, there was a significant *decrease* in sex crimes after erotic material was made easily accessible. Some studies, on the other hand, seem to show an increase in willingness to tolerate sexual abuse of women after exposure to pornography, but as these studies concern only changes in attitude rather than behavior, their implications are unclear.[40]

Since such empirical issues are too complex to be explored here, we will restrict ourselves to two comments. First, given our discussion of liberty, the burden of empirical proof is on proponents of censorship. In the absence of a strong empirical case, the rights of individuals to pursue the way of life that seems best to them should not be infringed upon. Second, even if use of pornography does increase harm, the case for censorship is not thereby proved. After all, exposure to all sorts of material can cause harm. In addition, the harm caused must outweigh the value of the liberty being restricted, as well as any good that the use of liberty in question may produce as a byproduct. For example, would we be justified in prohibiting football if new research were to show that attendance at football games caused somewhat of an increase in violent behavior among fans? Wouldn't we at least have to consider whether the harm was sufficiently weighty to override both the right of football fans and players to direct their own lives and the enjoyment derived from watching and playing the sport?

Finally, even if all these issues were resolved in favor of censorship, we would need to fill in our definition of pornography precisely enough to make it applicable in law. For example, what are the criteria of pornographic intent, or lack of artistic or literary merit? If we rely on community standards, how are we to tell what they are? What if they are emotional and based on prejudice rather than reason? Works which are now recognized as of great merit were once attacked as obscene and pornographic. If we are to censor, our standards must be precise enough so as not to exert a chilling effect of freedom of thought and discussion.

Perhaps proponents of censorship might shift their strategy at this point. Rather than relying on the harm principle, particularly since it is difficult to demonstrate that pornography does directly cause sexual abuse, they might appeal to the offense principle instead. We may censor pornography, they might argue, because it is repulsive and obscene.

The trouble is that since pornography is so widely used in our society, it is difficult to demonstrate that it is obscene, repulsive or offensive to the general population. Censorship can too easily become the weapon of choice of one group of the population simply trying to impose its standards of taste on others. Moreover, as we have seen in our earlier discussion of offense, it is far from clear that even an overwhelming majority of society has the right to prevent an individual from enjoying grossly offensive material *in private*.

The offense principle may be used to restrict the sale and advertising of pornography so that those who are offended by it can reasonably avoid exposure to what disgusts them. But it is doubtful if it can justify outright censorship of pornography. Have we any more right to censor pornography because of its allegedly revolting character than a racially divided society would have for prohibiting interracial social contact because it offends a racist majority?

Perhaps it is not the offensiveness of pornography but its immorality that justifies censorship. Can legal moralism of the kind defended by Lord Devlin justify censorship? Does pornography threaten the public morality of civilization? Certainly, a case can be made that it does. Arguably, pornography disrupts the idea that sex should be a special private expression of love between two people. On this view, by reducing sex to a purely physical act, done purely for immediate pleasure, the value of sex as an expression of intimacy and love, and its usefulness as a bond holding the family together are undermined. It encourages us to view immediate self-gratification as a crucial goal, desensitizes us to tenderness by its frequent emphasis on violent dominance and submission, and replaces expression of affection by crude physical release. Intimacy, love and the family are reduced in value and a public morality based on such goods is swept away by one based on sexual gratification, often through degradation of the object of one's sexual attention.[41]

Such a view is of considerable interest, but clearly faces some of the problems discussed earlier. For one thing, it needs to be shown and not just asserted that exposure to pornography really does cause us to disvalue intimacy, love, and the family, and replace them by reduction of sexual partners to objects for physical gratification. However, the moralistic critics of pornography may not be making an empirical point about the allegedly immoral effects of pornography. Rather, their point may be that regardless of its effects, pornography expresses an immoral view of human relationships and this immorality alone may be grounds for its prohibition.

Opponents of censorship might retort, though, that this approach begs an important question. Perhaps, rather than expressing an immoral view of human relationships, pornography expresses or encourages a different morality of sexuality. In terms of our earlier discussion of public morality, pornography may be an expression of a non-traditional sexual morality or ideology. That is, it may represent an attempt to change the public morality in this area.

Thus, as Fred Berger points out in an influential essay, pornography of at least some kinds may be connected with an ideal of sexual liberation which views affection, intimacy and tenderness either as inessential to good sex or as middle class hangups which just get in the way of sexual gratification.[42] Should the state be permitted to prohibit the graphic expression of such an ideology simply on the grounds that others find it immoral? Could a similar principle be applied in the area of thought and discussion without allowing for the possibility of severe repression? Once again, if our earlier discussion is sound, the proponent of censorship on grounds of legal moralism faces important objections.

Recently, another rationale for censorship has been proposed based on the model of discrimination. That is, it can be argued that because pornography so frequently pictures the degradation, domination and violent abuse of women, it ought be regarded as an invidious form of sex discrimination.[43] In fact, because so much of pornography pictures violence against women, it reduces women to the level of non-persons who can be used or abused according to the whims of males. On this view, since pornography appeals mostly to males and conveys the impression that women are primarily objects for the sexual gratification of men, pornography invidiously discriminates against women. Therefore, it ought to be illegal on grounds of equal protection and non-discrimination.

While some form of this position may turn out to be ultimately defensible, it, like the other arguments for censorship, faces severe difficulties. In particular, it does not justify wholesale censorship of pornography, as defined here. At most, it justifies censorship of that (predominant) subclass of pornography which contains violence or abuse of women or, on an even broader interpretation, of pornography which shows men dominating women. It does not justify censorship of "non-sexist" pornography, or pornography in which plain sex rather than domination and submission is the main focus.[44]

Moreover, since it may be very difficult to define the difference between permissible and impermissible forms of pornography in a way that is precise, any attempted censorship may be far too risky. How are we to legally define "domination" for purposes of censorship, for example? Vagueness in a law is a serious defect. Those whom a too vague statute attempts to regulate cannot know in advance what is expected of them. Punishing them for violating a statute whose meaning is unclear is unfair. Moreover, the statute cannot do the job intended of it if those to whom it applies cannot discern its purpose. Finally, a too vague statute allows too broad an interpretation. If a statute imposing censorship is too vague, it allows self appointed guardians of the public's morality a wedge to limit access to art and literature which expresses an ideology they want to surpress.

Perhaps most important, however, if the reason for censoring pornography is not the explicit portrayal of sex for purposes of arousal but rather the degrading of women, wouldn't that principle apply in other areas as well? That is, since it is the domination of women, rather than the display of sex for purposes of arousal, that is objected to, isn't a dangerous precedent being set? The state has been given the right to censor material which portrays women, or members of other groups, as being subordinated or violated. In the absence of a clear account of "subordination" or a clear way of distinguishing works with literary, political or artistic merit from others, the door has been opened to regulation of a good deal of expression and thought. Thus, may novels or movies which show women in positions of subordination also be censored? The more an ordinary novel portrayed women as dominated by men, the more subject to censorship it might be regardless of the intent of the author or lack of sexually explicit content. Allowing such a precedent may be too great a risk to take, it risks narrowing the scope of individual liberty far too much.

Finally, the idea that the behavior of some women in pornographic portrayal of sex degrades all women needs to be critically examined. Suppose a pornographic film shows a woman enjoying being violently abused. Why should this imply that women as a class enjoy being treated in such a way any more than the portrayal of a male abuser implies that men as a class enjoy violently abusing women? If the latter claim is mistaken, why isn't the former mistaken as well? Is the idea of individuals representing a group sufficiently clear to be made the basis for legal censorship?

These are complex questions which deserve more extended treatment than they can receive here. Debate over the proper answers is likely to be heated and inconclusive. We suggest, however, that the burden of proof remains on those who would resort to censorship to avoid insult or alleged discrimination. It is one thing to point out that certain material is degrading and insulting but quite another to say that no one should be legally permitted to obtain it.

Accordingly, the attempts to justify censorship of pornography by appeal to the harm principle, the offense principle, legal moralism and the value of equal protection all face severe objections which can be made in the name of personal liberty. While we agree that much of contemporary pornography, particularly that which pictures the violent abuse of women—and which suggests that women enjoy being the objects of such treatment—is open to important moral objections, we question whether censorship is justified. The price a free society may have to pay for its liberty is tolerating the enjoyment by many of its citizens of what others find immoral, degrading and grossly offensive. To censor on the grounds find immoral, degrading and grossly offensive. To censor on the grounds of immorality or offensiveness alone, is to place the liberty of all of us in danger, since the most cherished views of each of us may be found immoral or offensive by others. Liberty, if it is to protect us when we need it, must protect what we disapprove of, or find insulting or degrading, as well.

Liberty and Authority

We see no reason, then, to abandon a modified form of the harm principle. Each person is to be viewed as possessing a prima facie right to liberty. This right protects freedom of thought and action, so long as no direct harm to others results. According to our own theory, such harm would be constituted by depriving others of their liberty or by violating their rights to the prerequisites of an at least minimally decent human existence. The right to liberty, as so understood, significantly limits the scope of the state's authority. States may override the right to liberty only in order to protect and implement other rights, and when such a policy has been arrived at by a just adjudication procedure suitably constrained. Accordingly, with the exceptions noted, and in the absence of "clear and present danger," the right to liberty cannot be overridden on paternalistic grounds, to enforce the moral beliefs or personal tastes of the majority, or to suppress unpopular or allegedly dangerous ideas.[45] In some cases, it will be controversial whether constraints on democracy have been observed or whether conditions for exceptions are met. But while we cannot consider all "hard cases" here, at least ground rules for dealing with such difficult cases have been suggested.

THE PRIORITY OF LIBERTY

The right to liberty is one among several fundamental rights that the good state ought to protect and implement. However, these rights can conflict. In such cases, where one's rights claims must remain unfulfilled in order that another's can be implemented, the choice is to be made by democratic procedures, as outlined in Chapter Five.

Influenced by John Rawls's work (see our discussion of the lexical ordering of his two principles of justice in Chapter Four), philosophers have been paying increasing attention to what has been called the *priority of liberty*. Within the liberal tradition, liberty has always been assigned an especially fundamental place. Thus, we have already seen that in Locke's political philosophy, basic rights were rights to liberty from interference by others. Nozick's contemporary libertarianism seems to recognize only the right to negative liberty. Even those whose work defends economic redistribution, writers such as Rawls and Tawney, either give priority to liberty or argue that economic equality contributes to greater liberty.

In our view, when the right to liberty conflicts with rights to material prerequisites of a minimally decent human life, there are no grounds for a priori assigning priority to the former. However, we point out that since poverty, ignorance, and ill health can constitute barriers to liberty, or at least conditions that rob liberty of its value, there is no *necessary* conflict between liberty and economic redistribution. Liberty and equality can conflict, but they need not necessarily do so.

However, there is an implication of our position for the priority of liberty that bears mentioning. That is, it seems wrong, from a natural-rights perspective, to trade away the right to liberty for wealth, once one has already obtained material prerequisites of a minimally decent human existence. While the notion of a minimally decent human existence is vague, what we intuitively have in mind is this: Once people have reached a certain degree of wealth such that not only are subsistence needs provided for, but decent medical care, education, clothing, diet, and housing are available, then the right to liberty increasingly takes priority over securing of greater and greater affluence.

In Chapter Four, we saw that John Rawls argued for a similar position. Unfortunately, Rawls was not able to show that his rational contractors would arrive at such a conclusion without importing controversial psychological assumptions into the argument.

Our position, however, is not based on psychology. Rather, our point is that once a reasonable degree of affluence is obtained, additional wealth does not contribute to human dignity or respect for persons to the degree that loss of liberty diminishes such values. This is not a psychological assertion about what *causes* what. Rather, it is a *moral* claim to the effect that autonomy and the freedom to carry out one's choices are more *significant* constituents of a meaningful human life than is great affluence.

But aren't we just expressing our own personal preferences here? Are such preferences rationally binding on everyone? In response, we would point to two considerations. First, would anyone really say that a society of affluent slaves who, while wallowing in luxury, were always at their master's call, led a life in which the values of human dignity and respect for persons were exemplified? Unfortunately, not everyone is committed to the values of human dignity and respect for persons but those who are may find our intuitions acceptable. Second, as Mill argued, liberties are essential for *rational inquiry*. Liberty is required to safeguard access to information, to protect critical discussion, and to allow for the formulation and communication of new points of view. How can citizens in a democracy evaluate foreign policy, for example, if it actually is determined by covert intelligence operations that are not exposed to public scrutiny or evaluation? Once the material prerequisites of a minimally decent human life have been secured for everyone, loss of additional wealth is less likely to hinder inquiry than loss of liberty. Accordingly, as affluence increases, there seem to be good reasons for weighing liberty more and more heavily relative to competing values. These reasons may be overridden on occasion, and perhaps properly so, but they seem at least sufficient to shift the burden of proof to those who would constrain liberty in particular cases.

CONCLUDING REMARKS

Rights arise from the equal claims of individuals to some level of possession of a fundamental or primary good. Liberty is such a good. However, the right to liberty, like other fundamental rights, is a prima facie right. In cases of conflict, it sometimes is proper that it give way. But the right to liberty should give way only to other claims of *right*, not to the maximization of utility, the glory of the nation state, the claims of religious orthodoxy or current standards of offensiveness or personal preferences and tastes of the majority. Where liberty clashes with other rights, the other rights usually are those to the economic or material prerequisites of an at least minimally decent human existence. In such cases, the conflict is to be adjudicated by the democratic process suitably constrained by requirements of justice, compromise and desire to reconcile competing claims without allowing any one kind of right to be completely subordinated.

NOTES

[1]John Stuart Mill, *The Subjection of Women, 1869* (London and New York: Longmans, Green and Co., 1911), pp. 42–43.

[2]This point is made by William A. Parent, "Some Recent Work on the Concept of Liberty," *American Philosophical Quarterly* 11, no. 3 (1974): 151.

[3]Joel Feinberg, *Social Philosophy* (Englewood Cliffs, N.J.: Prentice-Hall, 1973), p. 7.

[4]Isaiah Berlin, "Two Concepts of Liberty," in Berlin's *Four Essays on Liberty* (New York: Oxford University Press, 1969), pp. 121–22.

[5]Ibid., p. 122.

[6]Ibid.

[7]Berlin seems to have adopted such a position recently. See, for example, his remarks in the introduction to *Four Essays on Liberty*, p. xlviiff.

[8]Ibid., p. 131.

[9]Ibid., p. 133.

[10]On this point, see C. B. Macpherson's discussion in *Democratic Theory: Essays in Retrieval* (New York: Oxford University Press, 1973), chap. 5.

[11]This is suggested by Feinberg, *Social Philosophy*, pp. 12–14.

[12]Gerald C. MacCallum, Jr., "Negative and Positive Freedom," *Philosophical Review* 76, no. 3 (1967): 314.

[13]See the arguments of chap. 3, in the section on "Justification."

[14]John Stuart Mill, *On Liberty*, 1859. Passages quoted are from Currin V. Shield, ed., (Indianapolis: Bobbs-Merrill Library of Liberal Arts edition, 1956), p. 13. All subseqeunt quotations from *On Liberty* are from this edition.

[15]We follow here a suggestion of Brian Barry's in *Political Argument* (New York: Humanities Press, 1965), p. 176f.

[16]James Fitzjames Stephen, *Liberty, Equality, Fraternity* (London: Smith, Elder & Co., 2d ed., 1874), p. x.

[17]Mill, *On Liberty*, p. 101.

[18]Ibid., pp. 99–100.

[19]See, for example, George Gilder, "In Defense of Monogamy," *Commentary* 58, no. 5 (1974): 31–36, for what can be read as an application of Devlin's position to the so-called new sexual morality.

[20]Lord Patrick Devlin, "Morals and the Criminal Law," from Devlin's *The Enforcement of Morals* (New York: Oxford University Press, 1965), reprinted in Richard A. Wasserstrom, ed., *Morality and the Law* (Belmont, Calif.: Wadsworth, 1971), p. 34.

[21]Ibid., p. 37n, pp. 39–41.

[22]Ibid., p. 33.

[23] H. L. A. Hart, *Law, Liberty and Morality* (New York: Random House, 1966), p. 51.

[24]Devlin, "Morals and the Criminal Law," p. 38.

[25]H. L. A. Hart, "Immorality and Treason," *Listener*, 30 July 1959, as reprinted in Wasserstrom, *Morality and the Law*, p. 54.

[26]Ronald Dworkin, "Lord Devlin and the Enforcement of Morals," *Yale Law Journal* 75, as reprinted in Wasserstrom, *Morality and the Law*, p. 69.

[27]Feinberg, *Social Philosophy*, p. 39.

[28]Mill, *On Liberty*, pp. 13–14.

[29]We have been unable to track the source of this remark but first heard it on a tape of a debate on suicide prevention between Dr. Thomas Szaz and an unidentified opponent. The opponent was the source of the remark.

[30]Thomas Szaz, M.D., *The Myth of Mental Illness* (New York: Dell, 1961).

[31]See Marvin Kohl, *The Morality of Killing: Sanctity of Life, Abortion and Euthanasia* (New York: Humanities Press, 1974), especially his discussion of euthanasia, on this point.

[32]Mill, *On Liberty*, p. 71.

[33]Thus, Gerald Dworkin has argued that paternalistic interference is justified if rational, autonomous persons would consent to it in the given circumstances. The limits of paternalism are set by what might be thought of as an ideal or hypothetical contract. See Dworkin's "Paternalism," in Wasserstrom, *Morality and the Law*, pp. 107–26.

[34]Mill, *On Liberty*, p. 21. Most liberals would agree that speech may be interfered with to prevent a "clear and present" danger from arising. But care must be taken not to construe "clear and present" so broadly that legitimate protest is silenced. In any case, the goal here is to prevent a dangerous *action*, not to interfere with communication as such.

[35]Ibid., p. 21.

[36]Ibid., p. 24

[37]James Fitzjames Stephen, *Liberty, Equality, Fraternity*, 1st ed., (New York: Holt and Williams, 1873), p. 49.

[38]Mill, *On Liberty*, p. 141.

[39]The relationship of pornography to obscenity is discussed thoughtfully by Joel Feinberg in his essay, "Harm, Offense, and Obscenity" in Burton M. Leiser, ed., *Values in Conflict: Life, Liberty and the Rule of Law* (New York: Macmillan Publishing Co., 1981) particularly pp. 238–239. We have found his discussion particularly useful, especially his critique of attempts to analytically link the pornographic and the obscene.

[40]For discussion, see Fred Berger, "Pornography, Sex and Censorship" in David Copp and Susan Wendell, *Pornography and Censorship* (Buffalo: Prometheus Books, 1983) pp. 83–104 as well as the empirical studies reprinted on pp. 213–321.

[41]For discussion of writers who hold such a view, see Berger, "Pornography, Sex and Censorship." An easily accessible example of one version of such an argument is to be found in Irving Kristol's "Pornography, Obscenity and the Case for Censorship," *The New York Times Magazine*, March 28, 1971.

[42]Berger, "Pornography, Sex and Censorship," p. 89ff.

[43]The case that pornography unjustly victimizes women is argued by a number of writers. Ann Garry's "Pornography and Respect for Women" in Copp and Wendell, *op. cit.*, pp. 61–82, is a particularly useful presentation of such a view.

[44]Garry discusses the possibility of "non-sexist" pornography in "Pornography and Respect for Women."

[45]Of course, the "clear and present danger" doctrine can be misused to suppress dissent through too broad an interpretation of what is a clear and present danger.

SUGGESTED READINGS

Benn and Petters, R. S. *The Principles of Political Thought: Social Foundations of the Democratic State.* New York: The Free Press, 1965. Chapter 10.
Berger, Fred R., ed. *Freedom of Expression.* Belmont, CA: Wadsworth, 1980. Classic articles on censorship.
Berlin, Isaiah. *Four Essays on Liberty.* New York: Oxford University Press, 1969. See particularly the essay "Two Concepts of Liberty."
Feinberg, Joel. *Harm to Others: The Moral Limits of the Criminal Law.* New York: Oxford University Press, 1984.
———.*Social Philosophy.* Englewood Cliffs, New Jersey: Prentice-Hall, 1973.
Hart, H.L.A. *Law, Liberty and Morality.* New York: Random House, 1966.
Mill, John Stuart. *On Liberty.* 1859. (Widely available in a variety of editions.)
Nielsen, Kai. *Equality and Liberty.* Totowa, N.J.: Rowman and Allenheld, 1985.
Oppenheim, Felix E. *Dimensions of Freedom.* New York: St. Martin's, 1961.
Wasserstrom, Richard, ed. *Morality and the Law.* Belmont, California: Wadsworth, 1971. Contains articles oy Devlin, Dworkin, Hart, and others which were discussed in this chapter.
Wolff, Robert Paul. *The Poverty of Liberalism.* Boston: Beacon Press, 1968. Chapter One, "Liberty."

Articles

Daniels, Norman. "Equal Liberty and the Unequal Worth of Liberty" in Norman Daniels, ed., *Reading Rawls: Critical Studies of A Theory of Justice.* New York: Basic Books, 1975, pp. 253-81.
MacCallum, Gerald C., Jr. "Negative and Positive Freedom." *The Philosophical Review,* Vol. LXXVI, No. 3 (1967), pp. 312–34.
Marcuse, Herbert. "Repressive Tolerance," in Robert Paul Wolff, Barrington Moore, Jr., and Herbert Marcuse, *A Critique of Pure Tolerance.* Boston: Beacon Press, 1969.
Parent, William A. "Some Recent Work on the Concept of Liberty." *American Philosophical Quarterly,* Vol 11, No. 3 (1974), pp. 149–66.
Wertheimer, Alan. "Social Theory and the Assessment of Social Freedom." *Polity,* Vol 7, No. 3 (1974), pp. 334–60.

Seven
LAW AND ORDER

Up to this point, our discussions have not included any consideration of how citizens who violate the laws of the state should be treated. Our efforts resemble a football coach who spends all his time constructing plays for the ideal game but who ignores questions of rule violations and inadequate performance on the playing field. If the theory of the state is to be complete, some attention must be paid to how a state ought to deal with citizens who violate its laws.

The legal apparatus of the state, particularly the penal institutions, have the responsibility for determining when violations of the law have occurred, for apprehending violators, and for taking measures that encourage both violators and nonviolators to obey the law. Recently, legal institutions in the United States have become highly controversial. The appropriate methods of apprehending criminals and the treatment of criminals have become items of considerable public concern. Charges of police brutality are a recurring phenomenon. Other questions have arisen concerning such practices as wiretapping, decoys to entrap potential criminals, and the use of police informers. Moreover, concerned citizens have focused on apparent injustices in our practices of punishment. The tragic results of prison rebellions and media exposes of conditions in prisons have raised serious questions about the purpose and organization of prisons.

171

Some psychologists and other social scientists have challenged the legitimacy of the institution of punishment. Other social scientists have conducted studies that indicate great discrepancies in the sentencing of criminals by judges and also show that members of certain races or social classes receive discriminatory treatment.

It would take us far beyond the scope of this book to discuss all these issues in detail. Rather, we shall focus our discussion on two issues, the legitimacy of punishment and the legitimacy of civil disobedience. Our discussion of these issues begins after some introductory remarks on the nature of a legal system and the necessity for an institutionalized system of coercive rules in the democratic state.

WHY LAW?

One might ask why it is necessary to have a set of coercive rules in the just state.

By far the most common argument for the necessity of law is based on the psychology of human nature. There is general agreement that people are political animals, that they need social-political organizations for their protection and self-realization. Such institutions are clearly advantageous. However, to be effective, institutions require rules and sometimes these rules work to the disadvantage of some individuals participating in the institution. On these occasions, the person whose aim is thwarted by the rule is tempted to ignore his obligations to obey the rule and to yield to immediate self-interest. To overcome this propensity, the rules of the state are backed by sanctions (punishments). Human nature requires that a state have a system of coercive rules to insure that its citizens obey the rules and regulations.

For example, H.L.A. Hart argues that coercive rules are necessary since there are always some persons in the community who will try to avoid obeying the law. Hart declares that coercive rules must contain some restrictions on the free use of violence, theft, and deception to which human beings are tempted, but which they must repress, if they are to coexist in close proximity to each other.[1]

Human frailty causes another problem that needs legal correction as well. In ancient Athens, legal decisions were made by vote in a case-by-case manner. There was not a strong stable body of written law. As a result, decisions were often made in the heat of passion or on irrelevant grounds. The classic case of error in this regard was the sentencing of Socrates on the charges of atheism and corrupting the youth. Plato's response to this state of affairs was an elitist political philosophy in which only the wise would be rulers. Aristotle saw that Plato's solution was dangerous since it is difficult to identify the wise and to insure that power will not corrupt them.

Aristotle's own solution was a stable body of law, especially a constitution, which would establish correct procedures of law and rule out other procedures as legally illegitimate. In other words, a body of law is a practical check on human passions and prejudice, making it less likely that miscarriages of justice will occur.

Of course, to argue on behalf of the need for law is not to argue that law is sufficient as a form of social control. The law and morality have considerable overlap, but they do not coincide. We cannot say, "If it's not illegal, it's not immoral," just as we noted in Chapter Six that we could not say, "If it's immoral, then it should also be illegal." The most cogent set of reasons why the law is not sufficient as an instrument of social control has been developed by Christopher Stone.[2] The first problem Stone calls "the time lag" problem. The law is primarily a reactive institution; that is it reacts to a harm that has occurred. Laws are passed after the damage has been done. But, for example, the harms caused by the adverse side effects of drugs which damage the gene pool, or the poisoning of the environment are severe and perhaps irreversible. What is needed is some way of preventing the damage in the first place. We cannot look to the law for that.

Second, there are limitations connected with the making of laws. Most decisions of public policy are inordinately complex. Consider nuclear power in the era of energy crisis. It is clear that the waste disposal problem has never been addressed satisfactorily and that the accident at the Three Mile Island facility near Harrisburg, Pennsylvania, raises serious questions about plant safety. Nonetheless, electrical energy is heavily dependent on oil, coal is a serious air pollutant, and the widespread use of solar power is not immediately technically or economically feasible. Given this dismal range of alternatives, how stringent should the regulation of nuclear power plants be? There simply is no consensus on the value issues in such a decision. As a society, we cannot agree on how the various issues are to be weighted. Without a majority consensus on the value issues, regulations that will be stable and enforceable are extremely hard to provide.

Another difficulty concerns the assignment of responsibility—of tracing the line of causal connections so that we can determine who has been injured and who has caused the injury. The adversary model of law presupposes the ability of a judge or jury to make that kind of determination. But many social issues do not easily fit into that model. As Stone says,

> The food we will eat tonight (grown, handled, packaged, distributed by various corporations) may contain chemicals that are killing us, or at least reducing our life expectancy, considerably. But (a) we cannot know with certainty the fact that we are being injured by any particular product; (b) it is difficult determining who might be injuring us—that is, even if we know that our bodies are suffering a build-up of mercury, we are faced with an awesome task of pinning responsi-

bility on any particular source of mercury; (c) we would have a difficult time proving the extent of our injuries . . .[3]

What such an example shows is that in many cases we cannot have
much confidence in our ability to trace the causal connections. Causal analysis works best in those cases where it is relatively easy to talk of *the* cause of
some specific event. As you move away from that paradigm, causal analysis
becomes less effective.

Third, there are problems with vagueness. Some vagueness problems
are inherent in language itself. However, when society attempts to draft
laws to apply in situations in which there is no consensus on what ought to
be done and in which it is difficult to determine causes and effects, the
vagueness problem is much more serious. Harried lawmakers are forced to
use broad, general terminology. Since the law cannot be directed to a
specific cause and a specific effect, useless generality is to be expected.
Besides, the legislator must satisfy the demands of those who "want something done" yet at the same time must draft a law that could receive a
majority vote. Platitudinous generalities are ideal in such a situation.

However, the legislative compromise soon becomes the administrators' nightmare. These vague laws must be fleshed out with regulations. But regulations that evolve from the idiosyncratic views of individual
bureaucrats rather than from a background of legislative intent are often
cumbersome, inconsistent, and trivial. As a result the entire climate
becomes poisoned and the broader and more important moral questions
are lost in the daily battles between the government and the governed.
Hence, we should not look at the law as the sole means of social control.
Nonetheless, the law does work well as a device for controlling much
behavior. In some cases, we use the law as a guide—to get a driver's license
or close a real estate deal. In such cases, the coercive element of law is
missing. The law also works best in controlling individual behavior that
seriously threatens other individuals or society itself. Any human society
requires a set of legal institutions.

WHEN IS A LAW REALLY A LAW?

Before deciding such questions as whether we should punish violators of
the law or whether civil disobedience is ever legitimate, we should know if
any command made in the name of the state is properly a law. In other
words, must a rule issued in the name of the state have certain characteristics before it legitimately can be called a law? The answer to this question is not as simple as it might seem. Indeed, one of the oldest disputes in
legal philosophy focuses on the different kinds of answers given to this
question. On the one side, the legal positivists argue that the conditions that

determine when a system of rules is to count as law are provided by the larger political framework of which the law is a part. For the positivist, the law is that set of rules that is in fact backed by the coercive power of the state. On the other side, the natural-law philosophers insist that in addition to the *political* criteria, the system of rules must meet *moral* criteria as well. The natural-law position is summarized by the dictum "An unjust law is not a law." The positivist position can be summarized by the dictum "The law as it is must be distinguished from the law as it ought to be."

Although philosophers revel in such semantic disputes, neither their academic colleagues in other disciplines nor their students usually understand the importance of some of these verbal debates. However, the debate about the nature of law does have important practical consequences. Since most citizens feel morally obliged to obey the law, it is important to know what counts as law and what does not. If individuals or groups can become identified with the law or with the source of law, there is a predisposition on the part of others to obey them. This psychological disposition is present even if the rules that emanate from the individual or group strike one as unjust or unfair. Such situations can present difficult problems. For example, after the collapse of Nazi Germany, trials were held to assess the legal guilt of certain Nazi officials. These trials raised an important question. Is a subordinate obeying the order of a superior who speaks in the name of law guilty of a crime if that order is immoral and illegal in decent states? Such a question raises the conceptual issue as to what is really a law and what is not. The fate of individuals rests on the answer given to that question.

A complete assessment of the conflict between natural-law philosophy and legal positivism lies beyond the scope of this book. However, a brief description of some of the considerations that incline one toward one definition or the other will accomplish two purposes. It will provide some of the conceptual underpinning for our answer to the two main questions of this chapter. It also will show that disputes that are apparently verbal often have important consequences for action.

On behalf of his view, the natural-law philosopher claims that the natural-law definition is required if one is to have adequate justification for the law. For the natural-law philosopher, it is not enough that a rule is sanctioned by the state. If we are to have an obligation to obey a law, the law must be morally justified as well.

We believe that this defense rests on a confusion, however. The basis for condemning a law is confused with the meaning requirements for law. A law that requires the segregation of a minority race might be justly condemned; indeed it might be our moral duty to disobey it. We can still call such an immoral rule a law, however. What went wrong is that legal justification was confused with moral justification. Since what counts as legal justification is defined by the legal system itself, it makes no sense to ask for legal justification of the law. Moral justification certainly can be demanded, however. One of the classical legal positivists, Jeremy Bentham made just this distinction. Against Blackstone, he argued that the law as it is must be distinguished from the law as it ought to be. Nonetheless, the legal system as a whole was to be judged against the moral principle of utility. From our perspective, we would judge a legal system on how well it protected natural rights and supported just political institutions. We agree with the positivist critics that to claim that a rule is a valid law is not to claim that we ought to obey it.

Second, natural-law theorists argue that their definition enables them to solve the practical difficulty of legally punishing someone for obeying an unjust law. For example, during the Nazi regime in Germany some heinous acts had been committed in the name of law. After the fall of the Nazi regime, some justification was needed to punish the perpetrators of these acts. With adoption of the natural-law conceptual scheme, a justification was at hand. The "law" to which the defendant appeals was not really a law at all, and so cannot be used as an excuse.

The legal positivists argue that the problems created by the Nazi regime are best resolved by using a retroactive law. Indeed, they could argue that even the natural-law theorist uses this approach, albeit in a roundabout and confusing way. Consider the natural-law theorist's strategy. Such a theorist first argues that the statute to which the defendant appeals was not really a law at all. On what basis can the natural law theorist say that? The appeal is to a moral principle—a moral principle that both acquires the force of positive law and supersedes the former positive law. But isn't this to elevate a moral principle into a positive law and to apply it retroactively? Essentially the natural-law philosopher solves the problem in the same way as the positivist.

The third argument on behalf of the natural-law definition maintains that without the moral test as part of the meaning of law, citizens will fail to condemn or disobey morally unjust laws. In the name of law and order, they will become participants in immorality and injustice by obeying and enforcing unjust laws. To prevent this occurrence, some moral tests should be made part of the meaning of law.

Traditional legal positivists like Jeremy Bentham and John Austin have a major rejoinder to this point, however. They argue that if each citizen could test the law against his own moral principles before he considered it genuine law, the philosophical foundations for anarchism would be provided. To test every law against individual conscience is to pave the way for chaos.

A recent fourth argument by Ronald Dworkin defends an analysis of judicial reasoning which has much in common with natural law theory. Dworkin has argued that in applying such contested notions as "equal protection of the law," judges have the obligation not simply to apply their own personal values, but to apply interpersonal legal standards of equality.

To apply their own standards would be to put the judiciary in conflict with democracy. Why should one judge's personal values outweigh those of the majority? But where do such interpersonal standards come from? The judge, according to Dworkin, must do what political philosophers do; namely, try to construct the best political theory consistent with the text of the Constitution and the most defensible precedents concerning the nature of equal protection. This theory, like the theories in this book, is irreducibly normative. Judges *qua* judges must make value judgments and so the law is necessarily value laden.

But can't positivists reply that Dworkin's theory has as much in common with positivism as it does with natural law philosophy? After all Dworkin has not shown that these interpersonal standards are morally correct. That would take an independent argument—like this book's arguments presented on behalf of a Constitutional democracy. The "moral" tests cited by Dworkin are those presupposed by binding legal norms; not necessarily those derivable from a correct moral theory. Hence the positivist contention remains intact. What counts as law is one thing, whether the law is morally correct is another.

Hence, we are confronted with two conceptual schemes that claim different practical results if adopted. The positivist argues that the natural-law conceptual scheme has anarchy as its practical consequence. The positivist might point to the illegal demonstrations at the South African embassy to support his views. Natural-law philosophers argue that under the positivist conceptual scheme, the ethical imperative of obedience to law is abused by the state in that citizens are co-opted into obeying and defending unjust laws. For example, natural law philosophers can point out that perpetrators of heinous deeds could, under positivism, use the excuse, "I was only following orders" as a justification for their acts. After World War II, some Nazis attempted to excuse their treatment of Jews in death camps in just this way. So did some of the U.S. servicemen in their attempt to justify the massacre at Mai Lai during the Vietnam War.

Despite these differences we believe that the gap between the natural-law philosopher and the legal positivist is not nearly as large as often believed. Both are concerned with the justice of law. Neither believes that a law issued according to the rules of the legal system is ipso facto just. Neither believes that every law is automatically entitled to obedience simply because it is a law. On these fundamentals, both traditions are in agreement.

While we do not know of any formal definition of law that is fully satisfactory, our discussion suggests that the general point of the positivists, that satisfaction of tests for legal validity does not guarantee satisfaction of tests for moral validity, seems justified. Therefore, the issues of morality and legality should be kept distinct. We also believe the positivists are basically right in viewing legal institutions as one member of the set of political institutions. Hence, we define a system of law as a set of coercive rules backed by the authority of the state.

Since we have indicated a preference for the neopositivist's definition of law, we must show that the adoption of that definition will avoid the evil consequences which the natural-law philosopher predicts, namely, that the citizens will obey the law like sheep, irrespective of the justice of its contents. We believe that individuals will not behave like sheep so long as they take a natural-law position on the question of justification. The activities of a state must be justified on moral grounds. Indeed, the purpose of political and social philosophy is to provide just the moral foundation required for evaluation of the political order.

PUNISHMENT

Many persons have accepted without question the idea that the appropriate means for dealing with criminals is to punish them by a fine, imprisonment, or both. In breaking the law, they hold, criminals deserve to be harmed in some way. With this attitude toward punishment already strongly internalized, many will find it strange that philosophers have felt a need to justify the institution of punishment. They will find it even stranger that many philosophers and social scientists think that our current practices of punishment cannot be justified. The arguments against punishment take many forms but there are some common threads running through them. One group of critics argues that it is society rather than the law-breaker that is responsible for crime. Since in this view society is responsible for the conditions that cause crime, punishment is an injustice inflicted on the law-breakers. Another group of critics is less interested in who is responsible for crime. What interests them is our response to crime; they argue that some form of *treatment* is more appropriate than punishment as a response to criminal acts. Before addressing these critics of punishment, let us begin our discussion by considering the two traditional philosophical arguments in favor of punishment—the utilitarian and the retributive arguments.

The Utilitarian Justification

If one were an act utilitarian, one would say that an individual is to be punished if—and only if—his individual punishment would lead to better consequences than his nonpunishment. Better consequences in this case are determined by seeing if the pain or harm of punishment is offset by the force that the punishment has in reducing the pain or harm of crime. Punishment is alleged to reduce crime by removing criminals from society, by reforming criminals, and most importantly by deterring other potential criminals. On utilitarian grounds, punishment is justified if the benefits of reducing crime outweigh the pain of the punishment.

The obvious objection to this approach has been dubbed the "punishment-of-the-innocent argument" as discussed in Chapter Two. The counterexample involves a town plagued with a rash of heinous murders. The populace is approaching panic. A drifter known by the authorities to be innocent is arrested and executed to stem the panic. This action would be justified punishment on act-utilitarian grounds, yet most of us would insist that this is not an act of justified punishment at all. Even if the argument is not foolproof, it has been so persuasive that utilitarians have constantly tried to reformulate their positions to avoid it. (For a possible act utilitarian response see p. 40).

The common utilitarian response is to give up act utilitarianism for rule utilitarianism. According to this view, it is the institution of punishment or the rules of the institution of punishment that are to be justified on utilitarian grounds. Individual acts of punishment are justified by appealing to the rules of punishment; the rules of punishment are justified on utilitarian grounds. It is then generally assumed that the legal rule that allows for punishment of the innocent would not pass the utilitarian test, even if individual acts of this kind would. We do not think this assumption has been or can be established.[4] However, our chief argument is the familiar one used throughout this book. The utilitarian theory of justification for the state and the institutions of the state is inadequate because it does not take account of the rights of the individual citizens. The reader may wish to return to the arguments in earlier chapters for the details of our position. With respect to justification, utilitarian theory is not sufficient to justify individual acts of punishment or the rules of the institution of punishment.

Perhaps utilitarianism will serve us better if it answers a different question. It may be relevant, not in determining who should be punished, but rather in determining how much a person should be punished. Jeremy Bentham, whatever his intention, spent most of his utilitarian analysis on this question. Bentham argued that the goal of punishment was *deterrence* and that in determining the amount of punishment this end must be kept in mind.[5] Punishment should, so far as possible, (*a*) inhibit one from committing a crime; (*b*) dispose one to commit a lesser rather than a greater offense; (*c*) dispose a criminal to commit no more mischief than is necessary; and (*d*) keep the amount of punishment necessary for deterrence as small as possible. Bentham's position may be summarized as follows: The first rule of punishment is "that the value of punishment must not be less in any case than what is sufficient to outweigh that of the profit of the offence." However, another rule of punishment must always be kept in mind: "The punishment ought in no case to be more than what is necessary to bring it into conformity with the rules here given."

Some illustrative comment might prove useful. It is easy on Bentham's account to see why the punishment for a serious crime is more than for a lesser crime. On utilitarian grounds, a serious crime is defined as one that produces more bad consequences than most other crimes. Now if the function of punishment is deterrence, you need more punishment to assure that the more serious crimes will not be committed. We must not be overzealous, however. It is often suggested that kidnapping, rape, and armed robbery be made capital offenses. To make them capital offenses, however, may well violate Bentham's condition that punishment dispose a criminal to commit no more mischief than is necessary. So long as murder, kidnapping, rape, and armed robbery are all capital offenses, there is no utilitarian reason why a criminal should not kill any of his victims of the three latter offenses. If he is caught he is no worse off and if he kills his victim the chances of his being caught and successfully prosecuted are reduced. On utilitarian grounds, the punishment for kidnapping, rape, and armed robbery should not be death.

Subject to certain significant retributive constraints that will be discussed shortly, we basically accept the utilitarian strategy of basing the amount of punishment on considerations of deterrence. We believe that rules fairly similar to Bentham's should be adopted by a democracy. Our main quarrel is with the utilitarian basis of punishment itself. The focus of this quarrel may be seen by contrasting utilitarianism with its chief rival, retributivism.

The Retributive Theory of Punishment

One of the major classical retributive theorists is Immanuel Kant.[6] It is useful to begin with his theory because it contains most propositions that retributivists defend and because it is so uncompromising. The basic propositions of Kant's theory are the following:

1. Punishment can be inflicted only on the ground that a person has committed a crime.
2. Judicial punishment can never be used merely as a means to promote some other good for the criminal.
3. If a person commits a crime, that person ought to be punished. In fact, it is immoral if the criminal is not punished.
4. The degree and kind of punishment are determined by the crime committed.

One should note that to Kant the commission of a crime is a sufficient condition for the infliction of punishment. Kant's comment in this regard might be considered by some as quite shocking:

Even if a civil society were to dissolve itself by common agreement of all its members . . . the last murderer remaining in prison must first be executed so that everyone will duly receive what his actions are worth and so that the bloodguilt thereof will not be fixed on the people because they failed to insist on carrying out the punishment. . . .[7]

Those guilty of a crime must be punished if justice is to be done. Some retributivist theorists, but not Kant, give proposition 3 an additional twist. They argue that criminals not only ought to be punished, but indeed have a right to be punished. Sometimes this is expressed by saying that the criminal has willed punishment or that he has contracted for it. One way of explaining this proposed condition is to take the overall perspective of the present book. We view political institutions as means for implementing individual rights and for resolving conflicts of rights. Presumably individuals concerned with these rights would choose to live in such a society as we have described. However, in accepting the benefits of such a society, justice requires that one accept its obligations as well. Thus, there is a sense in which the criminal has willed punishment and indeed even has a right to it. Hence, we add yet another item to our list of propositions that retributivists might hold.

5. If a person commits a crime, the person has a right to be punished.

Our list of five propositions indicates that retributivists may come in many forms and share the label "retributivist" with varying degrees of enthusiasm. A less extreme retributivist would defend fewer conditions. Our interest is not the verbal one of deciding how many or what propositions one must uphold if he is to be called a retributivist. Rather we wish to discuss the plausibility of the retributivist conditions to discover if any are acceptable. Since proposition 5 is not an essential element of contemporary retributivist views, we omit it from our discussion.

Acceptance of the first two propositions of the retributivist theory is essential if penal institutions are to be considered just. The first condition requires that a person be found guilty of a crime before being punished. The second condition requires that punishment be meted out in response to the crime and not inflicted simply to promote the good of the criminal. The first condition rules out the use of punishment (perhaps of innocent persons) simply to benefit society. It also protects persons from preventive detention and from any other device that would in effect punish them before a crime was actually committed. The second condition protects a criminal from imprisonment, beyond the terms of his sentence, on the grounds that continued imprisonment is in that criminal's best interest.

Condition 3 is also acceptable so long as it is understood that condition 3 does not make punishment obligatory. What condition 3 does is to say that it creates a presumption that punishment is appropriate or justified without having to show that any given instance of punishment also promotes utility. If a person makes a promise, he or she ought to keep it. However, sometimes the obligation to keep a promise must yield to a higher moral obligation. As it is with promisekeeping, so it is with punishing.

Proposition 4 brings the utilitarian-retributivist conflict into sharp focus. The utilitarians argue that the amount of punishment should be determined by consequences and hence the amount of punishment should only be great enough to provide deterrence. The retributivists have another answer, which goes back at least to Aristotle. Aristotle argued that the purpose of legal justice was to right wrongs. For Aristotle, this meant the reestablishment of a kind of equality.[8] A crime has upset the moral order and the punishment is designed to equalize the offense and set the moral order right. In this way one can speak of the punishment fitting the crime. This equality condition has also found expression in the popular notion of "lex talionis," an eye for an eye, a tooth for a tooth. Despite the expression "an eye for an eye," the equality condition is seldom interpreted to mean that there should be some kind of exact equality. Although you could punish a murderer by taking his or her life, many crimes can't have equivalent punishments—embezzlement, contract violation, and often libel to name but a few. The point of the equality conditon is that more serious crimes should be punished more severely. An embezzler who steals $1,000,000 should not get a less severe sentence than a shoplifter who steals a coat worth $100.

We reject this retributivist proposition on two grounds. First, we object on practical grounds. In many cases the determination of equality is practically impossible. Consider crimes whose chief evil consequences are at least partially psychological, e.g., libel, slander, blackmail, even kidnapping—and perhaps rape. How are these crimes to be equalized? In fact, the legal system has established an elaborate system of fines and terms of imprisonment, which however justifiable on other grounds, seems artifical and ad hoc if justified on grounds of equalizing the harm done or of reestablishing equality in the moral order. Nor is the practical difficulty simply the problem of developing a good yardstick. Consider murder. One retributivist answer is that equalization entails the legal execution of the murderer. But what is equalized? To execute the murderer is to have two dead persons instead of one. The moral order has not been reestablished, unless one simply assumes that morality supports this kind of retributivism.

The murderer example brings home a significant point. The fact is that crime does upset the moral order and that in a significant sense the injury can never be undone. There is no way the moral indignity can be erased. Nonetheless, there is a sense in which the infliction of punishment must be equal: Given due allowance for the proper exercise of judicial discretion, similar kinds of crimes should be punished similarly.

Finally, retributivism places additional constraint on utilitarian considerations of punishment. Punishment should be appropriate for the crime. For example, a hard to detect but minor crime should not be punished harshly even should it be true that only a harsh penalty would have deterrent effect (due to the low probability of getting caught).

In summary we disagree with the retributivists that the state must punish criminals and we disagree with the retributivist on how the amount of punishment a criminal deserves is to be calculated. However, we agree with the retributivists in maintaining that the state has a right to punish criminals, that a person should only be punished if found guilty of a crime, and that punishment can never be used merely as a means for improving the criminal. Moreover, punishment must be appropriate to the crime and consistently applied throughout the criminal justice system.

We are now able to show how radically our point of view on punishment differs from those who propose treatment rather than punishment as the appropriate response in dealing with criminals.

Recent emphasis in the social sciences, especially criminal psychology and penology, has been on the rehabilitation of criminals rather than on measurements of guilt, responsibility, and the notion of making criminals pay for their crime. The tendency has been to drop all talk of punishment and to speak only of treatment.[9] Crime is considered a type of disease, like malaria or smallpox. The criminal is isolated from society until cured.

But the blurring of the distinction between crime and illness, punishment and treatment, is extremely unfortunate for many reasons. First, surrendering the language of guilt and punishment threatens human rights. How we talk does make a difference. Once crime is treated as a disease, it is easy to leave the term of treatment indefinite. Presently, one serves a fairly definite term for the crime of armed robbery. However, if committing armed robbery is like being afflicted with malaria, one is cured only when a group of specialists representing the state say one is cured. The danger to civil liberties presented by such a practice should be obvious.

Moreover, the favorable connotations of treatment make it easy for the state to abuse treatment. Since treatment is supposed to be humane, there is a temptation to avoid taking seriously the rights of the one being treated. The procedural safeguards of the criminal trial are not part of the operating procedures of hospitals. In this regard, it is instructive to note that it is common practice in the Soviet Union to commit dissident intellectuals to mental institutions as punishment for their intellectual heresies. By calling such people mentally ill, one may "treat" them without even the pretense of a fair trial.

Yet another danger is that those who emphasize the benefits of treatment have a propensity to "treat" people before a crime is actually committed. After all, if someone has a disease that manifests itself in a propensity to commit antisocial acts, shouldn't that person be treated at the earliest opportunity? Somehow the fact that the person has not actually committed the crime for which he is being "treated" gets lost in the shuffle.

Finally, the proportional relation that now exists between a crime and punishment would be lost if crimes were treated like diseases. As Herbert Morris has pointed out:

> With therapy attempts at proportionality make no sense. It is perfectly plausible giving someone who kills a pill and treating for a lifetime within an institution one who has broken a dish and manifested accident proneness. We have the concept of "painful treatment." We do not have the concept of "cruel treatment."[10]

A second reason to avoid blurring the distinction between crime and illness, punishment and treatment, focuses on the loss of individual responsibility that such a view presupposes. We usually do not blame one for becoming sick. Illness is something that happens to someone; it is not something that one does. By viewing crime as a disease, one implicitly adopts a model that denies human responsibility for crime. On this point, those who utilize the therapy model for treating criminal behavior are at one with those who view crime as caused by society rather than by the individual criminal. An example of this latter view appears in the writings of Benjamin Karpman. He says:

> It is our basic tenet that the criminal is a product of a vicious, emotionally unhealthy environment in the creation of which he had no hand and over which he had no control. In so far as society has done nothing or not enough to alleviate the developing anti-sociality of the child, it may truly be said that it deserves the criminals it has and that the criminal is society's greatest crime.[11]

This is not the place for us to argue the merits of the claim that human beings have free will. It is a presupposition of nearly all moral philosophy that human beings are at least responsible creatures. Surely one's background does have important ramifications on how people behave. In some cases of criminal action, we might agree that one's background is a decisive causal factor. However, in many cases we believe people are responsible for their actions. To treat them in any other way would undermine their self-respect and sense of human dignity. We can illustrate our point by again quoting from Herbert Morris:

> Alfredo Traps in Durrenmatt's tale discovers that he has brought off, all by himself, a murder involving considerable ingenuity. The mock prosecutor in the tale demands the death penalty "as reward for a crime that merits admiration, astonishment, and respect." Traps is deeply moved; indeed, he is exhilarated, and the whole of his life

becomes more heroic, and, ironically, more precious. His defense attorney proceeds to argue that Traps was not only innocent but incapable of guilt, "a victim of the age." This defense Traps disavows with indignation and anger. He makes claim to the murder as his and demands the prescribed punishment—death.[12]

Perhaps those remarks are sufficient to indicate why we reject the views of those who seek to substitute therapy for punishment and the views of those who would deny individuals all responsibility for their actions. In a just state, failure to obey the law is prima facie evidence that the lawbreaker is being unfair to his fellow citizens. He is not willing to play by the rules when they work out to his disadvantage. When faced with such acts of law breaking, an institution of punishment that respects individual liberty and whose rules for determining guilt and innocence are in accord with democratic procedures and the demands of justice is certainly justifiable. There is nothing ipso facto immoral about punishment. The rules of punishment reflect essentially political decisions. The social sciences, by investigating the effects of various rules of punishment on recidivism, deterrence, and so forth, may help us to make enlightened rather than unenlightened decisions. Whether the rules are just depends upon whether the rules conform to the canons of justice. The rules are also constrained by what we shall call the retributivist rule of legal justice: Punishment may be inflicted only on those guilty of committing a crime.

For similar reasons we have grave doubts about the moral legitimacy of suggestions for preventive detention. The idea behind preventive detention is to incarcerate people before they actually commit a crime. Consider the following scenario: An adult man is observed to daily lurk about the elementary school playground. Police obtain his identity, and on the basis of information obtained about him, he fits the profile of a child molester. To prevent his harming a child, he is incarcerated. The man's incarceration is a paradigm case of preventive detention.

There are less paradigmatic examples. Some have argued that persons who are likely to commit crimes if they are out on bail should be denied bail. In this case, the person has been charged with a crime; the person has done something—at least prima facie. But the person is being denied bail on the basis of what might be done. Others have argued that juveniles who are likely to be repeat offenders should be jailed rather than released to parents or guardians.

In other words, preventive detention involves incarcerating persons because they are likely to commit crimes even though they have not, or jailing persons for a crime for which others who commit the same crime have not been jailed on the grounds that the person who is jailed is more likely to commit additional crimes. In both cases, persons are being jailed for what they are likely to do rather than for what they have done.

We believe that the same arguments which apply against punishing the innocent apply here. However, that does not mean that we should stand idly by and allow persons to be victimized. Society may encourage potential child molesters to seek treatment so that they will not commit a crime. Society may keep the potential child molester under surveillance. Society should provide speedy trials and police protection for victims and witnesses. There is much that can be done without preventive detention. However, justice may have costs. Despite the protections outlined above, on occasion the failure to use preventive detention will mean that some people will be harmed who otherwise would not have been harmed. Perhaps this is one of those cases where there is a genuine conflict between justice and utility and we come down on the side of justice. As we said before, punishment may be inflicted only on those guilty of committing a crime.

In summary, the following propositions concerning punishment seem most defensible.

1. No one can be punished unless found guilty of committing a crime.
2. The rehabilitation of criminals should not be confused with the punishment of criminals. The rehabilitation of criminals should have deterrence as one of its goals. All compulsory rehabilitation must be confined to the term of the criminal's sentence.
3. The amount of punishment is determined by the judicial system. More serious crimes should usually receive more severe punishments. The effectiveness of various punishments on deterrence should also play a major role in determining the amount of punishment.
4. If the rules for the infliction of punishment are to be just they must be in accord with the principles of justice as outlined in Chapter Four and with the principle of legal justice (1) above.

Not all instances of law breaking fit this violation-of-fairness model. In the next section we consider civil disobedience, an example of law breaking that those who practice it claim to be just. This special kind of law breaking deserves special attention and it is to this topic that we now turn.

CIVIL DISOBEDIENCE AND PROTEST

Is the citizen, particularly the citizen of a democratic state, under an absolute obligation to obey the law, even when such a citizen believes the law in question to be unjust? One of the most important moral questions that any individual might have to face concerns the limits of obedience owed to the state. During the past quarter of a century, the question of civil disobedience has been a central question in political philosophy. During this period, many conscientious, moral citizens believed that the state had overstepped its legitimate moral bounds or had failed in its responsibilities for providing certain benefits. In the 1950s, the atmospheric testing of nuclear weapons by the United States and other atomic powers was considered dangerous to all inhabitants of the globe and thus became an object of protest. The distinguished philosopher Bertrand Russell was one of the leaders in the protest against such testing. During the early 1960s, the injustice of many state laws governing the relations between races, particularly between blacks and whites, was called to public attention. By using such techniques as the sit-in, Dr. Martin Luther King, Jr., and other black leaders sought to overturn various laws segregating the races. The black struggle for equal justice gained sympathetic support for a time from most Americans, particularly when television newscasts showed scenes of white policemen hosing, beating, and in other ways maltreating nonresisting black and white men, women, and children. With the active involvement of the United States in the Vietnam War, civil disobedience focused on resistance to the war. Indeed, doubts about the United States's moral position on this war became so widespread and resistance so broad-based, that an American President was denied an opportunity to seek a second term and the United States was forced to begin a slow, painful withdrawal from Vietnam. When the war in Vietnam finally came to an end and President Nixon abolished the draft, the protests came to an end. However, now that Selective Service registration is once again the law of the land, some young men have refused to register as an act of conscience. Moreover, the escalating arms race and the dangers of nuclear war have fanned renewed protests in the U.S. and throughout the world.

In light of such events, one might think that the question of civil disobedience is of only recent concern. This is not at all the case. The Greek dramatists were true craftsmen at raising the moral complexities of civil disobedience. Sophocles' *Antigone* represents the epitome of the Greek dramatists' concern. The towering figure of Socrates, however, provides a starting point for philosophical debate on the question. Rather than escape from a death sentence Athens had imposed upon him, Socrates insisted to the end that the state was entitled to obedience and hence submitted to the penalty with equanimity and even good cheer. Not all men and women have followed Socrates' acceptance of obedience. Henry David Thoreau and Mohandas K. Gandhi are but two of the many well-known figures to choose a different response to alleged state injustice. The debate on the legitimacy of civil obedience is a long, emotional, and as yet unresolved one. The end of the Vietnam War and the return of more placid university campuses will not bring the debate to an end. Philosophers and concerned citizens will continue to explore the questions civil disobedience raises. Eventually, a new set of events may bring civil disobedience to public attention once again.

The perspective of this book requires that civil disobedience be a prominent area of concern. After all, we have argued that a democracy constrained by a theory of natural rights and by specific principles of justice provides at best a just *procedure* for implementing rights claims, and for adjudicating conflicts that arise among them. However, just as criminal trials sometimes set guilty people free or even convict innocent ones, so a state operating according to just procedures sometimes creates unjust results. With this thought in mind, we must now confront the question of whether or not a citizen should break the law if he believes an injustice has been done by state action.

The Nature of Civil Disobedience

Perhaps the most effective way of beginning to deal with this question is to ask how civil disobedience differs from other kinds of law breaking. The act of bank robbery for profit normally should be distinguished from the act of refusing to keep classified material secret.

The key for distinguishing civil disobedience from ordinary law breaking is that the motivation for civil disobedience is one of moral concern. One breaks the laws as a moral protest against some action of the state. We shall define civil disobedience as the act of intentionally violating a valid law for the purpose of registering a moral protest against the state. By emphasizing "intentional," "valid law," and "moral protest," acts of civil disobedience can be distinguished from other acts of law breaking that superficially resemble civil disobedience. First, it is important to distinguish civil disobedience from accidental or unintentional violations of the law. Suppose someone aids a seriously ill person by driving him to the hospital in an unregistered car.[13] Even if the driver knows that driving an unregistered car is against the law, the driver is not engaging in civil disobedience. If an act of law breaking is to be an act of civil disobedience, the act of law breaking cannot be simply a byproduct or side effect of other actions.

Second, civil disobedience must be distinguished from law testing. Law testing occurs when one challenges a law to see if it is really a valid law. The strategy of the law tester is to have some superior court, e.g., appeals or supreme, declare the rule invalid or unconstitutional. If this strategy is successful, the law breaker has not really broken the law and is not a civil disobedient. Indeed, the protestor has performed a valuable legal service by expunging an invalid rule from the legal system. Much of the civil rights activity of the late 1950s and early 1960s was not civil disobedience at all. It was law testing, not law breaking. The strategy was to show that segregationist statutes and certain rules restricting voter registration and occupational choice were illegal under the Constitution, i.e., that such rules were not laws at all.

One possible difficulty for this characterization is presented by the mistaken law tester. The difficulty for the law tester is that of error. The highest court may decide that the law being tested is a valid one. In this case, the protestor did really break the law, but breaking it was not a case of civil disobedience. The law breaking was not intentional. Of course, this law breaker is no ordinary criminal either. Perhaps it is best to call such a person an unsuccessful law tester.

This distinction between the law tester and the civil disobedient is not merely verbal. The justification for testing a law is easier to establish than the justification of civil disobedience. For the former, the justification is within the legal system itself. The interested party is really doing nothing more than unmasking a fraud by showing that what pretends to be law is not really law at all. Even unsuccessful law testers are somewhat heroic; they suffer consequences, sometimes serious ones, for their unsuccessful stand. It seems to us a mistake to consider Martin Luther King solely as a prime example of a civil disobedient. Rather, another of his great contributions to American society was an unmasking of many frauds by showing that so many rules that had held a people in bondage were not really laws at all.[14] The civil disobedient, on the other hand, by intending to break a valid law has greater problems with justification. There is at least a prima facie obligation to obey the law and the civil disobedient must show that this prima facie obligation is overridden.

In our definition of civil disobedience, this prima facie obligation to obey the law is allegedly overridden by the fact that the state has passed an immoral law or is pursuing an immoral policy. The civil disobedient breaks the law to register his moral protest. Is such activity really justifiable?

The Justification of Civil Disobedience

There are several arguments designed to show that one should not break valid laws as a means of registering one's moral protest against the state.

One such major argument has its basis in the moral imperative that one ought to obey the law. Some critics of civil disobedience seem to believe that the mere validity of this imperative is sufficient to show that civil disobedience is not justified.[15] Of course, this is not correct. For such a position to be correct, the moral imperative that one ought to obey the law would have to be supreme, i.e., whenever this imperative was in conflict with another moral imperative, the moral imperative that one ought to obey the law would have priority. It is one thing to grant that "One ought to obey the law" is prima facie binding. However, any attempt to make it a supreme moral principle would need considerable additional argument. The civil disobedient accepts the prima facie obligation, but maintains that in certain cases the prima facie obligation is overridden by a higher ethical principle.

It is unfortunate that the defenders of the supremacy view of "One ought to obey the law" give no argument for their position. One implication of their view is that one of our political obligations overrides all our other obligations. In a significant sense, the state is supreme. On the other hand, if, as we argue, the moral claims of the individual are supreme, then those who defend the supremacy of "One ought to obey the law" are defeated at the outset. Since we hold that the state should supplement or protect the rights of individuals, the state is subservient to the individual. Moreover, even when the state is empowered to resolve conflicts among individual rights, the powers of the state in this regard are not unlimited. They are constrained by principles of morality, principles that are inconsistent with the supremacy of "One ought to obey the law." "One ought to obey the law" could only be prima facie because the law, if obedience is justified, must be in accord with the principles of morality and justice.

The critic of civil disobedience can salvage an important point, however. If "One ought to obey the law" is an ethical imperative and if moral-action guides have supremacy over other kinds of action guides, i.e., if the moral point of view is supreme, then the only kind of claim that can defeat "One ought to obey the law" is another *moral* claim. Nonmoral claims will not do. What is established is that the *only* basis for the justification of civil disobedience is a moral justification. What the critic has not done is to show that this moral justification is impossible.

Another argument against civil disobedience is based on a version of the principle that people ought to keep their promises. The argument basically appeals to the following considerations:

1. The individual is a member of society.
2. This society provides certain benefits.
3. In return for the benefits, the individual's role is to obey the laws and perform certain civil responsibilities.
4. Civil disobedience then is bad citizenship since the individual is not playing by the rules of the political game. He receives benefits without doing his share.

One of the classic statements of this position is presented by Socrates in the *Crito*. Socrates presents the arguments of the state by personifying the laws that speak as follows on behalf of Athens:

Although we have brought you into the world and reared you and educated you, and given you and all your fellow citizens a share in all the good things at our disposal, nevertheless by the very fact of granting our permission we openly proclaim this principle, that any Athenian, on attaining to manhood and seeing for himself the political organization of the state and us its laws, is permitted, if he is not satisfied with us, to take his property and go away wherever he likes. If any of you chooses to go to one of our colonies, supposing that he should not be satisfied with us and the state, or to emigrate to any other country, not one of us laws hinders or prevents him from going away wherever he likes, without any loss of property. On the other hand, if any one of you stands his ground when he can see how we administer justice and the rest of our public organization, we hold that by so doing he has in fact undertaken to do anything that we tell him. . . . You have been content with us and with our city. You have definitely chosen us, and undertaken to observe us in all your activities as a citizen, and as the crowning proof that you are satisfied with our city, you have begotten children in it. Furthermore, even at the time of your trial you could have proposed the penalty of banishment, if you had chosen to do so—that is, you could have done then with the sanction of the state what you are now trying to do without it. But whereas at the time you made a noble show of indifference if you had to die, and in fact preferred death, as you said, to banishment, now you show no respect for your earlier professions, and no regard for us, the laws, whom you are trying to destroy. You are behaving like the lowest type of menial, trying to run away in spite of the contracts and undertakings by which you agreed to live as a member of our state.[16]

Socrates' argument, as stated by the laws, can be paraphrased as follows:

1. In return for certain benefits, the citizen promises to obey the laws of the state.
2. Should the citizen feel the laws of the state are unjust, he can try to convince the state of its error by following certain procedures.
3. Should the citizen believe that this contract with the state is a bad one, e.g., that he does not benefit or that the laws are unjust, he is free to leave at any time.
4. Hence, the citizen has a contract with the state in which the individual citizen receives personal benefits in return for a pledge of obedience.
5. The contract is in effect a promise between the state and its citizens.
6. One ought to obey one's promises.
7. Therefore, one either ought to obey the laws of the state or go elsewhere. (Obey it or leave it.)

Let us begin our discussion of the argument by indicating where it applies and where it does not. First, it will not count if the contract analysis of the relation between the individual and the state is wrong. Second, this argument will have no force if the contract is entered under duress or if there is no escape clause. We are in essence defending a freedom condition that the contract must meet. Most people would agree to obey the laws of the state, indeed surrender all personal liberty, if they were hungry enough and if the state provided food and shelter. Consider a holdup victim who has promised the armed robber to tell the police nothing about his crime.

Suppose the victim then tells the police everything and as a result the robber is captured. Surely the thief has no right to say that the victim was morally unjustified in telling the police since in so doing he broke a promise. A contract made under duress is not a contract at all. In other words, since the state is supposed to provide great advantages for the individual, if the contract argument for obedience is to be accepted, then there must be some options for those who feel they are not receiving the advantages or do not want them. Socrates tries to provide these options by procedures for registering complaints and ultimately for emigration. Our analysis has tried to indicate the necessity for those conditions. This leads to our third and final point. The contract itself must be a moral one. If Smith promises Jones that Smith will murder Green, Jones cannot hold Smith in violation of his contract should Smith not murder Green. Similarly, any contract between an individual citizen and the state must be of a moral nature if the contract is to have binding force. The kinds of constraint put on a contract depend on the moral theory that one is holding. According to our theory, no contract is morally obligatory if it denies the natural rights of the citizen signees or resolves conflicts between rights by unjust procedures.

The individual citizen may also be excused from obeying the contract when the state has failed to live up to the provisions in the contract that apply to it. Thus, the illegal mass arrest of Vietnam demonstrators in Washington is a plausible example of a state not living up to its own obligation to protect the civil rights of its citizens. After all, a contract places responsibilities and obligations on both contractors. The systematic failure of one party to carry out its obligations removes the moral obligation on the other party.

We can now summarize the conditions that must hold if the critic of civil disobedience can appeal to the principle "You ought to keep your contracts." (1) the contract analysis of the relation between the individual and the state must be appropriate; (2) the contract is not made under duress and does have escape clauses; (3) the contract is one that is morally acceptable; and (4) the state lives up to its contract obligations.

A further complicating feature must now be discussed. How are disputes as to whether or not the contract is being violated to be resolved? For example, who is to decide if the state is living up to its contract obligations? If the authorities of the state are to give the definitive answer to this question, the citizen becomes subservient to the state. The citizen must submit and has no justification for civil disobedience. To allow the state supremacy at this point is to concede that the contract argument against civil disobedience is successful. Of course, one could argue, as would we, that ultimately it is the individual citizen who must decide if the contract is being violated. This maneuver would be quickly challenged by the opponents of civil disobedience on the basis of the following two arguments: (1) Since normative statements are not objective factual statements, the individual citizen has no objective basis for his normative judgments; (2) to allow each citizen to pass judgment on the laws of the state would create the grounds for anarchy. Let us consider each of these arguments in turn.

The argument from moral skepticism We have previously claimed that there is at least a prima facie moral obligation to obey the law and that this obligation can only be overridden by a superior moral obligation. Now the critic of civil disobedience could ask, what could such superior moral obligations be? The traditional appeals to individual conscience, the inner light, the law of God, and the public good all fail on the same ground. When conflicts arise between consciences, between different theological conceptions of God's word, between different conceptions of the public good, there seems to be no way of resolving these disputes. It is just the sincere conscience of one person against another. Thus, it is claimed that there is no way the civil disobedient can justify his civil disobedience as warranted.

This situation is even more awkward in a democratic state. If one opinion cannot be justified over another, then there is no reason to accept the view of the civil disobedient over that of the majority. At least, the majority has the force of greater numbers; one might as well obey the laws of the state.

This argument has been a rather popular one and goes back at least to Protagoras (ca. 490–420 B.C.). Indeed it is often held by philosophers when the philosophical climate reflects doubts that value judgments can be justified—doubts that are widely held these days. To discuss this issue at length by turning to the literature of metaethical theory would take us far beyond the scope of this book. It is obvious that we believe value judgments can be justified. For the sake of argument, however, let us accept the premise that conflicts of value cannot be objectively resolved. This admission will not allow the critic of civil disobedience to carry the day.

If you follow moral skepticism consistently, whatever is true of the value judgments of the civil disobedient are also true of those of his opponent. If moral judgments cannot be defended, then the moral judgment that we ought to obey the law cannot be defended either. It is a non sequitur to say that moral judgments cannot be defended; therefore, you have a moral obligation to obey the law. The fact that the civil disobedient lives in a democracy does not change this conclusion one iota. The civil disobedient may well have the overwhelming majority aligned against him, but they are in no position to provide reasons for their moral positions if we take moral skepticism seriously. There may be nonmoral reasons for following the majority if moral skepticism is true. However, there can be no moral reasons for following the majority if moral skepticism is true. Hence, the argument against civil disobedience from moral skepticism fails.

Civil disobedience and anarchy One of the most frequent criticisms of civil disobedience is that it provides the basis for anarchy. Indeed some alleged civil disobedients have argued from anarchistic premises. Thoreau is probably one of the best examples. Here are some remarks from his essay "Civil Disobedience."

> The only obligation which I have a right to assume, is to do at any time what I think right. . . . There will never be a really free and enlightened State, until the State comes to recognize the individual as a higher and more independent power, from which all its own power and authority are derived and treats him accordingly. . . . In fact, I quietly declare war with the State, after my fashion, though I will still make what use and get what advantage of her I can, as is usual in such cases.[17]

It is these explicit principles of anarchy that many critics of civil disobedience find so abhorrent. Moreover, they argue that anarchistic consequences are implicit in all acts of civil disobedience. Whether a citizen disobeys a law because of the belief that it is immoral or because of the belief that the state has violated its contract, he is putting his own authority against that of the state. But if the civil disobedient can do that, every citizen is so entitled and the state would be undermined. Anarchy would reign.

We believe the argument prophesying anarchy to be unsuccessful for two basic reasons. First, in a just democratic state the necessity for civil disobedience would not reach a level where anarchy prevailed. Most citizens would perceive that, on the whole, state decisions are just and given that states are of necessity imperfect dispensers of justice, most citizens would also agree to accept occasional injustices. In essence, as Rawls has argued, a just state is likely to be stable and a certain amount of deviation from perfect justice must be accepted.[18] In a reasonably just state the argument of anarchy is based on a false set of empirical premises. In an unjust state, the argument from anarchy is no defense at all. Given that the state is unjust, it is not at all clear that anarchy ought not to prevail.

Second, the argument from anarchy reflects a fundamental misperception of the role of civil disobedience in the just state. We take the position of several recent writers on the topic that genuine civil disobedience is supportive of the state. It strengthens the state rather than undermines it. Since this is our chief argument in defense of civil disobedience, we shall develop it in some detail. Our strategy, then, for answering the opponents of civil disobedience is to show that their most plausible arguments are based on a misperception of the act of civil disobedience itself.

Civil disobedience as a support for democratic institutions   In our view, the democratic state constrained by general and particular principles of justice may be generally reliable, but, nonetheless, imperfect in performing its function of implementing the natural-rights claims of its citizens and of resolving disputes among rights claims. In such a state justified acts of civil disobedience would not occur with great frequency. Nonetheless, in a state where the achievement of justice is at best imperfect, we believe civil disobedience has a central place.

First, civil disobedience gives an opportunity for individual citizens to make a moral appeal to their fellow citizens when they believe that the institutions or practices of a state have violated their rights. Civil disobedience is then a means for seeking a redress of grievances. The potential benefits of civil disobedience do not fall solely on the civil disobedient alone, however. There are also substantial potential benefits for the state as well. The civil disobedient may well be able to show that certain state actions are unjust. Hence, the disobedient will provide the catalyst for reform. Given that the purpose of the state is to provide justice, a civil disobedient who succeeds in pointing out an injustice in civil procedures is a good citizen and not an ordinary law breaker. Even if the civil disobedient should fail in the attempt to convince the state that an injustice has been done, the disobedient still fills the role of good citizen. Because of such disobedience the state is forced to reexamine its policies and to be ever vigilant against situations where state activities do create injustice. A state that is constantly challenged is more likely to be a just one. As rigid patterns of thought need to be challenged and reexamined if the best kinds of intellectual activity are to prevail, so must the patterns of the state be challenged if the ideal of justice is to be approached. The civil disobedient serves as the analogue of an intellectual gadfly. In this sense our view of civil disobedience is clearly in the tradition of Socrates. The civil disobedient is not an enemy of the state; rather, the civil disobedient is a good citizen:

> If you put me to death, you will not easily find anyone to take my place. It is literally true, even if it sounds rather comical, that God has specially appointed me to this city, as though it were a large thoroughbred horse which because of its great size is inclined to be lazy and needs the stimulation of some stinging fly. It seems to me that God has attached me to this city to perform the office of such a fly, and all day long I never cease to settle here, there, and everywhere, rousing, persuading, reproving every one of you. You will not easily find another like me, gentlemen.[19]

To take this perspective on civil disobedience, however, is to be committed to constraining the form civil disobedience must take if it is to be justifiable. If an act of disobedience is to be justified, it must be (1) public; (2) nonviolent; (3) the civil disobedient must be willing to take the punishment the legal system may impose for disobedience; and (4) the law being violated should be identical with or related to the policy or law against which the moral protest is lodged. To the extent that any of these conditions is violated, then to that extent is the act of civil disobedience in question harder to justify. It is hard to see how violations of the first three conditions can be justified at all.

If civil disobedience is designed to call attention to a possible injustice so that the state might correct its procedures, then the act of civil disobedience must be open and public. Such openness is an indication that the law breaking of a civil disobedient is nonetheless, a political act of good citizenship. Clandestine law breaking, on the other hand, is directed against the political community; it is antipolitical. In such cases, one breaks the rules of society and tries to go undetected. Such action if universalized would threaten the state itself. Willingness to break the law *openly* is one of the characteristics that distinguishes the civil disobedient from the thief in the night.

This perspective on civil disobedience as an act of good citizenship also enables us to defend the traditional prohibition against violence. Our argument here is twofold. First, violence can be seen as an attack on the democratic state itself. Its goal is not to appeal or persuade but to force. Second, violence does not promote the atmosphere for a public discussion and reexamination of state policy. Violence tends to precipitate still more violence. Violent civil disobedience is likely to provoke violent response. Violent clashes among the citizens of the state tend to undermine both the institution of law and the state itself. The violent society is best epitomized by Hobbes's state of nature. In the state of nature, there can be neither government nor law. In other words, the violent disobedience of a particular law tends to set in motion a causal chain that undermines the conditions that make a state possible and valuable. For these reasons, the state could consider violent disobedience of its laws to be an attack on the state itself.

We emphasize that if the justification of civil disobedience is to be found in the civil disobedient's intention of provoking a reexamination of a state policy with an aim toward improving justice, violence is self-defeating. Violence is unjust since it violates the rights of others, it makes public rational discussion impossible, and hence obliterates a civil disobedient's claim that his law breaking is morally superior to that of the ordinary criminal.

Similar remarks support our contention that in justified civil disobedience, the civil disobedient must be willing to take the penalty. This willingness to accept the penalty indicates that the person is not at war with the state nor with fellow citizens. Rather, the civil disobedient is accepting his position as one among equals. The civil disobedient gives evidence of not taking unfair advantage in the sense of receiving the benefits of the state without paying the costs.

Finally, the civil disobedient should believe there is a connection between the law being violated and the law or policy being protested against. To broaden the attack from the unjust law or policy to any law remotely connected with the offending law or policy is to attack the state itself. If, on balance, the state performs its functions adequately, protest should focus on the unjust laws or policies. In most cases, protest should not be a broad attack on the state. The policy must be wicked indeed if it justifies a broad attack on all the policies of the state. Of course, in some cases, policies may reach that level of wickedness; the Nazi policy of exterminating the Jews is a case in point. However, unjust laws or policies of a state may be attacked without attacking all the policies of that state. The point of limiting civil-disobedient acts is to prevent a confusion between civil disobedience and stronger forms of protest. If this confusion is to be avoided, there must be some connection between the law being broken and the law or policy being protested against. To the extent this condition is violated, then to that extent is the act of civil disobedience in question harder to justify?

Not all philosophers have accepted these constraints. In attacking a position that is somewhat similar to ours, that of John Rawls, Professor Brian Barry has said:

> The essence of Rawls's high-minded conception of civil disobedience is the slogan 'This hurts me more than it hurts you.' The protesters are to break the law, but do it with such delicate consideration for others that nobody is inconvenienced. Why, then, bother to break the law at all? As far as I can see from Rawls's account, any public form of self-injury would do as well to make it known that one believed strongly in the injustice of a certain law: public self-immolation or, if that seemed too extreme, making a bonfire of one's best clothes would be as good as law-breaking. Civil disobedience á la Rawls is reminiscent of the horrible little girl in the 'Just William' stories whose all-purpose threat was 'If you don't do it I'll scream and scream until I make myself sick.'[20]

We think this attitude quite mistaken, however. Constraints on civil disobedience are the marks that are presented to establish that the law breaking in question is justified and hence stands apart from ordinary acts of law breaking. These constraints provide evidence that the intention of the law breaker is really a moral one. By adopting these constraints, those who claim that civil disobedience is unjustified can be answered. The type of civil disobedience under consideration here does not promote anarchy, nor do those practicing it claim any special status for their own moral views. Rather, civil disobedients only ask for an opportunity to present their case outside established channels and for this privilege they pay special costs.

Finally, if we view civil disobedience as an integral part of the political structure, the contract argument against civil disobedience is circumvented. The necessity for civil disobedience is accepted in a democratic state that provides at best imperfect justice. By interpreting civil disobedience as an act of good citizenship, we establish the grounds for its justification.

Toleration of Civil Disobedience in the Just Society

By construing civil disobedience as an act of good citizenship, constraints are placed on how the law breaking is to be conducted. However, constraints should also be placed on how the just *state* should treat acts of civil disobedience. We have already seen that one of the factors that justifies an act of civil disobedience is the readiness of its author to submit ultimately to the dictates of the legal order. By so doing, the disobedient demonstrates ultimate allegiance to democratic equality. However, it does not follow from this requirement that the government must *choose* to prosecute such conscientious law breakers. Persons who refuse to register with the Selective Service or who block the gates of companies that manufacture military goods need not challenge the government's *right* to prosecute and secure legal penalties. What they deny is that the government should exercise that right. Our earlier discussion of civil disobedience provides much of the rationale for an argument to the effect that the government should not always exercise its right. If civil disobedience, properly conducted, really is an act of good citizenship, then it is supportive of the state. A certain amount of civil disobedience makes the state more sensitive to possible injustice. To the extent that civil disobedience really does provide this positive function, one has an argument in behalf of the state not always exercising its right to punish civil disobedients.

Several objections have been raised against not prosecuting civil disobedients. One argument against not prosecuting is that it would simply be unfair not to prosecute. Equals would have been treated unequally. Some, but not all, law breakers would escape prosecution. Moreover, such failure to prosecute would allow the conscientious disobedient to secure the advantages of general compliance with the law by others without requiring that the same burdens also be shouldered.

In response, Ronald Dworkin has reversed the argument from fairness by turning it *against* those who favor automatic prosecution of conscientious disobedients. Since justice and fairness prohibit the similar treatment of dissimilar cases, they prohibit treating the *conscientious* law breaker as a criminal. The latter violates the law for purely personal gain, or to carry out personal desires, while the former does not so act. The criminal violates clearly valid law while the conscientious disobedient normally does not.

Accordingly, since the two kinds of cases are different, prosecutors *may* exercise discretion and choose not to prosecute conscientious disobedients:

> A prosecutor may properly decide not to press charges if the law-breaker is young or inexperienced, or the sole support of a family or dependent . . . or for dozens of other reasons. . . . If motive can count in distinguishing between thieves, then why not in distinguishing between draft offenders?[21]

Another objection argues that failure to prosecute civil disobedients would encourage the practice of law breaking. If the government were to choose not to prosecute a significant number of such persons, then an incentive for refraining from such disobedience would have been removed. Acts of conscientious disobedience would increase until the legal order itself was undermined. Everyone would feel perfectly free to disobey whatever laws they personally regarded as wrong.

However, this argument assumes without warrant that prosecutors and judges will not take into account the effect of toleration on the legal system. Our arguments show only that toleration is sometimes *permissible,* not that it is *required.* Presumably, one of the conditions under which it is justifiable is that it will not encourage law breaking so massive as to threaten the legal and political order. (Here one might note that the acts of protest and demonstrations of the late 1960s and early 1970s did not lead to even greater numbers of such acts in the late 1970s.)

A far more serious charge, at least on our view, is that the exercise of discretion in determining whether or not to prosecute (or, when exercised by a judge, to levy severe penalties) is arbitrary and unfair. Different prosecutors (and different judges) may exercise discretion differently, even when faced with similar cases. How discretion is exercised might well depend on the personal moral judgments of the individuals involved. Hence, exercise of discretion encourages inequality before the law. Whether a particular conscientious disobedient is prosecuted or not would seem to depend more on the luck of a draw of prosecutor than on the merits of the case.

This surely is a powerful objection. (Indeed, one of the strongest objections to the death penalty is the arbitrary way judges and juries have exercised their discretion in assigning it.) However, if certain additional factors are taken into account, this objection may prove less than decisive.

For one thing, the arbitrariness implicit in the use of discretion can be minimized. Where prosecution stems from one agency, such as the Department of Justice, all prosecutors can be instructed to refrain from prosecuting certain kinds of cases. Even where unassociated agencies are involved, the law itself can carefully circumscribe the conditions under which discretion may be exercised and the grounds on which disobedience is to be tolerated. Of course, some residual unfairness may remain. However, such unfairness may be *outweighed*. It surely is the case that a judicial system that allows for some discretion is superior on grounds of justice from one that does not. Even if the law could be applied mechanically to cases, which is doubtful, it surely is desirable to leave some room for flexibility. Only then can the nuances of individual cases be taken into account.

In conclusion, we do not think any of the arguments against the toleration of civil disobedience outweigh the justice of at least some toleration. Usually, civil disobedience is an act of good citizenship that yields positive benefits to the state. Sometimes, leniency in punishing civil disobedients may be a small price to pay for the benefits gained.

In this chapter, the role of conscientious disobedience in a democracy has been examined. We have emphasized not only that such disobedience can sometimes be justified but that it serves a valuable *moral* function in a democratic society as well. Since just procedures need not lead to just results, there is a continual need to reexamine the results to which such procedures lead. By contributing to such constant reevaluation, the civil disobedient and the conscientious refuser better the legal and political orders to which we all belong.

NOTES

[1]H.L.A. Hart, *The Concept of Law* (Oxford: Clarendon Press, 1961), pp. 189–95.

[2]Christopher Stone, *Where the Law Ends* (New York: Harper and Row, 1975).

[3]Ibid., p. 104.

[4]One theoretical argument against this position is provided by David Lyons. He tries to show that ultimately rule utilitarianism reduces to act utilitarianism. See David Lyons, *Forms and Limits of Utilitarianism* (Oxford: Clarendon Press, 1965).

[5]Jeremy Bentham, *Principles of Morals and Legislation* (1789), chaps. 13 and 14.

[6]Immanuel Kant, *The Metaphysical Elements of Justice*, trans. John Ladd (Indianapolis: Bobbs-Merrill, 1965), pp. 99–108, 131–33.

[7]Ibid., p. 102.

[8]Aristotle, *Nicomachean Ethics*, bk. 5, chap. 4.

[9]See Karl Menninger, "Therapy, not Punishment," in Jeffrie G. Murphy, ed., *Punishment and Rehabilitation* (Belmont, Calif.: Wadsworth, 1973), pp. 132–41.

[10]Herbert Morris, "Persons and Punishment," in Jeffrie G. Murphy, ed., *Punishment and Rehabilitation* (Belmont, Calif.: Wadsworth, 1973), p. 48.

[11]Benjamin Karpman, "Criminal Psychodynamics: A Platform," in Jeffrie G. Murphy, ed., *Punishment and Rehabilitation* (Belmont, Calif.: Wadsworth, 1973), p. 131.

[12]Herbert Morris, "Persons and Punishment," p. 40.

[13]This example is from R. B. Brandt, "Utility and the Obligation to Obey the Law," in Sidney Hook, ed., *Law and Philosophy* (New York: New York University Press, 1964), p. 51.

[14]Of course, Martin Luther King and other civil-rights advocates did engage in civil disobedience and indeed would have engaged in additional civil disobedience if the laws they were testing had been upheld.

[15]For example, this seems to be the position of Louis Waldman, "Civil Rights—Yes: Civil Disobedience—No" in Hugo Adam Bedau, ed., *Civil Disobedience: Theory and Practice* (New York: Pegasus, 1969), pp. 106–15.

[16]Plato, *Crito*, trans. Hugh Tredennick, in Edith Hamilton and Huntington Cairns, eds., *The Collected Dialogues of Plato* (New York: Pantheon Books, 1961), pp. 36–37.

[17]Henry David Thoreau, "Civil Disobedience," in Thoreau's *A Yankee in Canada* (Boston: Ticknor and Fields, 1866), pp. 125, 151, 145.

[18]John Rawls, *A Theory of Justice* (Cambridge, Mass.: Harvard University Press, 1971), pp. 567–77, and chap. 6, pp. 331–91.

[19]Plato, *Apology*, trans. Hugh Tredennick, in Edith Hamilton and Huntington Cairns, eds., *The Collected Dialogues of Plato* (New York: Pantheon Books, 1961), pp. 16–17.

[20]Brian Barry, *The Liberal Theory of Justice* (Oxford: Clarendon Press, 1973), p. 153.

[21]Ronald Dworkin, "On Not Prosecuting Civil Disobedience," *New York Review of Books*, 6 June 1968, reprinted in Jeffrie G. Murphy, ed., *Civil Disobedience and Violence* (Belmont, Calif.: Wadsworth, 1971), p. 113, with permission from *The New York Review of Books*, © 1968 Nyrev, Inc.

SELECTED READINGS

Bentham, Jeremy. *Principles of Morals and Legislation in the Utilitarians.* Garden City, N.Y.: Doubleday, 1961.
Dworkin, Ronald. *Taking Rights Seriously.* Cambridge, MA.: Harvard University Press, 1977.
Fuller, Lon L. *The Morality of Law.* New Haven: Yale University Press, 1969.
Golding, Martin P. *Philosophy of Law.* Englewood Cliffs, NJ.: Prentice Hall, 1975.
Hall, Robert T. *The Morality of Civil Disobedience.* New York: Harper & Row, 1971.
Hart, H.L.A. *The Concept of Law.* Oxford: Clarendon Press, 1961.
———. *Punishment and Responsibility: Essays in the Philosophy of Law.* New York: Oxford University Press, 1968.
Honderich, Ted. *Punishment: The Supposed Justifications.* Baltimore: Penguin Books, 1969.
Kant, Immanuel. *The Metaphysical Elements of Justice.* John Ladd, trans. Indianapolis: Bobbs-Merrill, 1965.
Van den Haag, Ernest. *Political Violence & Civil Disobedience.* New York: Harper & Row, 1972.

ARTICLES

Barnett, Randy E. "Restitution: A New Paradigm of Criminal Justice." *Ethics,* Vol. 87 (1977), pp. 279–301.
Cohen, Marshall. "Liberalism and Disobedience." *Philosophy & Public Affairs,* Vol. I (1972), pp. 283–314.
Dworkin, Ronald. "On Not Prosecuting Civil Disobedience." *The New York Review of Books,* June 6, 1968.
Farrell, Daniel M. "Paying the Penalty: Justifiable Civil Disobedience and the Problem of Punishment." *Philosophy and Public Affairs,* Vol. 6 (1977), pp. 165–84.
Schoeman, Ferdinand D. "On Incapacitating The Dangerous." *American Philosophical Quarterly,* Vol. 16, No. 1 (1979), pp. 27–35.
Wertheimer, Alan. "Should Punishment Fit the Crime?" *Social Theory and Practice,* Vol. 3 (1975), pp. 403–23.
———. "Punishing the Innocent—Unintentionally." *Inquiry,* Vol. 20 (1977), pp. 45–65.
———. "Deterrence and Retribution." *Ethics,* Vol 86 (1976), pp. 181–99.
Woozley, A.D. "Civil Disobedience and Punishment." *Ethics,* Vol. 86 (1976), pp. 323–31.

Eight
AN EVALUATION
OF PREFERENTIAL
TREATMENT

Systematic and pervasive discrimination directed against whole groups of people is a particularly serious and abhorrent form of social injustice. In our own society, racial minorities and women are among those who in varying degrees have been and continue to be victims of such systematic injustice. What should the response of society be to such injustice in its own domain?

While some would say that the just society simply should stop discriminating, others respond that that is not enough. In addition to eliminating discrimination, the state may be required to take affirmative action to insure that the victims of past discrimination can take their full place as equals in society. A particular form of affirmative action which has proven especially controversial is preferential treatment. Adherents of preferential treatment argue that the proper response to systematic discrimination is to extend special preference to members of victimized groups in the distribution of jobs, as well as in the selection of applicants to scarce positions in medical and law schools, and other graduate and university programs.

Preferential treatment has been the subject of considerable debate in the political arena and in the courts. White males such as Marco DeFunis and Allan Bakke have argued, before the Supreme Court, that preferential treatment in favor of racial minorities is a form of invidious reverse discrimination which deprived them of equal protection of the laws. In the 1978 *Bakke* decision, a divided Supreme Court claimed, by a 5-4 majority, that racial preference is not in itself unconstitutional. But, by a different 5-4 majority, that same Court decided that the particular form of racial preference extended by the University of California Medical School, from which Bakke was rejected, was not constitutionally permissible.[1] The Constitutional status of preferential treatment is still far from clear, in spite of the *Bakke* decision, precisely because the Court was so divided that no clear and widely accepted principled basis for the ruling emerged. Controversy over preferential treatment has continued well into the 1980s, especially since the Justice Department under President Reagan has been far more reluctant to support it against legal challenge than Justice Departments under previous administrations.

Is preferential treatment for blacks, Asian Americans, Hispanics, women, and other victimized minority groups justified? Are charges that it is simply a new form of invidious reverse discrimination warranted? In this chapter, we will consider whether society's responsibilities to the victims of social injustice require preferential treatment in their favor. But before turning directly to the substantive issues at stake, a number of preliminary points, often ignored in the heat of political debate, need to be clarified.

DISTINCTIONS AND CLARIFICATIONS

Debates over affirmative action often are doomed to inconclusiveness because different forms of affirmative action policies are not distinguished. To begin with, it will prove useful to distinguish policies of *nondiscrimination, affirmative action,* and *preferential treatment.*

A policy of distributing scarce positions among applicants is one of nondiscrimination if race, religion, sex, or ethnic background are not taken into consideration in the selection process.[2] Affirmative action, on the other hand, requires more than such neutrality. In addition, it requires the taking of positive steps to promote more adequate representation of members of victimized groups within the applicant pool, and presumably among those selected. It is important to see that affirmative action need not include preferential treatment in selection. Instead, it might encompass such relatively uncontroversial features as open advertising of positions, inclusion in advertisements of a statement of employer interest in securing applications from minorities, and greater internal efforts to insure that applications of minority group members are not dismissed for the wrong reasons.

Preferential treatment, on the other hand, is a form of affirmative action which requires that positive weight be given to race and/or sex in the selection process. The degree of preference can be *weak* if it is used only to break ties between otherwise equally qualified candidates or it can be *strong* if used to favor a less qualified candidate.

Given these distinctions, a number of points follow: First, to be against preferential treatment is not necessarily to be against all forms of affirmative action. Thus, opposition to the former should not be equated with opposition to the latter. As we have seen, preferential treatment is only one form affirmative action may take.

Second, to be for preferential treatment is not necessarily to be for quotas. Preferential treatment requires only that positive weight be given to race or sex; not that a fixed number of individuals of a particular race or sex must be hired. Thus, even if individuals are given special credit for belonging to a particular group, it does not follow that they will be more attractive candidates, all things considered, than nonmembers. Indeed, one can read Justice Powell's opinion in the *Bakke* decision as an argument to the effect that racial preference can, under some conditions, be constitutional, but that quotas cannot.

Finally, preferential treatment, even of the strong variety, does not necessarily involve selection of the *unqualified*. Indeed, to our knowledge, no serious proponent of preferential treatment favors selection of the unqualified. Rather, preferential treatment is to be applied within the pool of qualified, often highly qualified, applicants.

Linguistically, it is important not to automatically equate preferential treatment with reverse discrimination, at least if the word "discrimination" is used to suggest the making of arbitrary or inequitable distinctions. Whether preferential treatment is a form of unjust discrimination must be settled by substantive argument; not by arbitrary linguistic stipulation.

THE REVERSE DISCRIMINATION ARGUMENT

Its opponents maintain that preferential treatment ought to be condemned as a form of invidious discrimination in reverse. Stated formally, their argument, the Reverse Discrimination Argument or RDA, looks like this:

1. Invidious discrimination *against* racial minorities and women is unjust.
2. Present forms of preferential treatment *in favor of* women and minorities do not differ from past invidious discrimination against minorities and women in any morally relevant way.
3. Relevantly similar cases must be evaluated similarly.
4. Therefore, present forms of preferential treatment in favor of women and minorities are unjust.

The reasoning in this argument appears to be valid; *if* the premises are warranted, the conclusion must be warranted. Therefore, proponents of preferential treatment who want to reject the conclusion of the argument must reject one of the premises. But which one?

Premise 3 certainly seems to be acceptable. As we have seen, the principle of universalizability which it expresses is simply a requirement of practical consistency and so is required by the commitment to reason itself. Moreover, premise 1 is accepted by all parties to the debate. Proponents of preferential treatment must show, then, that there is a morally relevant distinction to be made between preferential treatment and invidious discrimination. But how are they to proceed?

It will not be enough merely to show that preferential treatment has good consequences. For if invidious discrimination violates the fundamental rights of the victims, those rights constrain how we may permissibly pursue the greatest good for society. Would we accept an argument in favor of racial discrimination against blacks in the segregated South of the early twentieth century to the effect that benefits to the white majority outweighed burdens imposed on the minority? If we reject that form of argument in the case of discrimination against racial minorities, in all consistency, must we not also reject it when employed in favor of preferential treatment? If so, appeal to such projected consequences of preferential treatment as better medical and legal care for the minority community, and alleviation of racial problems, only has force after the RDA is defused.

Can the RDA be defused? Those who answer in the affirmative generally employ one of three strategies. First, they may argue that preferential treatment is required by considerations of compensatory justice. Second, they might argue that preferential treatment is required to honor the rights of citizens in the future. Preferential treatment, in other words, is *required* by concern for individual rights. Finally, and perhaps most interestingly, they may deny that preferential treatment violates the rights of those disfavored, once those rights are properly understood. On this last view, premise 2 of the RDA rests on a misunderstanding of what the requirements of justice really are in the area of equal protection. We will consider each of these approaches in turn.

COMPENSATORY JUSTICE AND PREFERENTIAL TREATMENT

According to the argument for compensatory justice, preferential treatment in hiring and admissions is justified as compensation for past discrimination against group members as such. Often cited here is the familiar analogy of a race between two runners, one of whom is chained to a heavy weight. Surely, if the race is stopped in the middle and the chain cut, it would not be fair simply to let the race resume. Since the previously chained runner already is far behind, fairness requires that the effect of an unfairly imposed handicap be negated. Likewise, advocates of preferential treatment argue that, given past discriminatory practices, implementing equal opportunity is simply not enough. The inequalities resulting from past discrimination would be perpetuated into the future. Compensatory preferential treatment in favor of victimized-group members is required in addition.

If the compensatory approach is correct, the RDA misses the mark. Preferential treatment is designed to compensate victims of injustice, not to stigmatize, degrade, or disadvantage anyone. Moreover, compensation is owed to the victims of injustice; they have a right to it. So premise 2 of the RDA is simply mistaken. Let us examine this compensatory argument in some depth.

The Compensatory Paradigm

Perhaps the classic account of compensatory or corrective justice is found in Book V of Aristotle's *Nicomachean Ethics*. It will be helpful to briefly consider Aristotle's account, for compensatory defenses of preferential treatment diverge from it in several significant, and perhaps questionable, ways.

According to Aristotle, principles of compensatory justice apply when one party has wronged another. Such principles call for *provision of redress by the wrongdoer to the victim*. Moreover, the penalty imposed on the former, and thus the benefit supplied to the latter, should be proportional to the difference created by the original wrong. The goal is to restore the relative position of the affected parties to what it would have been had the original injustice never occurred.

This Aristotelian paradigm seems intuitively sound. The wrongdoer should not profit from nor should the victim be disadvantaged by injustice. Moreover, it does fit an important class of cases involving discrimination. For example, if an employer unjustly discriminates against black employees in promotion and award of salary, the major elements of the Aristotelian paradigm apply. There is an identifiable wrongdoer and an identifiable victim. There is an identifiable act (or acts) of injustice. The kind and amount of redress which is required is relatively clear. The employees should be paid the difference between the pay they actually received and the larger amount they would have received had the rules been applied equally to all. (Perhaps they also should receive an additional sum to compensate for stigmatization brought about by the employer's discrimination.) The victimized workers are not receiving preferential treatment but are only getting what they deserved, i.e., what they would have received under a policy of nondiscrimination.

How does the Aristotelian paradigm fit preferential treatment? Unfortunately, the fit is not a close one.

Evaluation of the Compensatory Argument

Preferential treatment departs from the Aristotelian paradigm in at least three important ways. First, in many programs, preference is made on the basis of race, sex, and other forms of group membership rather than on individual victimization. Second, compensation is not provided by wrongdoers but by arguably innocent third parties. Finally, compensation is not proportional to injury. Let us consider each point in turn.

Critics of the compensatory defense should admit that victims of discrimination deserve compensation. But they can go on to point out that if the reason for preferring a victim of discrimination to a nonvictim is the injury suffered, then the formal principle of justice requiring that similar cases should be treated similarly implies that *any* victim of injustice should receive equal preference, regardless of race, sex, or other group characteristics. The only relevant group, from the point of view of compensatory justice, is that composed of and only of the victimized.[3] Perhaps all black persons and all women are members of such a group, but if so they deserve compensation *qua* victim and not *qua* black or woman.

This implies that compensatory justice should be *neutral* with respect to race or sex rather than race or sex conscious. Preferential treatment violates this criterion and so, according to its critics, is an improper form of compensatory action.

In addition, consider how the *costs* of preferential treatment are distributed. Thus, unlike the case of the Aristotelian paradigm, which assigns the costs of redress to the wrongdoer, preferential treatment assigns the cost to arbitrarily selected white males, none of whom may actually be guilty of discrimination.[4] Critics of preferential treatment argue that it is unfair to expect such innocent third parties to pay such a price.

Proponents of preferential treatment sometimes reply that although such white males may not be guilty of actual discrimination, they are the innocent beneficiaries of discrimination against women and minorities.[5] On this view, whites, and white males in particular, share in the benefits that accrue to the majority from discrimination against minorities. These benefits include but are not restricted to competitive advantages brought about by generally superior education and a sense of esteem and self-worth that has never been undermined by the pervasive message that one belongs to an allegedly inferior and stigmatized group.

However, while this reply deserves serious consideration, it probably is not a fully satisfactory response to critics of preferential treatment. For one thing, even if all white males are beneficiaries of injustice, preferential treatment still does not inflict the costs equitably. Some arbitrarily selected whites are denied admission to graduate training, a job, or a promotion while others are unaffected. Second, it may not be true that all white males are net beneficiaries of injustice. While each white male arguably may have benefitted just from being white, some may be worse off than they otherwise would have been because of earlier discrimination directed against their own ethnic group. In some cases, where the loss outweighs the gain, they too may be entitled to compensation under the Aristotelian paradigm. Finally, while it sometimes is the case that innocent beneficiaries of injustice are required to compensate victims, that is not always the case. If my store does better than yours because yours is closed by arson, it is far from clear that I, rather than the arsonist or an insurance company, am the one who should compensate you for the injury.

Accordingly, it is far from clear that preferential treatment fits the second requirement of the Aristotelian paradigm; namely, that compensation should be made by the wrongdoer. It is plausible to maintain, then, that preferential treatment assigns burdens in an arbitrary and inequitable fashion.

At this point, it may be objected that almost any social policy assigns burdens in such a way. After all, if a new highway is built through town, displaced homeowners may be compensated but the other benefits and burdens may be distributed in a highly arbitrary way. You and I may live near the highway, but you may mind the noise of traffic while I do not. My business, a gas station, may be helped but yours, a rest home for the elderly, may not.[6]

We shall pursue this point in the next section, when we consider the argument that preferential treatment does not violate anyone's rights. For now, we note only that while ordinary social policy may inflict costs arbitrarily, we are not talking about a normal cost here. Rather, we are talking about disqualification at least partly on the basis of race or sex. That is why the appeal to compensatory justice is so important; it is designed to show that reverse discrimination is not at issue. But once the compensatory rationale is dropped and appeal made to ordinary considerations of policy, there is no especially compelling value, such as the claim to rectification, which might justify race-conscious policies. On the other hand, if the compensatory defense is appealed to, some rational connection must be demonstrated between the wrongdoing and the imposition of burdens.

Finally, there is a third area in which preferential treatment departs from the Aristotelian paradigm. Consider a plausible principle of compensatory justice that might be called the Proportionality Principle, or PP. According to the PP, the strength of one's compensatory claim and the amount of compensation to which one is entitled is, *ceteris paribus*, proportional to the degree of injury suffered. A corollary of the PP is that equal injury gives rise to compensatory claims of equal strength.[7] Thus, if X and Y were both injured to the same extent, and both deserve compensation for their injury, then, *ceteris paribus*, each has a compensatory claim of equal strength and each is entitled to equal compensation.

Now, it is extremely unlikely that a hiring program which gives preference to blacks and women will satisfy the PP because of the arbitrariness implicit in the search for candidates on the open market. Thus, three candidates, each members of previously victimized groups, may well wind up with highly disparate positions. One may secure employment in a prestigious department of a leading university while another may be hired by a university that hardly merits the name. The third might not be hired at all.

The point is that where the marketplace is used to distribute compensation, distribution will be by market principles, and hence only accidentally will be fitting in view of the injury suffered and compensation provided for others. While any compensation may be better than none, this would hardly appear to be a satisfactory way of making amends to the victimized.

"Compensation according to ability" or "compensation according to marketability" surely are dubious principles of compensatory justice. On the contrary, those with the strongest compensatory claims should be compensated first (and most). Where compensatory claims are equal, but not everybody can actually be compensated, some fair method of distribution should be employed, e.g., a lottery. Preferential hiring policies, then, to the extent that they violate the PP, *arbitrarily* discriminate in favor of some victims of past injustice and against others. The basis on which compensation is awarded is independent of the basis on which it is owed and so distribution is determined by application of principles that are irrelevant from the point of view of compensatory justice.

Compensation for groups? Perhaps the discussion so far shows that preferential treatment does not fit the Aristotelian paradigm of compensatory justice. Such a result is important because the Aristotelian paradigm expresses widely accepted principles of fair compensation; principles that are at the basis of much of the law of torts. However, we should not conclude too quickly that the compensatory defense fails. Perhaps departures from the Aristotelian paradigm can be justified.

Thus, it might be granted that *if* we could apply such ideal principles of compensation, the discussion so far would be conclusive. Ideally, similar injury warrants similar compensation, compensation should be provided by wrongdoers and compensation should be proportional to injury. Ideally, each compensatory claim should be assessed on its own merits, regardless of race, ethnicity, or sex.

However, it might be replied that in the present state of affairs, it is highly unlikely that ideal principles of compensatory justice can or should be applied. Matters are just too complex to permit case-by-case treatment. Consider the factors that might have to be weighed, for example, in providing reparations to black persons on an individual basis:

Compare, in this context, the circumstances of a Mississippi share-cropper, a Harlem welfare mother, a Fisk University professor, a successful jazz performer, an unemployed young man living in a Chicago slum, a political leader in Detroit, and a kindergarten child in a predominantly white suburban school. Each would have to prove the amount of his or her damages as an individual . . . an attempt to individualize the compensation awarded in a program of black reparations would have to weigh so many imponderable elements that . . . the recoveries might in the end be more capricious than accurate.[8]

Influenced by such considerations, James Nickel argues that with respect to black persons in the United States:

if the justifying basis for such [preferential discrimination] is the losses and needs resulting from slavery and discrimination, there will be a high correlation between being black and having those needs, and because of this . . . race can serve as the administrative basis for such a program.[9]

Nickel allows that "this may result in a certain degree of unfairness" but replies that "it can help to decrease administrative costs so that more resources can be directed to those in need."[10]

What we have here is a pragmatic justification for preferential treatment in nonideal situations. The argument is that given a statistical premise to the effect that a significant proportion of members of a particular group have been unjustly victimized, we are justified pragmatically in acting as if all have been victimized. Much work needs to be done on the precise formulation and assessment of this kind of argument. For now, the following comments may be helpful.

The unfairness Nickel mentioned takes two forms. First, some blacks who have not been severely victimized would receive compensation. Second, nonblacks who have been seriously injured by unjust acts or practices would not receive compensation. Nickel suggests that such residual unfairness can be outweighed by the resulting increase in efficiency in distribution of compensation. But that this *can* be so does not show that it *is* so. Indeed, if there are a significant number of severely injured persons who are not group members, there will be a *decrease* in efficiency. Aid will not be provided for many of those with the strongest compensatory claims at all, since many will not be members of victimized groups. Rather, it will go to group members instead. So, at the very least, Nickel's conceptual point needs to be supplemented by data on the extent of residual unfairness involved and the resulting implications for efficiency. He is not entitled simply to assume that his proposal will increase efficiency when in fact it may actually decrease it.

Moreover, if the reason for going to group classification is to channel resources to the victimized more efficiently, we ought to be reasonably certain that the proposed classification does the job. It is by no means self-evident for example, that classification by race, sex, or ethnic background is any more efficient or easier to apply than an alternative classification based on some index of income, educational, and health deficiencies. Such a socioeconomic approach would provide compensation to seriously deprived members of all groups. And, as there is likely to be a high correlation between serious deprivation and being treated unjustly, at least in the affluent countries, the social indicators approach seems morally more acceptable and no less efficient than Nickel's proposal.

Finally, even if these points can be answered, a more serious difficulty remains. That is, the administrative approach can also be used to justify disadvantaging women and minorities when it promotes efficiency to do so. For example, it would appear to justify an employer's refusal to interview any women for a job that required great strength on the grounds that most women lacked the strength to be able to do the job.

Such examples need not be merely hypothetical. In the important sex discrimination case of *Frontiero v. Richardson*, the Army attempted to justify imposition of different requirements on claims by male and female soldiers concerning dependents on pragmatic, efficiency-related grounds.[11] Under the relevant military statutes, a serviceman could claim his wife as a dependent without regard to whether she was in fact dependent upon him for any amount of support. However, a servicewoman could claim her husband as a dependent only after showing that he was in fact dependent upon her for over one-half of his support.

The Army's justification for this distinction was that, in fact, most women are dependent upon their husbands for support. Therefore, it would be inefficient to check into each particular claim. However, since most husbands are not dependent upon their wives, "it would be more economical to require married female members claiming husbands to prove actual dependency than to extend the presumption of dependency to such members."[12] Given the social situation at the time, and the fact that about 99 percent of the uniformed services were then male, the army's factual claim about efficiency may well have been true. Even if the claim was controversial, it arguably was not the Court's business to decide what was or was not efficient.

The problem, then, is this: If proponents of the compensatory defense of preferential treatment want to justify using racial criteria to assign benefits and costs on grounds of administrative efficiency, how are they to avoid assigning equal weight to efficiency-related arguments when they count *against* women and minorities? On the other hand, if they would agree that administrative efficiency does not justify disadvantaging individual women or minority group members, doesn't consistency require them to say the same thing about preferential treatment?

In *Frontiero*, the Supreme Court rejected the appeal to administrative efficiency to justify disadvantaging individuals because of sex. As Justice Brennan declared in writing the majority opinion,

> although efficacious administration of governmental programs is not without some importance, 'the Constitution recognizes higher values than speed and efficiency.' . . . On the contrary, any statutory scheme which draws a sharp line between the sexes *solely* for the purpose of achieving administrative convenience necessarily commands 'dissimilar treatment for men and women who are . . . similarly situated' . . . and therefore involves the 'very kind of arbitrary legislative choice forbidden by the Constitution.'[13]

If Brennan's point is sound, why can't it be argued with equal force that preferential treatment distributes compensation in such a way as to treat similarly situated people differently? Why should the white male victim of injustice be treated differently than other victims? Why should costs of eliminating discrimination be assessed against one white male but not another? Why should the equally victimized receive different compensation; compensation which is not proportional to injury?

At this point, proponents of the compensatory approach may agree that the version based on administrative efficiency has its problems. They may go on, however, to depart from the Aristotelian paradigm in a more radical way.

A second reply—collective compensation   A second kind of reply is that the kind of objection raised against compensatory preferential treatment is misdirected. If the concern was with compensating *individuals,* then it would be correct to point out that group membership is irrelevant to the justification of compensatory claims. But perhaps we should be concerned with compensating *groups* as *collective entities.*

Such a position has been defended by Paul Taylor. He maintains that

> if there has been an established social practice . . . of treating any members of a certain class of persons in a certain way on the ground that they have the characteristic C, and if this practice has involved the doing of an injustice to C-persons, then the principle of compensatory justice requires that C-persons as such be compensated in some way.[14]

Taylor's point is that although possession of C *was* morally irrelevant to how a person should be treated, it *became* relevant because of the application of the unjust discriminatory practice itself. On this basis, Taylor concludes that even an individual C-person who has not been victimized "nevertheless has a right (based on his being a member of the class of C-persons) to receive the benefits extended to all C-persons as such." Compensatory benefits are not to be provided for individuals as such "but rather are directed toward any member of an 'assignable' group . . . who wishes to take advantage of, or qualify for, the compensatory benefits offered to the group as a whole."[15]

The basic idea here is that compensatory justice covers the claims of major social groups as well as those of individuals.[16] If a group has been victimized by injustice, compensatory justice requires that the *group* be restored to the position it would have held were it not for the original wrongdoing.

Although the shift from individual to group compensation may prove fruitful, it marks a major departure not only from the individualistic assumptions which permeate much of Anglo-American ethical theory, but from a basic principle which has dominated our legal system; namely, that the fundamental rights guaranteed by the Constitution are rights of *individuals*. Perhaps a group approach to compensatory justice eventually can be made plausible. Nevertheless, there are serious problems which any advocate of the group approach will have to face.

Consider, for example, the following problem: Suppose a group G is composed of individuals $i_1, i_2 \ldots i_n$. If we speak of G being injured as a group, we might mean only that each individual member $i_1, i_2 \ldots i_n$ has been injured. In this sense, the group has been injured as an *aggregation*. On the other hand, we might speak of G being injured not simply as an aggregation but as a *collective entity*. Here injury to the group is not in principle reducible to injury to the individual members. Whether the concept of irreducible injury to a group is intelligible is itself a controversial issue. Taylor, however, seems committed to such a concept of collective injury. For, if by injury to the group he means only injury to individual members, the earlier objection would still hold. Compensation would be for injury and anyone, member or not, would be entitled to similar compensation for similar injury.

However, if collective and not aggregative injury to a group is at issue, another problem arises. Professor Taylor assumes that since compensation ought to be made to the group, each individual member is entitled to receive compensatory benefits. But such an assumption surely is questionable. What Taylor needs are premises that indicate how compensation intended for a group should be distributed among the members. But he supplies no such premises. And, it is at least plausible to think that if a group has been injured as a collective, compensation ought to be made to the collective as well, and not to individual members as such. Thus, suppose a particular religion as such has been unjustly discriminated against, perhaps by imposition of a tax burden not imposed on similar groups. Surely, compensation ought to be made to the religion as a collective entity, perhaps by granting it special tax benefits in the future, and not to each particular adherent. If not, we have not been told why not.

Accordingly, those who talk of compensating a group face a logical dilemma. Either no group exists as such, for the group is only an aggregation of individuals, or else the group is a collective entity, in which case it remains to be shown how compensating individuals compensates the collective. What is needed is a principle specifying the relation between collective compensation to groups and distribution of that compensation among individual members. In the absence of such principles, the shift from individual to group compensation is at best seriously incomplete.

Of course, it may be possible to supply the missing premises. For example, one can argue that in the case of black Americans, one restores the group to its rightful position by favoring individual members precisely because of the psychological links holding the group together. It is because black Americans, like members of other ethnic groups, tend to identify with one another's achievements that the success of some can encourage others to have aspirations that otherwise would have never seen the light of day. Moreover, members who are not directly advantaged can share in the satisfaction of achievement by other members of the group. Finally, successful group members can represent the group's interests in the professions, business, and government.

While such a view might eventually be made plausible, it sounds suspiciously like a "trickle-down" theory to us. Some individual members of the group, selected arbitrarily from the point of view of compensatory justice, will benefit directly from preferential treatment while others, selected equally arbitrarily, at best benefit only indirectly and to a lesser extent. Although the group arguably is restored to the place it would have held had there been no injustice, individuals within the group are treated arbitrarily. An individual who has been less significantly harmed by discrimination than another can benefit far more. (Similarly, costs are still assessed arbitrarily. Arbitrarily selected individuals, not groups are disadvantaged by preferential treatment.)

Perhaps more important, how are we to identify the groups to be compensated? Should relatively affluent and well-educated groups, such as Jews and Asian Americans, be eligible for compensation in light of a past history of discrimination? Or if we say that they have already overcome the effects of past injustice, should we say the same of blacks of West Indian descent, who do as well as the national average in terms of employment, income, and years of education?[17] It is tempting here to say that preferential treatment is needed only for those groups who have not yet "made it" in

America. But can such a move be made within a *compensatory* framework, the goal of which is paying what is due for *past* wrongs? In other kinds of cases, we do not deny that the victim of another's negligence is owed compensation just because she is wealthy and does not need to be compensated.[18]

We suggest that until a plausible theory of group compensation is provided, the burden of proof is on its advocates, at least when there is danger of conflict with important individual rights. In summary, preferential treatment should not be based on the relatively unclear idea of group compensation, at least when fundamental individual rights are thereby put in danger.

We conclude, then, that the shift from individual to group compensation, conceived of either in statistical or collective terms, does not avoid the problems of the compensatory justification of preferential treatment. If preferential treatment on the basis of race is justifiable, it is probably not justifiable through appeal to compensatory justice.

NONCOMPENSATORY DEFENSES OF PREFERENTIAL TREATMENT

Preferential treatment can be defended on grounds other than compensatory ones. Hence, even if the compensatory defense is inadequate, other defenses might be stronger. We will examine the most significant of these noncompensatory approaches to see if they fare better than the appeal to compensatory justice.

The Appeal to Merit and Efficiency

Advocates of the meritocratic approach argue that there are meritocratic reasons for hiring or admitting members of especially victimized groups. This argument is often applied to the university. There, it is argued, women and blacks, in faculty positions, can serve as role models for women and black students. Because of past discrimination, overt and covert, few members of such groups occupy university positions of authority and influence. But for women and black students rationally to attain to such positions, they must be able to see that people like them can succeed. If they are presented with female and black faculty, they are given living proof that discrimination can be overcome. Of at least equal importance, they may identify with such models and hence secure the special stimulation that will enable them to succeed.

In addition, it is maintained that women and minority faculty can play special roles in advising and counseling women and minority students. Surely it is disconcerting for black students on a largely white campus to be confronted with an entirely white faculty and administration. They might feel, with some justice, that other blacks are especially likely to understand their special problems as whites cannot. Moreover, members of victimized groups, because of their atypical experiences, are likely to have special viewpoints on many matters and so add an important sort of diversity to the intellectual community.

Similar arguments can be made in support of preferential admission to professional and graduate schools, as well as to undergraduate colleges. Such institutions always have tried to select a diverse student body. Surely, if preferential selection of a student from a sparsely populated state, or one who is skilled at basketball, is justified, so too is the giving of priority to women and minority candidates. Moreover, professional schools should serve the community as a whole. Minority-group members and women have been underrepresented in the professions, however. Hence, preferential admission of minorities and women to law and medical schools is a justified means of providing adequate legal and medical care to women and especially to poverty-stricken ghetto areas.[19]

These arguments, if acceptable, show that there are reasons having to do with the *merit* of the candidates for hiring or admitting minorities or women. On this view, such a practice is not preferential at all; the best candidates are being hired or admitted. Even though a minority group member or woman might be slightly less qualified in a particular case than a white male, there are additional nonstandard qualifications that put the white male at a competitive disadvantage *on the merits*.

Evaluation   In dealing with the arguments just cited, it is especially important to distinguish what they show from what they may seem to show but do not.

Consider, for example, the argument that preferential selection of black applicants to law school is justified in view of the need for lawyers to serve the black community. Surely, if this argument shows anything, it shows that *anyone,* regardless of race, who will practice in the black community—or perhaps in *any* area where lawyers are needed—should receive special consideration. The relevant consideration is not race but willingness to practice in certain areas rather than in others. Of course, as a matter of fact, blacks may be more anxious to practice in and help serve the black community than others. But if a nonblack is equally willing to help, he or she should receive consideration equal to that of otherwise similarly qualified black candidates. Likewise, a policy designed to equalize distribution of physicians throughout the United States may admit more minority-group members than would have been the case if only standard qualifications had been considered. But it will preferentially admit others as well and, in any case, the basis of assigning preference will not be race.

Indeed, there surely is something dubious about the assumption that only blacks will be willing to serve the black community, only women will serve women, and so forth. It is even more dubious to think the state should help promote such a segregated society by allowing preferential selection on a group basis. As Supreme Court Justice William O. Douglas wrote in his dissenting brief in the DeFunis case in which DeFunis, a white, charged he had been denied admission to the University of Washington School of Law on the basis of race:

> The equal protection clause commands the elimination of racial barriers, not their creation in order to satisfy our theory as to how society should be organized. The purpose of the University of Washington cannot be to produce Black lawyers for Blacks, Polish lawyers for Poles, Jewish lawyers for Jews, Irish lawyers for the Irish. It should be to produce good lawyers for Americans. . . .[20]

Similar points can be extended to the other arguments considered. If diversity is desirable, all who can equally contribute to a diverse intellectual community ought to receive equal treatment. If ability to motivate or serve as an example for students is a relevant quality, then that—and not race or sex—is the factor to be considered. Not all minority-group members or women are likely to be helpful to women or minority students. And in some cases, a white male may be best at motivating minority and women students. One ought not to assume that blacks identify only with blacks, Jews with Jews, women with women, and so on.

We conclude that arguments from merit and efficiency will in *some* contexts justify the hiring and admission of victimized-group members in cases where such persons would not be hired or admitted if only standard qualifications were considered. However, such persons are not hired simply because they are victimized-group members. Rather, they are hired because of their ability to do an important job well. But then any person who is equally qualified, in the expanded sense, is entitled to receive equal consideration regardless of group membership. Even though application of expanded meritocratic criteria may lead to increased hiring or admission of victimized-group members, it will at most be a contingent (although important) fact that group members are more meritorious in the expanded sense than others. No broad policy of preferential selection on a group basis is justified by the sorts of considerations examined in this section.

Moreover, one must take into consideration here the danger of creating two classes of faculty and students, namely, those who are most qualified in the standard sense and those who are most qualified in the expanded sense. Although the expanded notion of qualifications ought sometimes to be employed there is a danger of creating a double standard that may harm all affected in the long run.

The Appeal to Equality

Perhaps the strongest justification of preferential treatment seeks neither to rectify the past nor expand the notion of merit. Rather, it looks at the *consequences* of preferential treatment. Such a view need not be utilitarian but might be based on concern for rights and social justice. That is, it can be argued that preferential treatment even if it involves some present injustice, is necessary to bring about an egalitarian society. Thus, some might see it as a way of transferring wealth and power from groups that already have it to those that do not. Others might view it as a means for insuring that victimized-group members have a chance equal to others to develop and carry out rational plans of life. Preferential treatment, then, can be conceived as a mechanism for implementing equality of opportunity. Thus, one writer on the subject declares that:

> Women and blacks want to present themselves as qualified candidates and be assured of having a fair chance. . . . Past practices have shown they do not receive this fair chance and preferential hiring is a way of insuring that chance precisely because preferential hiring requires that the burden of the proof be placed on those who do the hiring— on those who have discriminated against women and blacks in the past—to demonstrate that they are no longer doing so.[21]

But does equal opportunity require preferential treatment? Why not simply enforce laws that prohibit discrimination? Then everyone would have the same chance and no one would receive special treatment.

Proponents of preferential treatment would reply that it is not enough to require everyone to play by the same rules if past discrimination handicaps some of the participants. Thus, some writers maintain that "the key to an adequate justification of reverse discrimination (is) to see that practice not as the redressing of past privations but rather as a way of neutralizing the present competitive disadvantage caused by those past privations."[22] Former President Lyndon Johnson's famous metaphor of the footrace (which we mentioned earlier) captures this point.

All of the above arguments defend preferential treatment as a key policy designed to attain desirable social goals of an egalitarian character. On this view, preferential treatment is needed as a means to make society more equal and more fair. Is this approach successful?

Social goals and reverse discrimination   The egalitarian goals which preferential treatment is alleged to promote do seem highly desirable.

Nevertheless, the egalitarian approach faces severe difficulties. The first major objection, which we will not pursue extensively here, is that preferential treatment may also produce *undesirable* goals. For example, it may exacerbate racial tensions and undermine the self-esteem of the recipients. However, even if the overall consequences of preferential treatment are harmful on balance, which is of course open to considerable debate, such a conclusion would show only that preferential treatment was bad policy, not that it was morally impermissible or that it wrongs anyone. Governments and institutions may adopt or even require the implementation of policies whose effects are debatable in the honest belief that more good than bad consequences will ensue in the long run.

However, policies may not be pursued, even for good ends, if they violate individual rights. And that is exactly the charge against preferential treatment. If preferential treatment is reverse discrimination, it should not be allowed simply to promote the overall best results, any more than we should tolerate invidious racial discrimination against minorities if it happened to promote the greatest overall happiness for a predominantly white society. In other words, the RDA stands as a barrier to the egalitarian justification of preferential treatment. It is arguably not just to employ discriminatory means in order to promote egalitarian goals.

Dworkin's Critique of the RDA

The view just expressed presupposes that preferential treatment violates individual rights. But does it? After all, the white males disadvantaged by preferential treatment cannot claim they have the right to go to law or medical school, or to certain jobs, for there are no such rights. Just how is preferential treatment like past invidious discrimination anyway? Ronald Dworkin, a distinguished professor of law and thoughtful commentator on values and social policy, has argued that advocates of the RDA simply are confused. Let us consider his argument in some depth.

In his book, *Taking Rights Seriously*, Dworkin has attempted to restore the primacy of individual rights in political and legal thought. In jurisprudence, Dworkin argues against what he takes to be the view of legal positivism that judges must use discretion in deciding difficult cases. Rather, he contends that judicial practice at its best involves the enforcement of preexisting rights. More broadly, Dworkin views individual rights as political trumps which persons may play in order to protect themselves against single-minded efforts to implement social and political goals.[23]

However, while Dworkin's theoretical account of rights seems designed to protect the individual, some of his applications of the theory to concrete cases are controversial, even among those sympathetic to his abstract defense of fundamental rights. In particular, Dworkin has used his account of rights to argue that white applicants disfavored by special admissions programs for minorities in law and medical school cannot legitimately complain that their rights have been violated. For, in Dworkin's view, special admissions programs for minorities do not violate individual rights to begin with. If Dworkin is correct in thinking special admissions programs violate no individual rights, important consequences would follow. In particular, whites disfavored by the programs could not claim that their equal rights were violated and so would have few if any grounds for claiming that special admissions programs for minorities are unconstitutional. The complaints of individuals such as a Bakke or a DeFunis could not be those of injustice and so would not raise constitutional issues of equal protection. Reverse discrimination would not be involved.

Instead, the only issues at stake would be resolvable by whatever principles normally apply to questions of pure public policy where no violations of individual rights are at stake. As Dworkin has claimed: "Racial criteria are not necessarily the right standards for deciding which applicants should be accepted by law schools. But neither are intellectual criteria, or indeed any other set of criteria. The fairness—and constitutionality—of any admissions program must be tested in the same way.[24]

In effect, Dworkin is claiming that those who equate special admissions programs for minorities with invidious discrimination in reverse are conceptually confused. Such critics are not clear about the nature of invidious discrimination.

Dworkin begins his account of fundamental individual rights by distinguishing between two kinds of rights to equality: "The first is the right to *equal treatment* which is the right to an equal distribution of some opportunity or resource or burden. . . . The second is the right, not to receive the same distribution of some burden or benefit, but to be treated with the same respect or concern as anyone else."[25] According to Dworkin, "the right to treatment as an equal is fundamental and the right to equal treatment is derivative." Thus, to borrow his example, "If I have two children, and one is dying from a disease that is making the other uncomfortable, I do not show equal concern if I flip a coin to decide which should have the remaining dose of the drug.[26] In this case, equal concern for each child, treatment of each as an equal, would yield an unequal distribution of the drug, or what Dworkin would call unequal treatment.

How does this distinction apply to the controversy over special admissions programs for certain minorities? According to Dworkin, such policies amount to unjust discrimination in reverse only if they violate individual rights. Now, a Marco DeFunis or an Alan Bakke has the right to go to law and medical school only if that right is derivable from correct application of an admissions policy which treats all the affected parties *as equals*. But since *any* policy ". . . will place certain candidates at a disadvantage . . . an admissions policy may nevertheless be justified if it seems reasonable to think the overall gain to the community exceeds the overall loss, and if no other policy that does not provide a comparable disadvantage would produce even roughly the same gain. . . . An individual's right to be treated as an equal means that his potential loss must be treated as a matter of concern; but that loss may nevertheless be outweighed by the gains to the community as a whole."[27] Dworkin is arguing that the charge of reverse discrimination is a red herring. The kind of distinctions involved in today's special admissions programs are far different from those characterizing past invidious discrimination against minorities. Thus, Dworkin acknowledges that "in the past, it made sense to say that an excluded black or Jewish student was being sacrificed because of his race and religion: that meant that his or her exclusion was treated as desirable in itself"[28] but adds that white males such as Bakke are "being excluded not by prejudice but because of a rational calculation about the socially most beneficial use of limited resources for medical education."[29] Since the disadvantage imposed on a Bakke or a DeFunis is counted equally in the process of social cost accounting, each has been treated as an equal. Since each has been treated as an equal, the rights of each have been respected. Since no rights have been violated, no reverse discrimination has been practiced and so, we are told, neither Bakke nor DeFunis has a case.

An evaluation of Dworkin's argument   The crucial notion in Dworkin's attempt to distinguish preferential treatment from invidious discrimination is that of treatment as an equal. As he officially explicates it, it is a right to both equal *respect* and equal *concern*. As he applies it, however, it is equal concern that does all the work. The policymaker is constrained to assign equal weight to the needs and interests of all affected by the policy.

So understood, the right to treatment as an equal looks suspiciously like the utilitarian requirement that everyone count for one and only one in computing social benefits and burdens.[30] It is compatible with such a requirement that some individuals be disfavored when the individual's loss is "outweighed by the gains to the community as a whole." If this is all there is to taking rights seriously, one wonders why the emphasis on rights is important to begin with.

Dworkin's perspective, in discussing the *DeFunis* and *Bakke* cases, is indeed that of the utilitarian legislator. As a consequence, the right to treatment as an equal, as he applies it in the discussion, does not satisfy the minimal requirement that he himself endorsed: namely, the rights have a certain threshold weight against the pursuit of collective goals. For the right in question is only the entitlement to be counted equally in determining which goals should be pursued. It does set limits on factors that may be considered in the policymaking *process* but sets no rights-based side constraints on the process itself.

Dworkin acknowledges that his approach is at least "parasitic on the dominant idea of utilitarianism"[31] and explicitly maintains that it is permissible to defend special admissions programs on utilitarian grounds.

However, he takes great pains to distinguish the kind of utilitarian arguments he regards as acceptable from those he does not. For the problem he believes he faces is that, given appropriate factual premises, utilitarian arguments might justify discrimination *against* disadvantaged minorities. It is worth a slight detour to show that Dworkin's distinction between acceptable and unacceptable utilitarian arguments fails, and hence that direct appeals to utility of the kind Dworkin endorses may well point in directions Dworkin would be loath to follow.

Dworkin's distinction arises from the difference between what he calls *personal* and *external* preferences. That you prefer clean rather than polluted air for yourself is a personal preference. That you prefer that people in the Northeast have clean air while those in the Sun Belt breathe dirty air is an external preference. Personal preferences express the speaker's own desires for satisfaction of his or her own wants and needs. External preferences express the speaker's desire for some particular distribution of goods, services, and opportunities to others.[32]

It is Dworkin's point that if the utilitarian allows external preferences to count in the calculus of social interests, the egalitarian character of utilitarianism is endangered. Utilitarianism traditionally is conceived of as egalitarian in the sense that each person's satisfaction or dissatisfaction is to count as much as any other's. But if external preferences are counted in, "the chance that anyone's preferences have to succeed will then depend not only on the demand made by the personal preferences of others on scarce resources but on the respect or affection they have for him or for his way of life."[33] In effect, the preferences of prejudiced individuals would count twice. Each such person's preferences for satisfaction of personal desires would have to be aggregated with his or her external preference that members of the victimized group be disadvantaged.

Utilitarian arguments are acceptable, then, only if they are independent of any appeal to external preferences. Appeal to external preferences is incompatible with showing equal respect and concern for all. In fact, we can now see the connection between Dworkin's view of individual rights and his qualified endorsement of utilitarian arguments. The right to treatment as an equal, at least as Dworkin applies it in his discussion of alleged reverse discrimination, simply requires that external preferences not be counted by the social policymaker. Basically, the function of that right is to set limits on the kinds of factors the utilitarian policymaker may consider!

Is the requirement that external preferences be disregarded defensible? In fact, utilitarians do not agree among themselves that external preferences are always to be discounted. Is it so clear, for example, that the desire of parents for their children's well-being is always to be ignored? Are the preferences of nonutilitarian members of the population for some ideal distributive principle to be cast beyond the pale of utilitarian consideration? We suspect there is no one answer to such questions which would prove acceptable to all utilitarians.

Suppose, however, that we accept the restriction on external preferences. Even so, the appeal to utilitarian arguments remains dubious. Utilitarian arguments might still support invidious discrimination, even if only personal preferences were counted.[34]

For example, suppose that in a particular society desirable jobs have been restricted to white males. Women and minorities demand in the name of equality that they too be given equal consideration for such positions. The white male majority, however, prefers to keep the restrictions in place. But this is not because of any external preference that women and minorities get the short end of the stick. Rather, each member of the white male majority reasons that his chances of securing desirable positions are reduced if the applicant pool is widened. So each white male favors keeping the old restrictions in place on purely personal grounds of self-interest. Given a large enough white male majority, such preferences might carry the day. The utilitarian legislator would have to count the losses of women and minorities as a matter of concern but might rationally conclude that such losses were "outweighed by the gains to the community as a whole."[35]

The problem with utilitarian arguments of the sort Dworkin considers acceptable is that they justify too much. If we would reject utilitarian arguments which, given appropriate empirical premises, would support discrimination against women and minorities, we must also reject parallel utilitarian arguments which justify disfavoring white males as such.

This point, it should be noted, counts not only against his conception of utilitarianism but against his conception of individual rights itself. Insofar as the right to treatment as an equal is taken merely to rule out consideration of external preferences, respect for such a right seems compatible with endorsement of the kind of discrimination against women and minorities just discussed. In the hypothetical example above, women and minorities were counted as equals; they were being excluded "not by prejudice but because of a rational calculation about the socially most beneficial use of limited resources. . . ."[36]

Is there another, perhaps more defensible conception of individual rights to be found in Dworkin's writing? Some of Dworkin's remarks at least suggest that treatment as an equal involves equal *respect* as well as equal *concern*. For example, he sometimes asserts that humans should be respected as beings "who are capable of forming and acting on intelligent conceptions of how their lives should be lived."[37] Insofar as Dworkin is suggesting here that there is a proper way for humans to be treated over and above what any calculation of social benefit might dictate, a nonconsequentialist conception of rights emerges.

Thus, it is plausible to think that basic rights, such as the right to freedom of speech, should be protected, not simply because of benefits accruing to the community from such protection, but because the autonomy of the individual is threatened in a particularly serious way where such rights are absent. For example, in the absence of free speech and open debate, individuals are deprived of the conditions under which reason functions most efficiently. Their range of intelligent choice has been circumscribed and thereby disrespect has been shown to their status as choosing autonomous beings.

This conception of rights as conditions for respecting persons equally as agents seems to us to be the most defensible of those considered. By emphasizing equal *respect* rather than equal *concern*, central importance is placed upon the agent's capacity to choose and act. Individuals are not regarded merely as loci of desires the satisfaction of which is to be maximized by the benevolent utilitarian legislator.

But for this very reason, this third conception of individual rights does not easily lend itself to Dworkin's analysis of benign discrimination. There is at least a prima facie incompatibility between equally respecting individuals as agents and dismissing an individual from consideration because of possession of immutable physical characteristics. The former implies emphasis on an individual's character, choices, and capacities, while the latter excludes these as irrelevant.

This suggests that what lies behind the charge of reverse discrimination is that preferential selection by race severs the link between a person's fate and a person's character, talents, choices, and abilities on the basis of possession of immutable physical characteristics. Qualities central to one's status as a person capable of forming and acting on an intelligent conception of how his or her life would be led count for less than the color of one's skin.

If, as we suggested in Chapter Three, natural or human rights are best understood as conditions which must be protected if humans are to be respected as rational and autonomous agents, then there are grounds for finding the RDA to be plausible. Even though preferential treatment does not stigmatize those disfavored by it in the same way as past racial discrimination stigmatized black Americans, or does not cause the same degree of injury, it still is open to the charge of disrespecting persons as such. By conferring or withholding benefits on the basis of race, or similar group membership, it requires that factors about individuals such as their choices, decisions, aptitudes, talents, and character—features that reflect their status as rational and autonomous agents—do not determine outcomes. People are deprived on the basis of race of the kind of respect due them as persons.

Before turning to our own proposals for affirmative action, we point out that proponents of preferential treatment have at least two responses to the above considerations still open to them.

First, they can argue that the above considerations are not decisive. Respect for persons, they might argue, is too vague a concept to decide such hard issues as the reverse discrimination controversy. Moreover, they might point out that preferential treatment does not totally ignore such features of the individual as character and motivation; rather, it uses race to decide between candidates who are each reasonably well qualified so that in the long run, all of us can be equally respected as persons.

This leads to a second response. Proponents of preferential treatment also can respond that in view of the systematic and pervasive injustices perpetrated against blacks and other minorities in our society, the RDA, even if plausible, is not sufficient to show that preferential treatment is unjustified. Rather, such critics could argue that especially since any reverse discrimination which may take place neither stigmatizes whites as a class nor harms them in any way comparable to the harms inflicted on minorities, it is less unjust than any alternative. That is, there would be even more injustice and violation of rights if we were to simply insist on nondiscrimination. Without affirmative action, including preferential treatment, the unjustly imposed handicaps of the past would continue to unjustly disadvantage the victims of past discrimination and their descendants for perhaps many more generations to come.

Such an argument appeals to what may be called a consequentialism of justice. Like utilitarianism, such a view requires that we adopt the policy with the best consequences. But unlike utilitarianism, it measures the goodness or badness of consequences in terms, not of happiness or unhappiness, but in terms of justice and injustice. We ought to adopt that policy which results in the greatest extension of justice in the long run, even if we have to commit some injustice along the way to get there.[38]

While we suggest that such a view may capture the intuitions of many Americans who are worried about the implications of preferential treatment, but who are troubled even more about the implications of doing nothing to remedy injustice, we think it ought not to be adopted too quickly. For one thing, the burden of proof surely is on those who claim that injustice is warranted in the name of greater justice to show beyond a reasonable doubt that the policy they recommend really will produce the goal they seek. After all, it is highly controversial whether preferential treatment really will promote a more egalitarian and integrated society or whether it simply will exacerbate existing racial tensions and resentments among groups. Perhaps more important, if a less objectionable alternative is available, one which carries less risk of involving injustice, surely it ought to be adopted.

In the next section, we sketch guidelines for an approach to preferential treatment which does not involve injustice. This approach should be of interest even to those who reject the RDA. Since it should be acceptable to many critics of preferential treatment, it might provide a more widely acceptable moral foundation for this form of affirmative action than proponents of preferential treatment have yet provided.

PREFERENTIAL TREATMENT WITHOUT DISCRIMINATION?

We have found no arguments for preferential treatment based on race, sex, or ethnicity that avoid serious criticism. Arguments that we have examined violate well-known principles of moral discourse, such as the requirement that relevantly similar cases be treated similarly. However, it is possible that policies of preferential treatment can be reformulated in such a way that they do not violate these canons. Let us briefly consider such an approach. If we are right, the choice is not just between preferential treatment and nondiscrimination. Instead, it may be between more acceptable and less acceptable forms of preferential treatment.

The Compensatory Element

Preferential treatment based on rectification for injustice might well be defensible if it were applied according to relevant criteria. This does not necessarily mean that such policies should be racially neutral or color blind; surely, there is a strong presumption that membership in certain victimized groups confers a compensatory claim (or at least a competitive disadvantage which ought to be rectified). However, it does not follow that those are the only such claims which should be considered. Other individuals, of any race or sex, may also have been victimized or may face severe disadvantages through no fault of their own. When choosing among qualified applicants for a position, it may well be permissible, when other factors are at least nearly equal, to take compensatory considerations into account. Moreover, in deciding who will be disadvantaged by such compensatory treatment, we ought to make sure that those who are asked to bear the costs do not have compensatory claims of their own. It does not follow, however, that we ought to do so along lines of group membership alone. We can benefit the most seriously victimized, regardless of race, while taking into account the special burdens of victimized groups when deciding who are the most seriously injured.[39]

Whether the majority of those who benefit are minorities or whether the majority of those who bear the costs are white males will depend upon the individual characteristics of those considered. Race may be one of the factors to be considered, insofar as it is an indicator of discrimination, but no one would be included or excluded a priori on such a basis.

While there certainly are problems connected with such an approach, such as how one kind of victimization is to be weighed against another, it still warrants consideration. Preferential treatment need not be considered a zero-sum game between white males and others; it can be reformulated to cut across such categories in a morally defensible way.

The Meritocratic Element

Standard meritocratic criteria of admissions and hiring ought to be reexamined and broadened where such an extension of standard criteria are justified. Once again, however, this can be done in such a way as to take race into account while recognizing that there are neutral reasons for extension that apply across group lines. (We argued this earlier in the section on "The Appeal to Merit and Efficiency.")

Avoiding Hard Choices

In addition, courts and other relevant institutions can try to avoid situations where women and minorities could be included only through excluding others because of their race or sex. For example, consider the question of whether a firm facing hard economic times ought to lay off those last hired, who may be disproportionately black and female, or violate seniority and fire senior white males instead. Proponents of preferential treatment may argue that the white workers might not have ever gained seniority had they faced competition from women and minorities earlier. Proponents of seniority might respond that it was not the workers who discriminated, and that the firm should not change the rules under which the workers have been employed in the middle of the game.

Perhaps we can avoid a zero-sum game here. Before deciding such a case, shouldn't the firm be required to show that no less compelling goal can be sacrificed in order to retain *both* the minority workers and those with seniority? Perhaps profit margins can be cut. Perhaps all workers, including management, can share a pay reduction so that more workers can be retained. If the employer is a town or other kind of municipality, perhaps nonessential services can be cut back before anyone is fired. Perhaps senior professors at a university should be asked to teach extra courses so that educational costs can be cut and more assistant professors, including women and minority group members, be retained. Such compromise may not always be possible, but perhaps the courts should aim first at reconciling differences through compromise and only last at deciding which group should bear the possibly avoidable costs of social policy.[40]

The Procedural Element

Admissions and hiring policies ought to be required to pass strict procedural tests to insure nondiscrimination. Some form of affirmative action, short of unjustified group preference, is required as a safeguard against future discrimination. Whether this need involve "numerical goals" is controversial, but there is at least the need to require hiring officers to demonstrate good faith efforts to find the best candidates.

SUMMARY

We have found that preferential treatment on the basis of race, sex, or similar group membership raises serious ethical questions and is open to the charge that it fails to respect persons in fundamental and important ways. We have suggested, however, that if preferential treatment is reformulated in ways that can apply across racial and other group lines, while still taking into account the special burdens facing members of victimized groups, it may avoid the charge of reverse discrimination. In our view, no individual should be sacrificed on the altars of egalitarian or compensatory ideals; and surely not when less obtrusive alternatives are available. The challenge posed by the reverse discrimination controversy is to promulgate rectificatory policies which acknowledge the force of claims to redress while avoiding arbitrary or inequitable treatment. Justice and equality demand no less.

NOTES

[1]*Allan Bakke vs. The Regents of the University of California,* U.S. Supreme Court, 1978.

[2]Actually, the issue of what counts as nondiscrimination is more complex than the text indicates. Depending upon how one wants to define "discrimination," race, religion, sex, and ethnic background arguably sometimes can be applied in nondiscriminatory ways. Thus, if one goes to a rabbi for information about Jewish religious practices, hires a black actor to play the part of a black in a movie or selects only women to play on a college women's basketball team, then, arguably, one is not discriminating in any invidious way. So, more precisely, a selection process is nondiscriminatory if it takes race, religion, sex, or ethnic background into account only when they are relevant to the qualifications of applicants. When such factors are relevant, or when the purpose of a job or institution is itself discriminatory, are matters for further discussion. While these issues are of importance, they are not directly relevant to our own discussion and so can be ignored in what follows, unless specifically mentioned.

[3]This point has been made by J. L. Cowen in his paper "Inverse Discrimination," *Analysis,* Vol 33, No. 1 (1972): pp. 10–12.

[4]At least, those who assign the costs do not base their assignment on claims that those disadvantaged actually have discriminated.

[5]Such a point is suggested by Judith Jarvis Thomson in her paper, "Preferential Hiring," *Philosophy & Public Affairs,* Vol. 2, No. 4 (1973) p. 383 and is criticized by Robert K. Fullinwider in his book, *The Reverse Discrimination Controversy* (Totowa, N.J.: Rowman and Littlefield, 1980) pp. 37–42.

[6]For discussion of a similar case, see Fullinwider, p. 39.

[7]The next four paragraphs of this section are reprinted from Robert Simon, "Preferential Hiring: A Reply to Judith Jarvis Thomson," *Philosophy & Public Affairs,* Vol. 3, No. 3, (1974), pp. 312–21, copyright © 1974, Princeton University Press, reprinted by permission of Princeton University Press.

[8]Boris Bittker, *The Case for Black Reparations* (New York: Random House, 1973), p. 88. Bittker ends up by defending the case for reparations in spite of the difficulty he raises in the quoted paragraph.

[9]James Nickel, "Classification by Race in Compensatory Programs," *Ethics*, Vol. 84, No. 2 (1974): 147–48.

[10]Ibid., p. 148.

[11]*Frontiero v. Richardson*, U.S. Supreme Court, 1973, reprinted in Joel Feinberg and Hyman Gross, *Philosophy of Law* (Belmont, Ca.: Wadsworth, 1980) pp. 365–69.

[12]*Frontiero*, in Feinberg and Gross, p. 365.

[13]Justice Brennan, *Frontiero*, in Feinberg and Gross, pp. 368–69.

[14]Paul Taylor, "Reverse Discrimination and Compensatory Justice," *Analysis*, Vol. 33, No. 6 (1973): 179.

[15]Ibid.

[16]Such a view is also discussed, from the point of view of constitutional law by Owne Fiss in his "Groups and the Equal Protection Clause," *Philosophy & Public Affairs*, Vol. 5, No. 2 (1976).

[17]Thomas Sowell, *The Economics and Politics of Race* (New York: Morrow, 1983) p. 186ff.

[18]After all, if the person whose car you negligently damage is more affluent than you are, you still owe the victim compensation for your carelessness.

[19]However, it can be argued with a good deal of justice that members of any sex or ethnic group who are willing to work in minority or poverty stricken areas should be given equal degrees of preference.

[20]Justice William O. Douglas in his dissent in *DeFunis v. Odegaard*, U.S. Supreme Court, 1974.

[21]Marlene Gerber Fried, "In Defense of Preferential Hiring," *Philosophical Forum*, Vol. 5, No. 1–2 (1973-1974): 315.

[22]George Sher, "Justifying Reverse Discrimination in Employment," *Philosophy & Public Affairs*, Vol. 4, No. 2 (1975): 163. However, Sher denies that his argument justified selection on a *group* basis.

[23]Ronald Dworkin, *Taking Rights Seriously* (Cambridge: Harvard University Press, 1977). Material in this section is reprinted from Robert L. Simon, "Individual Rights and Benign Discrimination," *Ethics*, Vol. 90, No. 1 (1979), pp. 88–97, by permission of the University of Chicago Press.

[24]Dworkin, p. 239.

[25]Ibid., p. 227.

[26]Ibid.

[27]Ibid.

[28]Ronald Dworkin, "Why Bakke Has No Case," *The New York Review of Books*, Vol. 24, (1977): 15.

[29]Ibid.

[30]This point has been suggested by Charles King in his review of *Taking Rights Seriously* in *Law and Liberty*, Vol. 3 (1973): 3.

[31]Dworkin, *Taking Rights Seriously*, p. xi.

[32]Ibid., pp. 234–35.

[33]Ibid., p. 235.

[34]This has been pointed out by Marshall Cohen in his review of *Taking Rights Seriously* in *The New York Review of Books*, Vol. 24 (1977): 37–39.

[35]Dworkin, *Taking Rights Seriously*, p. 227.

[36]Dworkin, "Why Bakke Has No Case," p. 15.

[37]Dworkin, *Taking Rights Seriously*, p. 272.

[38]While the arguments of Chapters Four and Five do suggest that some trade-offs among rights may not only be permissible but sometimes even may be necessary, it does not

commit us to the sort of utilitarianism of rights that the present objection suggests. That is, one can recognize the need for trade-offs without being committed to adopting the policy that maximizes protection of rights or minimizes their violation. Rather, one might want fairness in the distribution of benefits and burdens. For discussion of the need for trade-offs, see George Sher, "Rights Violations and Injustices: Can We always Avoid Trade-Offs," *Ethics*, Vol. 94. No. 2 (1984): 212–24.

[39]For example, we can give special weight, over and above that given to other forms of educational disadvantage, to those applicants for college admission who have attended schools which in addition to having poorly funded or otherwise weak educational programs are de facto racially segregated. Or, we can assume that all else being equal, the members of racial minorities, particularly blacks, have encountered special burdens of racial discrimination. Neither dictates that preference will be given to minority applicants over, say, disadvantaged whites, but each insures that their problems will receive special attention. In this way, we can have a "race conscious" policy which is not invidious in that (a) it does not exclude anyone from the competition, (b) it allows us to assign appropriate weight to the special difficulties facing all individuals, and (c) it does not require that members of any particular social group actually be selected.

[40]Here we adopt a suggestion made by Drew Days at a conference on civil rights, sponsored by the Center for Philosophy and Public Policy, the University of Maryland, October, 1984.

SUGGESTED READINGS

Bittker, Boris. *The Case for Black Reparations.* New York: Random House, 1973.
Cohen, Marshall, Nagel, Thomas, and Scanlon, Thomas, eds. *Equality and Preferential Treatment.* Princeton: Princeton University Press, 1977. Includes classic articles by Ronald Dworkin, Owen F. Fiss, Thomas Nagel, George Sher, Robert Simon, and Judith Jarvis Thomson.
Fullinwider, Robert. *The Reverse Discrimination Controversy.* Totowa, New Jersey: Rowman and Littlefield, 1980.
Goldman, Alan. *Justice and Reverse Discrimination.* Princeton: Princeton University Press, 1979.
Sindler, Allan P. *Bakke, DeFunis, and Minority Admissions: The Quest for Equal Opportunity.* New York: Longman Publishing Company, 1978.

Articles
Cohen, Carl. "Race and the Constitution." *The Nation*, Vol. 20, No. 5 (1973), pp. 135–45.
Ezorsky, Gertrude. "Fight Over University Women." *The New York Review of Books*, Vol. XXI, No. 8 (1984), pp. 32–39.
Goldman, Alan H. "Affirmative Action." *Philosophy & Public Affairs*, Vol. 5, No. 2 (1976), pp. 178–95.
Newton, Lisa. "Reverse Discrimination as Unjustified." *Ethics*, Vol. 83, No. 4 (1973), pp. 308–12.
Nickel, James. "Classification by Race in Compensatory Programs." *Ethics*, Vol. 84, No. 2 (1974), pp. 146–50.
Taylor, Paul. "Reverse Discrimination and Compensatory Justice." *Analysis*, Vol. 33, No. 6 (1973), pp. 177–82.

Nine
ETHICS
AND INTERNATIONAL
AFFAIRS

Do our moral obligations stop at the water's edge? Do individual citizens in the affluent nations have moral obligations to the disadvantaged millions of the Third World? Can one nation wrong another? What is the proper role of natural or human rights in foreign policy? Should states aim only at enhancing their national interest or should their pursuit of national interest be constrained by moral norms?

These and related questions suggest that at least some moral principles might apply across national boundaries. But what are these principles and upon whom are they binding? Do they apply only to individuals in interpersonal relations, or do they also apply to the conduct of such institutions as the state? For example, are states morally required to sacrifice their national interest in order to meet the demands of morality?

In this chapter, we will explore questions concerning the role of morality in international affairs. Does morality even have any significant role in the international arena? The political realists answer that it does not. Let us begin by considering their views.

THE CHALLENGE OF REALISM

Political realism is a view about the limits of morality in international affairs. Although it has distinguished contemporary adherents, it was also defended in other eras and was perhaps first described by the ancient Greek historian Thucydides.

In his *History of the Peloponnesian Wars*, Thucydides describes the "Melian dialogue" between the generals of imperial Athens and the leaders of Melos, an isolated island colony of Sparta. The Athenians demanded fealty of Melos but the independent Melians refused to submit. In Thucydides's account of the negotiations between the two sides, the Athenian generals put morality to one side. According to the generals, the reality of the situation is, "They that have . . . power exact as much as they can, and the weak yield to such conditions as they can get."[1] The Melians refused to surrender until required to do so by force of arms. Thucydides tells us that then "the Athenians . . . slew all the men of military age, made slaves of the women and children and inhabited the place with a colony."[2]

The Athenians, at least on Thucydides' account, are being "realists" in the sense of putting the interest of their city-state ahead of any moral considerations. Can such a dismissal of morality in international affairs possibly be justified?

Two Arguments for Realism

For analytical purposes, it will be useful to distinguish *descriptive* from *normative* political realism. The former is a descriptive doctrine about how nations do act while the latter is a normative doctrine about how nations should act.

> (DPR) Nations always do act in ways intended to maximize their national interest.
> (NPR) Nations always should act in ways intended to maximize their national interest.[3]

The realist arguments that we will consider are attempts to infer normative from descriptive political realism.

The first argument we will consider might be called the consequentialist argument for realism. According to this argument, which has been defended by such important contemporary writers as the late Hans Morganthau, if nations do act to promote their national interest, they will produce more overall good than if they pursue moral goals. Hence, they ought to act in ways intended to maximize their national interest.

As Morganthau fleshes out this argument, it states that if nations pursue their moral ideals in the international arena instead of realistically following their interests, their behavior will be unstable, unconstrained, and unpredictable. "What is good for the crusading country is by definition good for all mankind and if the rest of mankind refuses to accept such claims to universal recognition, it must be converted with fire and sword.[4] The fanaticism of Khomeni's Iran or the narrow but fervent anticommunism that some observers believe periodically locks U.S. foreign policy in a straightjacket might be two examples of the kind of crusading moralism against which Morganthau and other realists have warned us. On the other hand, the realists continue, if each state realistically calculates its own interests and restricts itself to their pursuit, its behavior becomes predictable, stable, and above all constrained. The kind of compromise which often is impossible on matters of deep moral difference becomes a matter of practical negotiation. Accordingly, peace, security, and toleration of national differences is best assured if every state avoids the pursuit of abstract moral ideals and pursues its own national interest instead. According to the consequentialist argument, then, if states do act to promote their national interest, they will promote the overall best consequences as well. Therefore, states should always aim at maximizing self-interest.

In addition to the consequentialist argument, realists often advance a Hobbesian argument as well, designed to show that it is morally permissible for states to promote their national interest, even when it might conflict with moral concerns.

According to the Hobbesian, since descriptive political realism is true, international affairs closely resemble the state of nature as described by Hobbes (see pp. 12-14). Just as individuals in the Hobbesian state of nature act egoistically in the pursuit of wealth and glory, so too do nations act egoistically in the pursuit of national interest. Accordingly, since each nation acts selfishly, no nation can have any reason to expect other nations to behave morally towards it. But then any nation which did act morally would be making itself vulnerable to predatory nations. As Morganthau maintains, "a foreign policy guided by universal moral principles . . . relegating the national interest to the background is under contemporary conditions . . . a policy of national suicide actual or potential."[5] Since morality does not require extreme self-sacrifice, although it may permit it, morality cannot require nations to sacrifice national interest to universal principles in a world where other nations are not prepared to do the same.

Are these arguments for realism defensible? While a thorough examination of realism requires more extended treatment than can be provided here, enough can be said to cast doubt on both the consequentialist and Hobbesian arguments.

A Critique of Realism

The consequentialist defense of realism amounts to the claim that better consequences will be promoted if nations act out of concern for national interest than if they act on moral principle. Realists who defend this argument, however, may have far too simplistic a view both of the concept of national interest and of the role morality might play in international affairs.

Is the Hobbesian argument defensible? Do international affairs resemble a Hobbesian state of nature in which states, rather than individuals, inhabit a lawless world governed only by the needs for survival and power? If so, what moral implications follow?

The claim that international affairs closely resemble a Hobbesian state of nature is controversial and has frequently been attacked, most recently by Charles Beitz in his book *Political Theory and International Relations*.[6] Beitz points to several disanalogies between the state of nature, as described by Hobbes, and international relations. In particular, he argues that for Hobbes, each individual in the state of nature is virtually self-sufficient, has a virtually equal capacity to kill any other individual and has no grounds for reasonable expectation that other individuals would adhere to any set of common norms. However, in the modern world, states are increasingly economically interdependent, small weak states do not represent serious threats to the greater powers, and general norms of international conduct, including respect for diplomatic personnel and fidelity to treaty, are generally observed.[7] While these factors are not sufficient to show that the international arena is similar to a well-ordered domestic society, for there are important differences of degree, they do cast doubt on the parallel with the "war of all against all" described by Hobbes.

However, even if international relations do resemble a Hobbesian state of nature more closely than writers such as Beitz would concede, the extreme conclusions of the realists do not follow. That is, the premises that (1) no nation can count on other nations to act morally towards it and (2) no nation is morally required to take extreme risks to its national interest do not entail (3) no moral requirements exist in international affairs. Rather, premises 1 and 2 establish at most that nations are not required to take severe risks, not that they are permitted to do anything which enhances their national interest to any degree. Similarly, an individual in a Hobbesian state of nature may not be morally required to unilaterally disarm. It does not follow that he is permitted to torture, rape, mutilate, or otherwise victimize others without provocation merely for his own momentary gratification.

So far, the assumptions of the realist that (a) international affairs are a Hobbesian state of nature and (b) that if international affairs are a Hobbesian state of nature, then anything goes, have each been criticized. Equally open to criticism are the realist's assumptions about the nature of morality and about the nature of the national interest itself, assumptions which underlie the consequentialist defense of realism in international affairs.

According to the consequentialist defense of realism, reliance on morality in world affairs will lead to dangerous and intolerant crusades in the name of ideals; only reliance on the common standard of national interest will insure predictability, restraint, and international stability. But at this stage of our inquiry, it probably is unnecessary to point out that the role of morality in world affairs need not be restricted to the kind of crusading moralism rightly rejected by the realists. As we have seen in our discussions in other chapters, moral inquiry need not be dogmatic, rigid, and intolerant. Willingness to compromise competing values, tolerance of differences, and sensitivity to the consequences of actions are themselves elements of a rational employment of morality in human affairs. It is far from clear that such a sensitive and rational morality will have the disastrous consequences predicted by realism if employed in the international arena.

Perhaps equally open to question is the assumption of the realists that the national interest constitutes a clear and objective standard for generating our own policies and predicting the behavior of other nations. We suggest that on the contrary, the idea of national interest is subject to various interpretations and is as open to debate and misunderstanding as are the basic concepts of morality and ethics.

In particular, the realist's argument assumes that the national interest will be understood the same way by all observers regardless of their own normative commitments or ideological frameworks. Only if there is a common understanding of a nation's interest will all observers agree in their predictions about what the nation's self-interested behavior will be. Only if predictions are reliable in this way will the behavior of states seem stable and rational and miscalculation be avoided. Imagine the damage if U.S. policy makers based a prediction that the U.S.S.R. would not go to war in response to a certain provocation on the calculation that war is not in the Soviet Union's national interest, when in fact the conception of national interest employed by the Russian leaders was very different from that postulated by American analysts.

In fact, conceptions of the national interest can differ along a variety of dimensions. What is to count as the nation; a majority of its citizens, a set of institutions and laws, or a geographic territory? Is the nation's interest to be identified simply with aggrandizement of power, or might ideal elements also enter in? For example, is the United States's national interest necessarily enhanced by an increase in military strength even if that results in reduced respect for democratic institutions throughout the world?

Disaster in international affairs, then, can arise not only from crusading moralism but also from one state basing its own foreign policy upon mistaken assumptions about how other states see their national interest. The idea of national interest seems to be a *contested* one: proponents of different ideologies may well advocate different conceptions of the national interest. If so, the idea of national interest, rather than providing a clear, predictable, and neutral basis for the generation, explanation, and prediction of policy, is itself at the center of debate over what policy should be. As the late Charles Frankel, a philosopher and former official of the Department of State, has told us,

> A national interest is not a chart pinned to the wall from which one takes one's sense of direction. The heart of the decision making process . . . is not the finding of the best means to serve a national interest already perfectly known and understood. It is the determining of that interest itself: the reassessment of the nation's resources, needs, commitments, traditions and political and cultural horizons—in short, its calendar of values.[8]

In short, since the nature of the national interest is open to interpretation and debate, the idea that it can serve as an ideologically neutral standard for justifying, explaining, and predicting the behavior of states seems mistaken.

While we have not considered all possible defenses of political realism, we hope to have shown that since the two principal arguments for realism are open to serious objection, realism itself is far from being an obvious choice. Given our initial intuition that Athenians violated the requirements of justice in warfare in their treatment of the Melians, the burden of proof would seem to be shifted to the realist. Accordingly, we will go on to discuss concrete moral issues in international affairs. Perhaps the most convincing refutation of realism, once its major defenses have been defused, is to show how morality might actually apply in the world arena. We will begin with a problem facing individuals as much as nations, the problem of famine and world hunger. What are our moral obligations to the severely disadvantaged in other lands?

WORLD HUNGER AND THE OBLIGATIONS
OF THE AFFLUENT

The terrible plight of the world's most seriously disadvantaged people raises many issues for public policy. Among those issues are those having to do with the millions of victims of famine and near starvation throughout the globe. Consider the parents who watch their children slowly starve during the almost hopeless retreat along dusty roads from an area struck by famine. Consider the millions whose health is damaged, whose rational capacities may be impaired, because of inadequate diet. What are the obligations of the more fortunate to alleviate such suffering?

Many of the issues raised by this question are empirical and conceptual as well as moral. For example, how extensive is world hunger? Such a question looks like a purely factual one, to be settled by empirical inquiry.

However, it also raises an important conceptual issue. How is "hunger" to be defined? By varying our criteria of undernutrition and starvation, we can come up with widely different figures as to the extent of world hunger.

It sometimes is charged that some nations and organizations try to minimize the problem by maintaining that serious starvation is not as widespread as many health organizations claim. On the other hand, some observers, such as Nick Eberstadt, argue that inflated figures hurt the poor.

> Food relief and development projects for seventy million people, spread across ninety countries, are a manageable undertaking, and with some international cooperation could be attempted fairly easily. If on the other hand, the number of starving were believed to be a billion the task might seem unmanageable or hopeless and for the governments involved politically dangerous to boot.[9]

As we will see, empirical and conceptual disagreement over the nature and extent of world hunger has implications for the moral analysis of the issue. What are the moral obligations of the more advantaged nations and peoples of the world in light of world hunger? At least one writer, biologist Garrett Hardin, has argued that the more advantaged not only have no obligation to help, but may well be morally required not to help. Let us begin by considering his views.

Lifeboat Ethics and the Tragedy of the Commons

Hardin uses two analogies, that of lifeboat ethics and that of the tragedy of the commons, to make his case. Hardin begins by asking us to imagine that after a shipwreck, we sit with fifty other people in a fairly well-provisioned lifeboat. We find our boat surrounded by one hundred other survivors, treading water and asking for provisions. Since ". . . they can all be seen as 'our brothers,' we could take them all into the boat, making a total of one hundred fifty in a boat designed for sixty. The boat swamps, everyone drowns. Complete justice, complete catastrophe."[10] Perhaps we could at least let an additional ten people into the boat, for after all its carrying capacity is sixty. Hardin replies that "If we do let an extra ten into the lifeboat, we will have lost our 'safety factor,' an engineering principle of critical importance."[11] Our own security would have been thrown into great danger.

The analogy to world hunger is fairly clear. If those of us in the affluent countries rescue the starving, we will all be swamped as world population grows and more and more people continue to need our aid. Those rescued will reproduce, so by saving some starving people now, we will be responsible for even more starving people later, until we are all overwhelmed by needs far too extensive to be met at all. By limiting suffering now, we would have produced even more suffering later. Aid would make the situation drastically worse, not better.

Hardin's argument is reinforced by the example of the tragedy of the commons.

> If a pasture becomes a commons open to all, the right of each to use it may not be matched by a corresponding responsibility to protect it. . . . the considerate herdsman who refrains from overloading the commons suffers more than a selfish one who says his needs are greater.[12]

In short, everyone has an incentive to overload the commons. If I refrain from overloading, I will be exploited by those with no scruples. Since everyone reasons the same way and no one wants to pointlessly sacrifice his or her welfare, everyone overloads and the commons is eventually destroyed. Similarly, the simple provision of aid, as if it came from a global commons, will simply encourage more and more irresponsible behavior on the part of the recipients, until the global commons is exhausted and we are all reduced to the level of the severely disadvantaged.

Are Hardin's arguments decisive? Should we apply his lifeboat ethic to world hunger? What are the real implications of the tragedy of the commons? Let us consider Hardin's position in some depth.

A critique of lifeboat ethics   Unfortunately for his perspective, Hardin's position rests on some very debatable factual and moral assumptions. For one thing, Hardin makes the empirical assumptions that if aid is given to disadvantaged nations so as to minimize or prevent starvation, population will rise and if population rises, the standard of living will fall still further. Each of these assumptions faces serious difficulties.

Even if aid is given to a developing country to prevent starvation, that aid can be accompanied by birth control devices and instruction. Aid does not have to be all of one type. Indeed, aid might be given only to those countries who are willing to implement birth control policies, or at least such states may be given priority in receipt of aid. (Such a selective policy might seem objectionable on humanitarian grounds, but one might want to go half way with Hardin here and reply that one should give aid where it will do the most good.)

Perhaps of greater importance, there is evidence which indicates that when a developing nation becomes better off, its rate of population growth tends to decrease.[13] This may be because children are considered a resource in a poor nation; they bring in income and care for parents in old age. In a poor country, it pays to have many children since only a few will survive to maturity. However, as the country becomes more affluent, a higher percentage of children survive, the family tends to have resources which it might rather invest elsewhere than in child care. There is less incentive to have many children as a form of old age insurance. The better off the developing country becomes, the less its population may grow.[14]

Finally, even if population in developing nations does grow, it does not necessarily imply that the standard of living will fall. Highly populated Japan, as well as the Benelux countries, have shown that efficient use of human capital can produce a high standard of living along with high population density.

Hardin, of course, might reply that while his empirical assumptions are not self-evident, neither are those of his opponents. Perhaps provision of aid will only generate more problems. Even a lowered rate of population growth in some developing nations may not be enough to help so long as the size of the population grows. Be that as it may, it is important to see that Hardin's predictions are highly controversial.

His moral assumptions are highly controversial as well. The moral theory upon which his argument seems to be based is some version of utilitarianism. It is because the alleged consequences of famine relief would be bad that Hardin rejects such aid. However, if, as we have argued, natural or human rights constrain the pursuit of utility, appeal to utilitarian consequences does not settle the case, particularly when Hardin's own predictions are open to question.

Thus, some proponents of an approach to morality which makes rights and justice more fundamental than utility may question whether those on the lifeboat—the citizens of the more affluent states—have any right to be there. Are their secure places the result of exploitation of the less affluent nations through colonialism, or just the result of the luck of being born in the right place at the right time? In either case, the fact that some are fortunate enough to be in the well-provisioned lifeboats does not mean they are morally entitled to their favored status.

A more moderate critic might acknowledge that many of those in the developed nations do have rights to their position, rights they have either earned, legitimately inherited, or which are natural rights. For example, the right to liberty may protect us against great interference with our lives, even if it is simply moral luck that we have enough to eat and someone born in Chad does not. (Similarly, even if I have healthy kidneys and you do not through accidents of birth, it does not follow that you can appropriate my kidneys without consent; you are blocked by my right to personal liberty.) However, the moderate critic will still want to argue that the idea of positive rights to a minimal welfare floor, which we have defended in Chapter Three, supports claims of entitlement of the starving. If there is a natural right to a minimally decent standard of living, the affluent will be morally obligated to make some contribution, even across national boundaries.

Is this kind of approach any more defensible than Hardin's? Let us go on to consider an argument for the view that the affluent of the world have stringent moral obligations to help relieve world hunger.

The Case for Sacrifice

Peter Singer, an Australian philosopher who has written on a wide variety of social issues, argues that individuals in the developed nations have extensive and demanding obligations to relieve starvation.[15] Singer argues from the following assumptions:

1. Suffering and death from lack of food, shelter, and medical care are bad.
2. If it is in our power to prevent something bad from happening, without thereby sacrificing something of comparable moral importance, we ought morally to do it.

Given these assumptions, Singer maintains that since starvation clearly is bad, then we ought to give as much as we can to prevent it, up to the point where deprivation would cost us more than what we give up would benefit the recipient.

It might be objected that the fact that many of the world's starving live far away and are citizens of other countries blunts our obligation, but Singer would deny this. After all, suppose I could save a child drowning in a nearby swimming pool by throwing her a life raft and save a child in an underdeveloped country by mailing a check for an amount I do not need. Why should the difference in proximity make a difference to the force of my obligation in either case?

Let us accept this point, at least for now, and consider assumption 2, which states that if it is within our power to prevent something bad from happening without thereby sacrificing something of comparable moral importance, we ought to do it. How is this principle to be defended?

Sometimes Singer seems to defend the principle by appealing to example. Thus, he points out that "if I am walking past a shallow pond and see a child drowning . . ., I ought to wade in and pull the child out" even if this means getting my new clothes muddy in the process.[16] However, this example does not support principle 2 since the sacrifice involved is relatively minor. It does not establish an obligation to sacrifice something significant let alone an obligation of the affluent to reduce themselves to near poverty to rescue the starving. To support 2, Singer would have to show that the rescuer has an obligation to risk his or her life to save the child. Since it is far from clear that such heroic action is morally required, Singer probably cannot defend 2 by appeal to example.

Perhaps it can be defended by appeal to the more general principle of impartiality. If everyone is to count as a fundamental moral equal of everyone else, we have no basis for favoring our own welfare over that of other people. If each counts for one and only one, preventing X from suffering a certain evil is morally required so long as the cost to me is less, even if only slightly less, than the evil I prevent by sacrificing my own interests. Otherwise, I am favoring myself and violating the principle of impartiality.

Looked at in this way, however, 2 looks suspiciously like a variant of utilitarianism, which might be called negative utilitarianism. Unlike standard utilitarianism, it does not require us to promote the good of others. But it does require us to aggregate the avoidance of evil so as to minimize total bad consequences of our acts or practices. If so, it is open to a number of the objections against utilitarianism which we discussed in Chapter Two.

In particular, Singer's negative utilitarianism seems to leave little room for individuals to live their own lives, carry out their own projects, and develop in ways they choose for themselves. Rather, it requires individuals to sacrifice control over the direction of their lives, so long as by doing so, they (perhaps only minimally) reduce the suffering of others. While such sacrifice may be heroic, it is far from clear that it is morally required.

A proponent of Singer's view might reply that our criticism of 2 rests on a question begging appeal to the intuitions of our readers. People in our culture, the critic might maintain, have been brought up to think of morality as relatively undemanding; as a set of constraints protecting individual liberty but not requiring much of the individual. Utilitarianism, however, attempts to *reform* this traditional moral perspective. A more demanding morality, the critic maintains, is more appropriate in a world where suffering is so frequent. To reject utilitarianism on the grounds that it is too demanding is to beg the question since the rejection is based on appeal to traditional moral intuitions which the utilitarian would reject.

This last ditch utilitarian defense is a thoughtful one, but we suggest that it does not carry the day. For one thing, utilitarianism itself sometimes is defended by appeal to the intuition that we ought to be benevolent towards others. Perhaps more important, if utilitarianism implies that individual autonomy and the capacity for persons to live their own lives are not significant, it is hard to see how individual freedom and liberty can be accommodated within a utilitarian framework. Finally, if morality is made so demanding that people psychologically cannot live up to it—or are called upon to sacrifice virtually all their nonmoral goals on the altar of moral goodness—morality will come to be seen only as an abstract ideal with no real bearing on human life. The "strains of commitment" of adherence to a strict utilitarian morality may be too great; a point Singer himself has acknowledged in recent writings.[17]

In any case, if, as we have argued, respect for the individual as a choosing autonomous person is itself a fundamental moral value, a utilitarian ethic of world hunger which does not take such a value into consideration is open to the charge of swallowing up the person in the long run pursuit of a better world. While, as we will argue, some sacrifice is required in a world where great suffering cries out for alleviation, it is doubtful that the more advantaged individual should be viewed simply as a mere means for the alleviation of suffering as Singer's variant of utilitarianism seems to require.

It also is worth noting that Singer's position, like that of Hardin, rests on factual assumptions about world hunger. In particular, his discussion seems to at least suggest that world hunger can best be dealt with by individual self-sacrifice on the part of the relatively affluent. If, as recent studies suggest, world hunger is paradoxically not due to severe food shortages but rather to the maldistribution of an adequate food supply, the best long-term solution may well involve political action at the state level designed to bring about institutional change in developing countries.[18] While this perhaps does not eliminate the need for interim help by individuals, it does call into question the assumption that we can make others better off by making ourselves collectively worse off. It is at least arguable, although perhaps self-serving, to maintain that the Western nations need to remain affluent in order to contribute to an expanding world economy and in order to retain the influence needed to promote reform in the distribution of food in the developing world.[19]

World Hunger and Natural Rights

Our discussion suggests that a position on world hunger more demanding than Hardin's but not quite so demanding as Singer's might be worth consideration. In particular, if people have the natural right to a minimally decent standard of living, that right, since it is natural, applies across national boundaries. On the other hand, if people possess natural rights to liberty, and exercise those rights as members of social organizations, they acquire special obligations within those institutions; obligations to children, spouses, co-workers, and fellow citizens. Those obligations may frequently conflict with obligations to aid those in other lands. Moreover, as autonomous persons, it is far from clear that we are obligated to sacrifice our own life plan in order to benefit others, although it might well be especially praiseworthy should we choose to do so.

Singer has suggested that those who find 2 too stringent may want to replace it with 2' below.

> (2') If it is in our power to prevent something very bad from happening without thereby sacrificing anything else morally significant, we ought, morally, to do it.

2' differs from 2 in that it allows a wider range of excuses for non-compliance; we may violate 2 only in order to preserve something of *comparable* worth but may violate 2' to preserve a morally significant but not necessarily comparable goal. The trouble with 2', however, is that it seems empty without some specification of just what has moral significance.

Perhaps the natural rights perspective can help here. As we developed that perspective in Chapter Three, it required that individuals be respected as autonomous, rational agents. Natural or human rights are fundamental conditions that must be protected if humans are to be respected in such a way. Therefore, obligations which arise from the rights of others have greater moral authority than moral considerations such as benevolence. It may be morally good to be benevolent; it is morally required that we honor our obligations. Among the obligations which the rights of others impose on us is the duty to promote the positive rights of others; human rights to minimally decent conditions of welfare without which humans cannot develop or function as rational and autonomous agents.

As Singer argues, it is hard to see why such an obligation should end at the water's edge. Perhaps the primary obligation to help the world's disadvantaged does fall on their own governments. But when such governments are unable or unwilling to help, it is difficult to see why a difference in citizenship alone should block our obligation to help.

On the other hand, the natural rights perspective recognizes that positive rights claims of recipients are constrained by the negative rights of potential donors. If humans are to be respected as rational and autonomous beings, each individual should be left free to develop and follow an autonomously selected plan of life, consistent with reasonable contributions to support the positive rights of others. Moreover, our obligations to our families and to those others to whom we have special obligations may limit our degree of responsibility to help alleviate world hunger or promote a more egalitarian distribution of wealth throughout the world. Singer may be on strong grounds, however, when he argues that a mere concern for luxuries, which is not necessarily wrong in itself, does not excuse us from meeting our obligations to those who suffer abroad any more than it excuses us from paying taxes at home.

Finally, it is important to remember that the most effective means of fighting world hunger may exist at the institutional rather than collective level. Perhaps the best contribution we can make requires not simply financial contributions, but rather political judgment at the institutional level. Although the proper response of individuals to a particular famine may be to provide relief, it is an open question whether the long-term solution to not only world hunger but underdevelopment in the Third World is redistribution. Development policies, which emphasize growth, also need to be considered. Although such programs may themselves raise questions of distributive justice, as when a developing country sacrifices its poorest people in order to save capital for future growth, some combination of development and redistribution may produce morally more defensible results than uncoordinated giving on the individual level alone.

However, the developed nations need to be careful about interference in Third World nations which can sometimes have unfortunate consequences. For example, market pressure on such countries to switch from crops which can be consumed at home to cash crops for sale abroad is viewed by many experts as one factor which contributes to poverty.[20] At the same time, internal maldistribution and corruption within the developing nations may result in foreign aid being diverted from those it was designed to help to the ruling elite. Ideological narrowness in the Third World, which may lead some developing nations to blindly reject market approaches to problems regardless of circumstances, may also unnecessarily retard development.

Accordingly, while individuals may have responsibilities to provide aid, action at the institutional level designed to create global systems of equitable distribution may ultimately be what a morally defensible approach to world hunger requires. Be that as it may, individuals do have obligations to make reasonable contributions, in light of their own situation, to maintain the positive rights of starving people abroad. These obligations may demand more sacrifice than most of us are willing to acknowledge, although we doubt if they require as much of us as Singer's position suggests. But while we do have a right, as autonomous rational agents, to a significant degree of freedom as to how we live our lives, this does not imply that our obligations to others stop at the water's edge.

NATURAL RESOURCES AND GLOBAL JUSTICE

Many of the world's less developed nations have maintained, in the United Nations and in other international forums, that a New International Economic Order, designed to more equally distribute the world's wealth, ought to be implemented. On their view, the current unequal distribution of wealth and resources between the developed nations and the Third World is inequitable and unjust. International treaties, including the proposed Law of the Sea Treaty, rejected by the United States in 1982, contain provisions calling for a shift of resources toward the underdeveloped nations.

Although the general topic of global justice extends far beyond claims to natural resources, entitlements to natural resources are a central area of concern. Should a nation that lies on rich oil deposits or fertile fields have an absolute and exclusive claim to the fruits of what may be nothing more than good luck? Should natural resources which lie outside national boundaries, such as mineral deposits in Antarctica, in the depths of the sea, or in outer space, be regarded as the exclusive property of the discoverers, or should they be regarded as part of a global commons, "the common heritage of mankind"?

Resource-rich nations may have enormous advantages over resource-poor ones. An individual born into a resource-rich country may, through an accident of birth, have a far longer, healthier, and more interesting life than an individual born into a resource-poor nation. Is such a situation fair or equitable?

In this section, we will explore two influential positions on ownership of natural resources. During the discussion, it will be important to keep in mind the distinction between natural resources which lie within national boundaries and those which do not, since different principles may apply in each case.

Locke and Libertarian Entitlements

Libertarianism, as understood here and discussed in Chapter Four, is the political philosophy which holds that it always is impermissible to interfere with personal liberty. For libertarians, the liberty to appropriate and exchange property is a particularly important one. But how does property get appropriated in the first place? An answer to that question might shed important light on claims to ownership of natural resources.

Many libertarians rely on a theory of appropriation proposed by John Locke, whose views we discussed in Chapter Three. According to Locke, as long as we are in the state of nature, we are entitled to our body, and our labor being our own, we can appropriate property by mixing our labor with it. Owners of justly appropriated property can freely exchange it among themselves through the market, or can voluntarily transfer entitlements by giving gifts.

If we view international affairs as something like a Lockean state of nature, with nations having rights logically parallel to those of individuals in Locke's theory, then nations can be regarded as being entitled to control resources just as individual persons have control over their bodies. Moreover, states or other collective entities, such as corporations, can appropriate resources lying outside their own national boundaries by mixing their labor (or that of their agents) with it. For example, an American mining consortium can come to own mineral deposits on the deep sea bed through deep sea mining. On this view, since it is the corporation which has invested the resources, technology, and labor into deep sea mining, it acquires an entitlement to the minerals at the mining site.

This position is a libertarian one, since entitlements to resources arise from individuals or collectives exercising their liberty over their bodies. If we could not collectively or individually appropriate property through our free actions, our liberty to control our lives would be significantly restricted. In addition, such free appropriation also may enhance efficiency since it rewards the productive and the enterprising.

A Critique of Libertarian Entitlements

Since the Libertarian Entitlement Theory has been examined in Chapter Four, the discussion here will focus on its application to appropriation of natural resources rather than on its overall validity.

To begin with, even adherents of the Lockean theory of appropriation sometimes will admit that it is vague at crucial points. How much labor must be invested in resources before one can claim them? Why, as Robert Nozick asks, doesn't the laborer lose his labor rather than gain property? For example, if you grew a tomato, made tomato juice from it, and mixed the juice with the Atlantic Ocean, you would lose your tomato juice rather than acquire the Atlantic.[21] Finally, how broad is your entitlement? For example, if you come to own a valuable resource, do you have a right to use it in ways that may harm your neighbors? For example, can you pollute at will simply because your mining operation is on your property? What are the limitations on Lockean entitlements generated by the rights of others?

These are general difficulties with the Lockean theory of acquisition. It is important to see that they count just as much against collective acquisition of property by a socialist state as against individualist acquisition by members of a capitalist one so long as either is defended on Lockean grounds.

Clearly, there is a problem, although not necessarily an unsolvable one, of explaining how property can be justly appropriated in the first place.[22] Rather than deal at length with the general problem, which might be resolved by revision of the Lockean approach, or by a more broad-based appeal either to the utility of various rules for acquiring property or their relevance to preservation of individual freedom, we will consider in depth a particular argument against full appropriation of natural resources. Proponents of this argument maintain that even if the Lockean or some other individualistic approach to appropriation of other kinds of property is correct, none of these approaches apply to natural resources.

Resource Egalitarianism and the Geologic Lottery

Resource egalitarianism is the view that natural resources are "the common heritage of mankind": that everyone in the world has an equal claim to benefit from their development. As so defined, resource egalitarianism contradicts the libertarian view since it denies that natural resources can be fully owned and totally controlled by the appropriators.

The first argument for resource egalitarianism which we will consider is based upon the "geologic lottery." That is, the resource egalitarian can argue that the location of natural resources throughout the globe is a matter of moral luck. The Saudis have done nothing to deserve the huge oil deposits in their territories, nor have Americans done anything to deserve the mineral deposits or fertile soil found within the continental United States. Location of resources is the result of a geologic lottery for which no human is responsible. Since no one is responsible for the location of natural resources, no one can claim to deserve control of them. Therefore, they must be regarded as the common heritage of mankind, to be developed and used for the benefit of all.

According to writers such as Charles Beitz, such a position would be endorsed from a global version of Rawls's original position; an initial situation in which the veil of ignorance (see Chapter Four) is extended to cover knowledge of citizenship.

> The fact that someone happens to be located advantageously with respect to natural resources does not provide a reason why he or she should be entitled to exclude others from the benefits that might be derived from them. Therefore, the parties would think that resources (or the benefits derived from them) should be subject to redistribution under a resource redistribution principle.[23]

Moreover, Beitz maintains that such an argument is more defensible than Rawls's similar treatment of natural abilities and talents: ". . . unlike talents, resources are not naturally attached to persons. . . . Thus, while we might feel that the possession of talents confers a right to control and benefit from their use, we feel differently about resources."[24]

Critique of the Lottery Argument

Is the lottery argument decisive? Before it is accepted, at least three kinds of objections need to be considered. First, it is important to be clear about exactly what the lottery argument establishes. Properly understood, it does not establish that ownership of or entitlement to natural resources is either morally or conceptually inappropriate. Rather, what it shows, at most, is that claims to entitlement or ownership cannot be based on personal or collective desert. However, if ownership is conceived of as a set of rules which, for example, promote utility if generally observed, or as a means of implementing the right to liberty, the appeal to the geologic lottery is beside the point.

Even ignoring this point, the lottery argument is open to further objection. In particular, it does not deal with the distinction between *actual* and *potential* resources. It is true that no one is responsible for the distribution of potential resources around the globe. No human, for example, placed huge oil deposits in the Middle East. However, oil deposits become an actual resource only given a technology which can utilize them. Given a less advanced technology than now exists, or a much more advanced one, today's valuable oil supplies might be virtually worthless.

What is the significance of the distinction between actual and potential resources? The point is this: Although no one is responsible for the initial distribution of potential resources, persons and collectivities such as nations can be responsible for turning potential into actual resources. An individual, by inventing a new technology, or a state, by supporting an enlightened policy with respect to science and education, can be responsible for the development of the technology which most efficiently utilizes the available resources. Since the lottery argument only applies to potential resources, it cannot be used to show a priori that claims to actual resources cannot be based on desert, although of course in specific instances the lottery argument may be found to apply even to actual resources after detailed examination of particular cases. It cannot be used to generally discredit desert claims; whether it has force in particular instances depends on the facts of the particular cases at hand.

This point has special application to natural resources found outside national boundaries, such as mineral deposits lying in the deep sea bed. For the ability to mine and develop such resources depends upon a complex combination of policies influencing technological development, education, and basic research in the sciences; precisely the kinds of things for which individuals and groups can plausibly claim credit.

It is open to the proponent of the lottery argument to reply that no one deserves the good luck to be born into the kind of society which makes efficient use of its human capital. Once this move is taken, however, we seem to be back with the general Rawlsian argument that no one deserves individual talents and capacities. For if a society's development is at least in part due to such factors, and if people have the right to pass on at least some of those benefits to their descendants and to their fellow citizens, then even if one does not deserve to be born into an advantaged position, one may be entitled to some (although perhaps not all) of the inherited initial advantages anyway. So unless the proponent of the lottery argument is willing to extend it from geology to the individual level, an extension which writers such as Beitz try to avoid (perhaps because of the disadvantages pointed out in Chapter Four), the appeal to the geologic lottery cannot be used as a general tool to undermine claims of entitlement or ownership to natural resources.

RESOURCE EGALITARIANISM AND POSITIVE RIGHTS

We have seen so far that there are difficulties both with an unrestricted Lockean entitlement approach to natural resources that special claims to natural resources never are justified because all such claims must be based on pure luck. Perhaps a view combining the best elements of resource egalitarianism and a libertarian entitlement theory might be worth considering.

While we are not able to present a full theory of how global justice might bear upon appropriation of natural resources, the account of natural or human rights sketched earlier does have implications in this area which may be worth consideration. The ground of such rights is the basic idea that humans are owed respect and concern as rational autonomous creatures. Part of such respect involves acknowledging the worth of human liberty; including the freedom to join and act as members of groups or institutions formed to secure goals that cannot be secured by individuals acting alone. Nations and corporations may at least sometimes constitute such groups. While there is a real problem as to whether unjust nations, those that fail to respect the status of their citizens as free and autonomous beings, should have the same rights and status as reasonably just ones, the liberty of individuals to participate in collectives is the ground for collective claims over natural resources.

Thus, if the function of government is to protect the rights and interests of its citizens, subject to moral constraints of not violating the rights of others, and this requires territorial integrity, nations have at least a prima facie right to control who has access to resources within territories. Similarly, if nations or corporations take risks to develop resources lying in previously inaccessible areas lying outside national boundaries, they may have claims to a profit based upon desert or upon compensation for investment (and the risks which go along with it).

However, none of this implies that such resources ought to be under the absolute control of the developer or the host nation. This is because in addition to negative rights, each individual has a positive right to a minimally decent standard of living. Although a nation's leaders arguably may have a duty to put the crucial interests of their fellow citizens first, this does not imply that they can ignore the natural rights of others. Thus, in our view, the affluent nations, and their citizens, are under an obligation to make reasonable contributions to an overall scheme of global justice designed to ultimately create a global welfare floor below which no citizen of the world will be allowed to fall. While such a global welfare floor is at present utopian, there is an obligation to take reasonable steps, in light of other pressing obligations and needs, to help make it a reality. One possible way of doing so is expecting those collectivities—nations or corporations—which develop resources lying outside national boundaries to pay an international tax on profits for such an end. Ideally, the demands of justice, while not so demanding as to unduly limit most individuals' life plans, do apply across national boundaries.

The Ideal and the Actual in International Affairs

The developed nations have received much criticism, not only from Third World countries but from many of their own concerned citizens, for not providing sufficient nonmilitary aid to less developed areas of the globe. It has been charged that less than 1 percent of the U.S. gross national product is devoted to such aid. This is a shockingly low total, even if one adds the U.S. contributions to those of the U.N. and the World Bank, contributions which the critics often ignore.

While we share the view that an increase in such nonmilitary aid is warranted—and warranted on grounds of global justice rather than charity—we do note that there is a difficulty in jumping too quickly from premises about what justice ideally requires to conclusions about actual policy.

In particular, if global justice is based on individualistic concerns, as it is in our account of natural rights or Beitz's attempt to apply Rawls's theory to international affairs, it is unclear just how it applies in a world of states. That is, global justice as so conceived justifies distributive principles for individuals but actual distribution in the real world is among states. The problem, of course, is that unjust states may use any wealth they receive for unjust purposes rather than apply it to alleviating the plight of individuals.

Thus, the proposed Law of the Sea Treaty, which in part would have regulated the development of undersea resources, and which was rejected by the United States in 1982 in spite of acceptance by virtually all the other nations of the globe, called for some redistribution of the benefits of deep sea mining to less developed nations. The U.S. rejection, based in part on professed adherence to a Lockean entitlement theory (and perhaps also on economic self-interest), was criticized by those at home and abroad who viewed the deep sea bed as a global commons to be developed for the benefit of all.

Although these criticisms are not without force, the Law of the Sea Treaty was at best an imperfect instrument of global justice. For it did not require either that recipient countries be internally just or use redistributed benefits in just ways. Indeed, given the sorry record of many such states, some of the benefits almost surely would have been used for unjust purposes. It is arguable that the U.S. should have signed the Treaty, although reasons other than those of global justice (such as the need for a stable international arena) seem most compelling. Given the defects of the entitlement theory, the Treaty surely was rejected for the wrong reasons. Nevertheless, in view of the distinction between the actual and the ideal, it is doubtful that acceptance of the Treaty was actually required by considerations of global justice.[25]

In view of these considerations, an enlightened foreign policy would have as one of its principle aims a negative one. We should not act so as to violate or contribute to violation of rights abroad. While implementation of a global welfare floor may be beyond our present powers in the actual world, we can try to avoid economic policies which exploit others or support of dictatorships which grossly violate human rights. We can also take reasonable steps, in view of the realities, to implement positive rights. Surely, we can and should do far more in this area than we are doing at present.

Nevertheless, as we have seen, rights can conflict. Although we should be suspicious of politicians who use the contested concept of national interest to justify any policy however gross, international realities may force unpleasant choices upon us. For example, should we continue support for a repressive but friendly dictatorship if the alternative may be its replacement by an at least equally repressive and hostile opposition?

Philosophy alone cannot settle such hard cases. What is required in addition is thorough knowledge of the facts and wise judgment concerning different policy alternatives. Nevertheless, moral principle is not irrelevant to international affairs. While the concrete application of moral principles to international affairs raises many difficulties, over which good and reasonable people may disagree, such principles do set constraints to which any justifiable foreign policy must conform.[26]

THE MORALITY OF NUCLEAR DETERRENCE

No discussion of the role of ethics in international affairs would be complete without considering what surely is the greatest threat to the continuation of the human race: nuclear war. Since the start of the nuclear arms race, the two nuclear superpowers, the Soviet Union and the United States, have relied on the policy of massive retaliation or mutual assured destruction (known, aptly in the view of many, as M.A.D.). A nuclear attack by one power would be deterred by the threat of massive nuclear retaliation by the other. In recent years, there has been talk among strategic experts, and some actual movement, towards a counterforce strategy in which nuclear weapons would be targeted at enemy weapons systems rather than cities, but massive retaliation is still the dominant doctrine of nuclear strategy accepted by the superpowers.

Is such a policy morally defensible? Could it ever be moral to use nuclear weapons? Is the strategy of counterforce morally superior to M.A.D.? Is unilateral nuclear disarmament the only moral policy? Or does the safety of the United States and the West, as well as the human rights of hundreds of millions of people outside the Soviet Union, depend on our continued reliance on the policy of massive retaliation?

Clearly, anything close to a full-fledged nuclear exchange represents a devastating threat, not only to the superpowers themselves, but to all life on earth. Although no one can be sure of what the consequences of such an exchange would be, it is important to keep in mind that in addition to immediate casualties of blast and fire storm, millions more would die lingering deaths because of radiation sickness. Disease and plague would take their toll among a weakened population. Hospitals, physicians, and medical supplies would be scarce at best, since many such persons and facilities are located in target areas or would be destroyed in the aftermath of an attack. The capacity of the land to produce food might be endangered by long-term irradiation of the soil. Recently, prominent scientists have argued that the huge clouds of dust raised by such an exchange might cause an extended "nuclear winter" which would threaten all life on earth. Even the effects of a smaller nuclear exchange directed at military targets would cause millions of civilian casualties, including that of noncombatants in other countries who would be affected by radiation from fallout and possible climatic changes.

In light of this, is there any moral justification for possession of nuclear weapons, let alone the formation and implementation of a policy of mutual deterrence, or even counterforce? American defenders of prevailing policy argue that until the Soviet Union can be induced to enter into verifiable arms control agreements, the policy of deterrence is morally justified. The threat of nuclear deterrence is needed not simply to prevent a Soviet nuclear first strike but also to prevent Soviet nuclear blackmail which would render us unable to defend our friends or our interests, and would perhaps subject millions to oppression. Defenders of deterrence often point to Western military weakness and failure of nerve as an impetus to Hitler's aggression. Perhaps if the West had been more resolute, the evils associated with World War II could have been prevented. Deterrence, in this view, provides the best chance for peace while appeasement will lead to Soviet domination and repression. Is such a view defensible? Let us consider criticisms of it in greater depth.

A Critique of Deterrence

Critics of deterrence advance several important arguments in support of their view. While we cannot consider all of them here, several are of special interest.

Often, a critique of deterrence starts out with the premise that the employment of nuclear weapons, at least on any large scale, is immoral and absolutely prohibited on ethical grounds. Such a principle is supported by at least the two following sorts of considerations. First, the damage from nuclear war is so terrible that no goal to be attained through the use of nuclear weapons could outweigh the harm caused. Indeed, if nuclear war would result in the destruction of civilization as we know it, it could not be a means to any goal whatsoever. Second, because of the widespread damage caused by fallout, the spread of disease among survivors, climatic change, and massive disruption of commerce, millions of innocent people in militarily uninvolved countries would die or suffer horribly. The critic of deterrence argues that given these consequences, the massive use of nuclear weapons cannot be morally justified.

Although such a claim may be more controversial than critics of deterrence sometimes allow, we shall accept it here and try to see what follows.[27] Proponents of deterrence might reply that even if the large-scale *use* of nuclear weapons is morally prohibited, it does not follow that the *threat* to use such weapons is prohibited as well.[28] Suppose, for example, that it is morally prohibited for me to kill an innocent child. Nevertheless, it might be permissible for me to threaten to kill the innocent child of a terrorist who is about to poison a major city's water supply if by so doing I could prevent the death of millions of other innocents. In this view, the policy of nuclear deterrence is designed to prevent both the tragedy of nuclear war and that of domination by repressive nations.

However, such a rejoinder is far from conclusive. The critic of deterrence might offer the following objections: First, the benefits of deterrence are either illusory or outweighed by the costs. Second, nuclear deterrence differs from the example above in that in order for deterrence to be effective, nations must form the conditional intention to actually use nuclear weapons if the other side attacks. To form the intention to kill millions of people, and perhaps destroy the human race, is morally wrong. Moreover, our hypothetical example does not involve formation of an actual intention to hurt the child. In any case, it involves sacrificing one to save millions; not the devastation that a nuclear war would generate. Let us consider each of these lines of attack separately.

The Consequences of Deterrence

Clearly, the policy of deterrence has many costs. These range from the opportunities which could have been taken had money spent on nuclear armaments and delivery systems been available for other purposes to the real fears of nuclear war generated among the population, especially children. In addition, there is the risk of accidental nuclear war or nuclear war launched deliberately by the superpowers. Do the alleged benefits outweigh these costs?

The benefits, of course, are alleged to be deterrence of Soviet nuclear or conventional attack, the preservation of world peace since 1945, and the preservation of American strength and influence in world affairs. But are these benefits more illusory than real?

Much here will depend on one's beliefs about the world. Critics will argue, with much force, that in the absence of deterrence, the chances of a surprise nuclear attack are less than the chances of (accidental or intentional) nuclear war under the policy of mutual assured destruction.

The claim that deterrence has kept the peace can be criticized in turn on the grounds that no causal connection has been demonstrated. True, there has been no world war since the policy of mutual assured destruction was adopted. But there have been smaller wars. Moreover, to say that deterrence causes peace may be as groundless as the claim that since the rise in population of the Sun Belt is correlated with increased publicity about the dangers of smoking, such publicity has caused the population shift to the South. Correlation does not entail causation.

Finally, the claim that deterrence prevents nuclear blackmail can also be questioned. As one writer argues:

> . . . there is little evidence that either side is prone to blackmail of this
> sort. On the Russian side, the military tradition is either to act or not
> act: threatening to act is not a standard feature of Soviet policy. The
> Soviets did not *threaten* to invade Hungary and Czechoslovakia; they
> simply invaded them. . . . As for the United States, the use of nuclear
> threats was eschewed in the Acheson era. . . .[29]

Indeed, it can even be argued that reliance on nuclear weapons generates a
kind of overconfidence that lulls us into weakness with conventional forces.
This *increases* the risk of localized wars, such as the Vietnam War, and
makes the use of nuclear weapons more rather than less likely since we may
leave ourselves with no other means of effective defense.

Are these criticisms decisive? We certainly think they deserve serious
consideration by all thoughtful people. However, there are competing considerations which also require equal consideration.

Are the chances of Russian surprise nuclear attack really reduced if
the United States unilaterally disarmed? Much here depends on one's views
of Russian intentions. While we find it hard to see what the U.S.S.R. would
gain from a massive surprise nuclear attack on the United States, other
than a great many cases of fallout-induced cancer in its own population and
possible famine caused by a grain shortage worse than at present, the
incentives to attack first conceivably may seem great in an international
crisis if the target is not prepared to retaliate. While the likelihood of such a
surprise massive first strike may not be great, even given a lack of deterrence, it is exceedingly difficult to say just what the probability might be
given the heat generated by a tense international confrontation.

We also can ask whether it is the case, as is maintained in the passage
quoted above, that it is not the Soviet style to engage in nuclear blackmail?
Is it arguable that, on the contrary, the Soviets have refrained from nuclear
blackmail precisely because of the nuclear arsenal of the West? Is it as
likely, for example, that the Soviets would have invaded Poland or
Afghanistan had the opposition in either country possessed a credible
nuclear deterrent?

In other words, the consequentialist case, both for and against deterrence, relies on a complex set of calculations and estimates about Soviet and
American intentions, the chances of accidental nuclear war, and the
destablizing effects of various policies. It is unlikely that the analysis of the
consequences can be sufficiently precise to support decisively either side.
This suggests the desirability of looking at alternatives to either continuation of deterrence policy or unilateral nuclear disarmament. Our discussion so far does suggest, however, that consequentialist considerations
neither conclusively support nor conclusively undermine the case for
nuclear deterrence. Perhaps the best that can be said here is that we should
be wary of relying uncritically on either the claims of the deterrence the-

orists or on those of their critics as to which kind of policy produces the best overall consequences. Because consequentialist calculations are likely to prove inconclusive, we might do well to consider other kinds of moral considerations which bear on the ethics of nuclear deterrence.

Nuclear Policy and Individual Rights

As we have seen, a major criticism made by opponents of nuclear deterrence is that such a policy is inherently immoral. It threatens millions of innocent human beings with death, and places the very future of the human race in jeopardy. As Douglas Lackey, a philosophical critic of deterrence policy, argues, our policy is ". . . to threaten *someone else* with death when the murderer actually strikes. An American counterattack would be directed against the Russian people, and it is not the Russian people who would be ordering an attack on the American people."[30] In other words, the policy of M.A.D. requires that each side hold the population of the other hostage for good behavior. But if no one has the right to hold anyone else hostage, which we surely would admit in the case of kidnappers or terrorists who threaten a city with nuclear blackmail, must we not come to the same conclusion about nuclear deterrence? Isn't it inherently wrong because it violates our right to freedom and well-being by making us hostages for the behavior of others; behavior for which in many cases we have minimal or no responsibility?

Is this critique decisive? A defender of deterrence might reply that a nation may not have actually formed even the conditional intention to use nuclear weapons in case of attack. Rather, the threat may work if the rival power believes there is a sufficiently high probability it will be acted on in the appropriate circumstances, even if no one knows for sure what would actually happen. But Lackey's point is that the threat of retaliation is itself immoral, even if no conditional intention to retaliate actually has been formed. Threatening the innocent is deemed inherently immoral.

Is it always wrong to threaten in such circumstances? Remember our earlier example of the threat directed against the innocent child of the terrorist who himself is threatening to kill millions. This threat does not seem immoral, especially if the antiterrorist forces do not know themselves whether they will carry it out if it fails to deter the terrorist.

Of course, the actual military situation is different. As noted earlier, the nuclear powers are not threatening one to save many, they are threatening virtually everyone. Moreover, it probably is unrealistic to say no actual intention has been formed. While it is true to say that we do not know for certain how people will behave if their country comes under nuclear attack, deterrence is credible in the first place only because retaliatory procedures are already in place, and people are already trained to carry them out.

The proponent of deterrence is not without response, however. If we sometimes have to balance the rights of some against the rights of others, perhaps deterrence achieves the best possible balance. If we were to unilaterally disarm, the probability of rights violations through the repressive acts of other nations might be significantly increased. If such a claim is true, the greatest expected preservation of natural rights (the loss of rights in case of nuclear attack times the probability of attack measured against the loss of rights in case of increased repression following unilateral nuclear disarmament times its probability) might be promoted by the deterrence policy. If we are willing to judge policies by the expected trade-offs of rights violations they are likely to promote, we cannot avoid the complex and indecisive consequentialist calculations we discussed earlier.

Perhaps, however, such a consequentialism of rights is itself immoral.[31] Perhaps it always is wrong to violate one person's rights in order to prevent the rights of others from being violated by third parties. If so, nuclear deterrence is wrong because it threatens innocents, regardless of the consequences.

That is a hard line to take. Our discussion in other chapters supported the view that rights must sometimes be balanced against one another. Suppose, however, that we reject such a view, if only for the sake of argument. Does it then follow that nuclear deterrence policy is morally forbidden?

Not necessarily. Perhaps the kind of threat constituted by deterrence does not violate anyone's rights in the first place.[32] Thus, no one's personal freedom is restricted by the threat. Soviet citizens and American citizens are not imprisoned by the threat of deterrence. Their movements are in no way restricted. They are being placed in great danger through no fault of their own. But it is at least arguable that any policy of national self-defense would have such an effect, given the destructive force of modern war. Surely, for example, it would have been permissible in 1938 for the British to have warned Germany of retaliation for aggression even though some of the citizens of Germany were not guilty of complicity with the Nazis and would have been innocent victims of the threat.

Be that as it may, the arguments developed earlier in this book suggest that we do have some positive obligations to others. If we have positive duties to protect the rights of others, then if unilateral disarmament would lead to widespread repression and rights violations, we have a reason to refrain from unilaterally disarming. Can we be absolutely forbidden from threatening retaliation for the evil acts of others but be permitted to stand by and refrain from trying to stop repression? If our earlier discussions have been sound, there may be no rigid distinction between our duty not to violate rights and our duty to preserve the rights of others. If so, the kind of consequentialist trade-offs discussed earlier may be impossible to avoid in the debate on nuclear policy.

The Search for Alternatives

Our discussion of nuclear policy has been inconclusive, which may be as it should, for there are unlikely to be easy answers in this area. However, it does suggest that a search for alternatives to both a continuation of present deterrence policy, on one hand, and unilateral nuclear disarmament on the other, is well worth considering.

While we cannot consider all reasonable alternatives here, given the deficiencies of deterrence, it is important that the superpowers be willing to take some risk to alter the present situation. The status quo is hardly free from risk itself. For example, the United States might take the lead in eschewing the development of weapons systems that could be knocked out by a surprise attack. Thus, the more we invest in weapons, such as nuclear submarines, which are relatively safe from a surprise attack, and the more we encourage others to do the same, the less incentive there is for a first strike. We can at least make sure that deterrence is more stable and efficient than at present. Once that state is achieved, the United States might unilaterally reduce the size of its nuclear forces and wait for an appropriate Soviet response. If no such response was forthcoming, we might try other alternatives.

We are not suggesting any one alternative here; we are only suggesting that there are policies to be explored which require neither blind adherence to the arms race nor unilateral nuclear disarmament. All reasonable alternatives, including a nuclear freeze, and various plans for arms reduction, need exploring.

CONCLUSION

In this chapter, we have argued that morality does play a role in foreign affairs. That role is not one of oversimplified moralism, rightly criticized by the realists, but of consideration of complex and often competing moral factors. Thus, in the area of international distributive justice, our discussion suggests that the rich nations of the North have far greater obligations to the poor of the South than is presently acknowledged, although these obligations are limited by the rights and deserts of their own citizens, and by the unfortunate realities of governance in many of the nations of the Third World. Whether our particular lines of argument seem convincing, however, is perhaps less important than our principal conclusion. Morality does not stop at the water's edge.

NOTES

[1]Richard Slatter, ed., *Hobbes' Thucydides* (New Brunswick, N.J.: Rutgers University Press, 1975) p. 379.

[2]Ibid., p. 385.

[3]The difference between descriptive and normative realism was first pointed out to me by Robert Holmes.

[4]Hans Morganthau, *In Defense of the National Interest* (New York: Knopf, 1951), p. 37.

[5]Ibid., p. 35.

[6]Charles Beitz, *Political Theory and International Relations* (Princeton: Princeton University Press, 1979), particularly pp. 27–66.

[7]Thus, the behavior of Iran in holding American diplomatic personnel as hostages was in part so shocking precisely because it violated a widely observed norm of international relations regarding the inviolability of diplomats which all states might be expected to find in their general interest.

[8]Charles Frankel, "Morality and U.S. Foreign Policy." *Headline Series.* No. 224 (1975): p. 52.

[9]Nick Eberstadt, "Myths of the Food Crisis," *The New York Review of Books*, Feb. 19, 1976, reprinted in James Rachels, ed., *Moral Problems* (New York: Harper & Row, 1979), p. 299.

[10]Garrett Hardin, "Lifeboat Ethics: The Case Against Helping the Poor," *Psychology Today.* 1974, reprinted in Rachels, p. 280.

[11]Ibid.,

[12]Ibid., p. 282.

[13]See, for example, William W. Murdoch and Allan Oaten, "Population and Food: Metaphors and Reality, "*Bioscience,* Sept. 9, 1975, reprinted in Thomas A. Mappes and Jane S. Zembaty, *Social Ethics: Morality and Social Policy* (New York: McGraw-Hill, 1982), pp. 372–79.

[14]See the discussion in Murdoch and Oaten.

[15]Peter Singer, "Famine, Affluence and Morality," *Philosophy & Public Affairs*, Vol. 1, No. 3 (1972).

[16]Ibid., p. 231. This example has been discussed by Brian Barry in his essay, "Humanity and Justice in Global Perspective," in J. Roland Pennock and John W. Chapman, *Ethics, Economics and the Law*, Nomos XXIV (New York: New York University Press, 1982), pp. 221–25. Some of Professor Barry's comments suggest the lines of our own criticism in the text, although we do not know if this sort of objection was precisely what Barry had in mind or if he would endorse it.

[17]See, for example, Peter Singer, *Practical Ethics* (New York: Cambridge University Press, 1980), pp. 180–81 where Singer acknowledges that the issue of how much can be reasonably demanded of others is more complex than indicated in "Famine, Affluence and Morality."

[18]See Amartya K. Sen, *Poverty and Famines: An Essay on Entitlement and Deprivation* (New York: Oxford University Press, 1981) for a defense of the thesis that inadequate food supply in the famine-stricken country is not the principal cause of famine.

[19]For discussion, see William Aiken and Hugh Lafollette, eds., *World Hunger and Moral Obligation* (Englewood Cliffs, N.J.: Prentice-Hall, 1977), particularly the essays by John Arthur, Joseph Fletcher, and Michael Slote.

[20]See the discussion in Henry Shue, *Basic Rights* (Princeton: Princeton University Press, 1980), especially pp. 42–51.

[21]Robert Nozick *Anarchy, State and Utopia* (New York: Basic Books, 1974). The tomato juice example is discussed on p. 175.

[22]For discussion of philosophical arguments concerning the justification of property, see Lawrence Becker, *Property Rights* (Boston: Routledge & Kegan Paul, 1977).

[23]Beitz, p. 138.

[24]Ibid., p. 139.

[25]For discussion of how the distinction between the ideal and the actual might bear on issues of morality and international affairs, see Robert L. Simon, "Global Justice and the Authority of States," *The Monist*, Vol. 66, No. 4 (1983): 557–72.

[26]Material in this section has appeared in Robert L. Simon, "Troubled Waters: Global Justice and Ocean Resources," in Tom Regan, ed., *Earthbound* (New York: Random House, 1984) pp. 179–213 and is reprinted with the kind permission of Random House.

[27]Some might argue that there are possible (although perhaps not probable) circumstances in which nuclear war might be the lesser of two evils. Suppose, for example, on threat of nuclear annihilation that a Nazi-like country demanded that the West surrender religious and racial minorities to it so that they could be exterminated. We suspect that some readers will think that no nation should give in to such a threat, even if refusing meant nuclear war. Of course, even if nuclear war arguably might be the lesser of two evils in some possible circumstances, it does not follow it is the lesser of two evils in any circumstances that are likely to actually develop.

[28]This point is discussed by Gregory Kavka in his article, "Some Paradoxes of Deterrence," *The Journal of Philosophy*, Vol. LXXV, No. 6 (1978): 285–302.

[29]Douglas Lackey, "Ethics and Nuclear Deterrence," in Rachels, pp. 430–31.

[30]Lackey, p. 439.

[31]Such a claim is put forward by Nozick, p. 28ff. and is criticized by George Sher in his article "Rights Violations and Injustices: Can We Always Avoid Tradeoffs?" *Ethics*, Vol. 94, No. 2 (1984): 212–24.

[32]Such a claim is defended by William H. Shaw in "Nuclear Deterrence and Deontology," *Ethics*, Vol. 94, No. 2 (1984): 248–60.

SUGGESTED READINGS
(Works on Ethics and International Affairs)

Aiken, William and LaFollette, Hugh, eds. *World Hunger and Moral Obligation.* Englewood Cliffs, N.J.: Prentice-Hall, 1977.

Beitz, Charles. *Political Theory and International Relations.* Princeton: Princeton University Press, 1979.

Brown, Peter and Maclean, Douglas, eds. *Human Rights and U.S. Foreign Policy.* Lexington, Mass.: Heath, 1979.

Hare, J. E. and Joynt, Carey B. *Ethics and International Affairs.* New York: St. Martin's Press, 1982.

Hoffman, Stanley. *Duties Beyond Borders: On the Limits and Possibilities of Ethical International Politics.* Syracuse: Syracuse University Press, 1981.

Nardin, Terry. *Law, Morality and the Relations of States.* Princeton: Princeton University Press, 1983.

Shue, Henry. *Basic Rights: Subsistence, Affluence and U.S. Foreign Policy.* Princeton: Princeton University Press, 1980.

Sterba, James, ed. *The Ethics of War and Nuclear Deterrence.* Belmont, Ca.: Wadsworth, 1985.

Walzer, Michael. *Just and Unjust Wars.* New York: Basic Books, 1979.

INDEX